MEDIA AND DIVERSITY

THEN, NOW AND BEYOND

MEDIADIVERSITY INSTITUTE

Content

Milica Pešić

Milica Pešić has been the Executive Director of the Media Diversity Institute since its start. She has designed and supervised multi-national, multi-annual diversity media development programmes in Europe, NIS, MENA, SEA, Sub-Sahara, West Africa, and the Caribbean. As a journalist she has reported for Radio Free Europe, the BBC, the Times HES, and TV Serbia. She holds an MA in International Journalism from City University, London. Prior to MDI, Milica worked for New York University, the International Federation of Journalists (IFJ, Brussels), and the AIM (Paris). She has co-designed an MA course in Media and Diversity taught at the University of Westminster (UK), and provided media consultancy for the UN, Council of Europe, UNICEF, Internews, Freedom Forum, and the IFJ.

25 IS ONLY THE BEGINNING

BEING BORN DIFFERENT

I discovered what it means to be different early in life. I was born left-handed, like a few relatives on my father's side. But they were old, lived in the countryside, and never went to school. In my family, my left-handedness was seen as proof that I was taking after my father's family as well as a sign that I was meant for something special in life.

Then I went to school, eager to learn all those great things about the world, mentioned in adult conversations or on the radio. *'Čuda prirode'* ('Nature's Wonders'), my favourite section in the Politika daily, had already opened some doors to the world waiting for me in school. Well, my teacher - a lady in her late thirties, very elegant and always smelling fragrant - saw only one thing about me: my left-handedness. She wanted me to 'correct it' and in order to convince me to do so she put me in the naughty corner, in front of the whole class, thirty-odd kids. The feeling of injustice, the shame, the hurt, the embarrassment I felt then is still vividly with me today. I recall it every time I talk to a member of any marginalised group I meet through my MDI work, every time I encounter a situation where someone is upbraided for being different. The little Calimero in me cries out each time - 'It's an injustice!' The unofficial motto of MDI.

My teacher did not succeed at first. She sent me to the headmaster, a grey-haired tired-looking elderly gentleman. I can't recall what he said or did. I can't recall what else my teacher said, but by fourth grade I was writing with my right hand, though I still did everything else with my left. Irony struck towards the end of that year, my last with that teacher, when it came out that her husband and my father had fought together in the same partisan platoon. She and her husband came for Sunday lunch; my poor mother had been preparing it for days. In the middle of dessert, my elegant teacher declared: 'Milica has been such a help. Really my right hand.'

YUGOSLAV CHILDHOOD

I grew up in a working class part of Belgrade, the capital of Yugoslavia which officially was a classless society. My best friend and neighbour Bozana went to the same primary school and was as fearless as I was when we joined the other kids to play our favourite games: 'Partisans and Germans' or 'Cowboys and Indians'. It was always Girls versus Boys. She was Macedonian, but that had nothing to do with anything in those days. Only Bozana and I dared to walk up the stairs to the fifth floor of an unfinished building, stairs with no banister rails yet. Bozena taught me to like margarine-spread bread with pickled cornichons, the only savoury food I enjoyed. Bozana was only a year older than me, but she was far advanced in another domain as well: fashion. She was the first to have a '*suskavac*', a dream nylon raincoat smuggled in from Trieste, a favourite shopping destination for the Yugoslav *'nomenklatura'* and communist contraband traffickers. And she knew so much about sex that I could barely follow her stories.

Like Bozana, my other friends were from all over Yugoslavia. Branko and Lola Croats, Dragan and Zoran Bulgarians, Dzeladin Albanian, Fiza was Roma, Skender (my first love) was Turkish... but, we paid little attention to ethnicity, let alone religion. I never heard my parents or any other adults mention ethnicity except as a distinction, to differentiate two persons with the same first name. One Vera was *Vera Bugarka*, Vera the Bulgarian, while the other Vera was referred to by her surname, *Vera Butuchi*. What we had in common was a great childhood and great poverty though at the time I didn't know we were poor. There was no one around who wasn't.

HOW DIFFERENT IS DIFFERENT ENOUGH?

In 1997, as a project coordinator for the International Federation of Journalists (IFJ), I was collecting material for a Reporting Diversity handbook, and in Hungary, I met NGO activists representing ethnic minorities. Among them was a Roma lady who, upon hearing that the main purpose of my project was to help journalists like me understand how damaging discrimination against people like her could be, looked at me, puzzled. 'You will never understand what it is like to be in my dark Romany skin', she said. 'I cannot be in your skin, but I *might* be able to identify with your feeling of injustice', I responded.

That was the moment I knew what I wanted to do for the foreseeable future—to advocate for those who have been marginalised, excluded, discriminated against, punished, tortured just for being different. And I wanted to pursue this goal by flexing my skills in the field I knew best—journalism. That was the year that I established MDI, first as part of New York University's *Center for War, Peace, and the News Media (CWPNM)* and then as an independent organisation with its own objectives and programmes and offices, first in the UK, and later in the South Caucasus, Western Balkans, and Belgium.

AH, PARIS!

I fell in love with journalism while studying comparative literature at Belgrade University. Every summer I would spend a couple of months in Paris, where I practiced my French, wrote stories for *Venac*, a Serbian literary magazine for teenagers, and spent endless hours having fun and discussing literature, politics, history, and culture with peers from all around the world. Paris was where I fully understood that even though we Yugoslavs lived in some ways behind an iron curtain, there were misunderstandings and misconceptions about each other on both sides of the information line. My Paris friends - French, Latin Americans, Algerians, Italians – and I would read French newspapers for examples of misconceptions about events in our respective countries while taking a more critical look at our own press as well. As befitted our youth, we believed that we were the intellectual elite of the future. It was with them, and in Paris, that I became certain journalism was what I wanted to do. I was fascinated with its power to inform--but also with its power to misinform as well.

MY FATHER

My father, who was tall and weighed around 100 kg, never talked about his prison experience, which happened before I was born. He was only 21 and a member of Tito's guard in 1948 when Tito broke with Stalin. He obviously didn't get the message behind the carefully formulated initial information about it in the Yugoslav press. He was sentenced to 27 months hard labour on the *Goli Otok* prison island for listening to Radio Moscow. When he left the prison, he weighed only 47kg. And his time there left its mark. In prison, the men in charge of cutting the bread for the others were among the most hated; everyone believed they were getting too little of this dietary staple. That's why my father, later in life, never cut the bread at the dinner table. Even though this should have been part of his traditional role as head of the family, he always waited for someone else to do it.

Despite his lingering trauma, however, my father never stopped believing in communism. He somehow always thought that the sentence he received was just because he had betrayed what he viewed, or I thought he viewed, as his church.

That he was deeply scarred by the experience became clear when I received my first official job offer as a journalist in *Tanjug*, the official Yugoslav news agency. Soon after I got the offer, it was withdrawn, with no explanation. My father was sure he was the reason. Soon after, I got a job with National TV, the only TV station in Serbia at the time. Off I went, straight to the prime-time news bulletin. I could only imagine what was going through my father's mind when, eight years later, in 1991, I joined the first serious anti-government demonstrations calling for a free TV Serbia and, with a group of colleagues, set up the *Association of Independent Journalists of TV Serbia*.

We tried to fight Milosevic's propaganda, which was then in full swing in preparation for the war that was soon to cost hundreds of thousands of lives. The price I paid was smaller – loss of a job, a beating by the police, arrest, hospitalisation. And then the decision to leave the country. Ethnic and religious hatred was spewing from every state-controlled medium, first and foremost TV Serbia. Muslims and Croats were not our brothers anymore, and Albanians were referred to only by derogatory names. In Trumpian terms, it was 'Serbia first'.

I tried to explain to my father how the media machinery worked. 'Why don't you do your job, why are you doing politics?' he would ask. 'I am not doing politics, I am producing the news! And the news involves politics. It's not the same thing as producing croissants!' I tried to explain. But no examples and no words could convince him that

Milosevic was wrong. My own father did not believe me. My father, who taught me that skin colour doesn't matter? My father, who claimed that what matters is how good a human being you are? What he saw on TV Serbia was--for him--the truth. This is how populism and propaganda work. They engage our emotions and ignore rational arguments or get us to bypass our normal cognitive functions. This is when I fully understood how toxic journalism can be and how important basic journalistic principles such as fairness, accuracy, and inclusion are. Many of the media content studies MDI has done over the years have shown that neither my father nor Serbia nor the Balkans are unique. Populism can thrive when framed around ethnicity and religion, even in the most democratic countries with the most professional media.

CHANGING IDENTITY

I came to Britain as a Yugoslav because that's how I was brought up, but for most of the people I met, I was simply a Serb, meaning a 'bad guy'. At a London event, the moderator, without asking how I wished to be introduced, referred to me as a Serb. I felt an immediate need to counter or subvert the audience's expectations of what it meant to be identified in this way--as Serbian. 'Well,' I replied mischievously, 'I *am* a Serb! A sexy Serb!' ('Ask the person you are going to talk to how they'd like to be introduced' is one of the first tips we give journalists when doing MDI training.)

From that day on, I embraced my Serbian identity, but ideologically I've never abandoned the Yugoslav idea. The experience taught me to become aware of how our identity or perception of it changes from culture to culture – it moves, shrinks, or becomes something we do not recognise ourselves.

When MDI worked in Indonesia, I was, as Ade Armando, Communication Professor, and my co-trainer put it, 'the first Western person who understands us'. I had never seen myself as a Westerner. At City University, London, my knowledge of the Russian language and my communist past warmed up the conversation with visiting Vietnamese journalism professors. It was similar in Syria and Egypt, where I was seen above all as coming from a country that had given the world the Non-Aligned Movement.

Meanwhile, Tony Blair became British Prime Minister. Soon multiculturalism would become a buzzword and diversity one of the basic values of *Cool Britania*. The BBC's Jeremy Paxman grills politicians. The BBC's Director-General admits the public broadcaster is 'hideously white'. The Guardian introduces the concept of *Open Journalism*. But, there were tabloids too, which frequently published extremely discriminatory articles. So much to learn for those who came from a strongly controlled media background. So much to share with those who work in what is nowadays called *captured media*. Initially, MDI only worked with journalists in the belief that once they learned how to be fair, accurate, and inclusive, the world would take on a new shape. We quickly learned that training journalists was just the start of our work and that, to achieve our goals, we needed to look beyond that approach, as important as it was.

THE VERY FIRST...

MDI's first 25 years have been about learning, discovering, innovating, inventing, and then sharing what we've learned. On that journey, we have been helped and supported by many wonderful individuals - experts who became our friends, our ambassadors, our loyal supporters. Each of the contributors to this book has brought us something new – a challenge, a suggestion, a goal to reach. The bottom line has been: freedom of expression is a fundamental human right to be enjoyed by all people regardless of race, ethnicity, religious beliefs, age, gender, language, sexual orientation, or physical and mental abilities, i.e. whatever makes people different from one another. Getting the media to include these diverse voices while looking for common ground is a core principle of our training programmes. Instead of fanning misunderstanding and conflicts, we want the media to provide space for inclusive debate on issues that impact all of us and that we all care about, no matter how diverse our backgrounds.

In compiling with book, I invited some of our most valued colleagues and friends to share with us their thoughts about diversity and the media then and now. Each of them has played a role in furthering MDI's goals over the last quarter century and helped us envisage our next steps. They have helped us shape MDI into a frontline, multi-stakeholder Freedom of Expression organization dedicated to remaining focused on our particular field of expertise, which is embodied in our name. This has not been easy—not in the 2010s, when *diversity* became a buzzword among much bigger media development organisations, which suddenly decided that they were experts on these issues, and not currently, when *diversity* has become a dirty word in the voices of the far right.

Remzi Lani, founder and CEO of the *Albanian Media Institute,* suggested that MDI's efforts should also include organisations that represent diverse groups and individuals, for they can help journalists get information not available from official sources. They can help journalists find stories and discover otherwise unsung heroes that were otherwise unknown. And we did.

John Owen, who at the time ran the *European Center* of the US-based *Freedom Forum,* hosted the very first European Reporting Diversity conference, which MDI organized. He opened his London office to us so we could develop our first Reporting Ethnic and other Minorities programme. That process resulted in our first major grant in 1999--one million euros from the European Commission. John's support as our Trustee, his financial backing, and his invaluable contacts helped us get our first core funding. Jean-Paul Marthoz, a journalist and author of more than 20 books on journalism, shared with us his passion for this magnificent profession. He inspired us to always challenge ourselves and never stop bringing journalists together no matter how different their views may be.

Boro Kontic and his *Mediacenter Sarajevo* where people of different ethnicities and religions worked together all through the Balkan wars, brought humour to our joint reporting diversity handbook he called *The Praise of Folly,* which celebrated sexual diversity at a time when LGBT communities were closeted across the region.

We learned quickly that criticising the media without doing it systematically and methodologically would not persuade editors to accept our evaluation of their work. Thanks to Professor Snježana Milivojević from Belgrade University, we developed our very first Media Monitoring Manual[1], which still forms the basis of our academic approach to media content. Her colleague Jovanka Matić, with whom she wrote one of the first books on TV Serbia's propaganda, encouraged us to always be curious about whatever new idea comes along.

When the Balkan wars were over, and we wanted to bring together editors from the region to discuss post-war professional challenges and spread the concept of diversity among them, it was Željko Ivanović, my dear friend, with whom I set up the first online feature agency in the Balkans, a brave man who founded *Vijesti*, the first independent newspaper in Montenegro, who hosted our Regional Post-Conflict Media Conference. Since that event, whenever our funding has allowed it, we have included media decision-makers among our 'stakeholders',

---

[1](2002). MDI MEDIA MONITORING MANUAL. Media Diversity Institute. https://www.media-diversity.org/mdi-media-monitoring-manual-2/

as the funders call the people we work with. Our work with editors was helped by Nick Carter, then Chief Editor of *Leicester Mercury* (UK). His idea of bringing community voices to his newspaper inspired our cooperation with outlets such as Georgian National TV, and Moroccan national radio, whose senior editor Safi Naciri became a local MDI co-trainer and loyal supporter.

We moved from the Balkans to the former Soviet countries, first to the South Caucasus in 2003, and then in 2007 to Russia, where we partnered with the *Russian Union of Journalists*. Their then 'foreign minister' Nadezda Nadia Azhgikhina, a poet, a journalist, a gender and media expert, introduced us to an unbelievably diverse world of post-Soviet Russia. Nadia brought us to places we never thought we'd work in – from Makhachkala to Archangelsk, to Ufa to Murmansk, Saratov, and Yekaterinburg, to list but a few. Along that road, we learned how colonial an approach Russia still had towards many of its minorities and how hard it would be for Russians who suddenly became minorities in newly independent states to embrace the new status, something which still resonates in the countries that were once part of the Soviet state.

Along the way, and again thanks to John Owen, we met Joy Francis. A tireless activist for racial equality who has significantly contributed to the racial diversity of British newsrooms and an avid advocate of inclusion in the media and publishing. Together with Nick Carter, Joy was among the first MDI lecturers at our MA in Diversity and the Media[2], which we developed and have been running in partnership with the University of Westminster since 2011. Joy became our trainer, our advisor, and our Trustee, encouraging us not only to register as a UK organisation but also to include Britain in our work. Unlike much bigger media development international organisations that only work internationally, we started scrutinising the British media for discriminatory content as well, making sure we didn't just take positive examples of diversity coverage from domestic media. And we continue this practice.

[2] MA PROGRAMME: DIVERSITY AND THE MEDIA. Media Diversity Institute. https://www.media-diversity.org/ma-programme-diversity-and-the-media/

PIONEERS NEED PIONEERING TOOLS

Our working with journalism academics actually started in 2001, when we added them to our stakeholders, having learned that the vast majority of Balkan newsrooms were not equipped with the skills needed to deal with ethnic or religious diversity. It was quite a concern for those of us who knew how regional propagandist media used those two specific categories of identity during the wars as the pretext and justification for the conflicts. Since then, we have worked with journalism academics from more than 100 universities – from the Balkans to the South Caucasus, Russia and the Baltic countries, the Middle East and North Africa, Nigeria, Indonesia, and China.

As pioneers in the field of diversity and the media, we realized we needed to develop our own training tools – from handbooks and manuals to training modules, not to mention a pool of effective trainers. Inspiration and support came from Rob Leavitt, who at the time was with the CWPNM. Rob conceptualised the Nigerian Reporting Diversity manual and made sure that best practices from both sides of the Atlantic were shared with journalists in the countries where we worked.

Rob introduced us to David Tuller, an American journalist and journalism trainer (and future public health academic), who had lived in Russia in 1991 when the Soviet Union broke apart and wrote the first book on Russian LGBT communities. In the early 2000s, David wrote several of our Reporting Diversity Handbooks[3] for journalists and developed our initial training modules. Our projects benefited from his professional experiences of working in different countries as well as personal experiences arising from the fact that he is gay and Jewish. David's work brought us praise from journalists and academics, who still reference the handbooks he wrote for MDI.

[3] Tuller, David. (2004). Reporting Diversity Manual. *Media Diversity Institute.* https://www.reportingdiversity.org/wp-content/uploads/2021/01/Reporting-Diversity-Manual-Balkan-EN.pdf

Over the years, we managed to put together a pool of more than 50 experts to whom we reach out whenever we develop or launch a new programme. We recently included in this pool Shada Islam, an award-winning Belgian journalist. Shada co-authored our latest Report Diversity! Guidelines to train media circles on inclusiveness and preventing gender Islamophobia[4]. Anne-Marie Impe, another Belgian journalist, brought us her Reporting on violence against women and girls[5] handbook for journalists. We found this to be such a valuable resource that we adopted it rather than developing our own.

CULTURAL TRANSLATIONS

In our work with academics, we have had immeasurable help from Professor Verica Rupar, who led us through the process of designing the MDI modules for the Master Course. Verica has done several studies for MDI, such as 'Reporting Ethnicity and Religion in the EU Media'[6] and authored our Inclusive Journalism handbook[7] for academics. With these and our other publications, our goal has been to ensure that their content would be a useful read for journalists, journalism students, and academics.

[4] White, Aidan (ed)., Islam, Shada. & El Marakeshy, Mariam. (2022). Report Diversity! Guidelines to train media circles on inclusiveness and preventing gender Islamophobia. *Media Diversity Institute.* https://www.media-diversity.org/resources/report-diversity-guidelines-to-train-media-circles-on-inclusiveness-and-preventing-gender-islamophobia/

[5] Impe, Anne-Marie. (2019). Reporting on violence against women and girls: a handbook for journalists. *UNESCO.* https://unesdoc.unesco.org/ark:/48223/pf0000371524

[6] Rupar, Dr Verica. (2012). "Getting the facts right: reporting ethnicity and religion". *Media Diversity Institute in partnership with the International Federation of Journalists and ARTICLE 19.* https://www.media-diversity.org/resources/study-on-media-coverage-of-ethnicity-a-religion-in-europe/

[7] Rupar, Dr Verica. & Zhang, Dr Chao. (2022, January) Inclusive Journalism Handbook. *Media Diversity Institute.* https://www.media-diversity.org/resources/inclusive-journalism-handbook/

Adapting these publications for use in different journalistic cultures has been possible due to journalism academics such as Haiyan Wang and Anbin Shi in China, and Professor Naila Hamdy in Egypt. Along the way, we learned that the people who have had the deepest appreciation of the work of organisations such as MDI have been those who have professional experience working in different journalistic cultures, such as Prof Ed Bracho of the University of Westminster (UK), who also taught at our Master's Course; Prof Zahera Harb, Head of the Journalism Department at City University (UK); and Dr. Diani Citri, who has helped us discuss with journalists and NGOs throughout Indonesia such highly sensitive issues as radical Islam, even at such places as Makassar, where the severed heads of 'infidels' were shown on the screens of local TV stations just months before we went there in 2008.

While we have always believed that the NGOs we work with can benefit from journalism publications, reading them became *a must* when, with the appearance of social media, these NGOs started producing their own media content. But with the help of experts such as Mike Jempson, founder of The Media Wise Trust (UK), who authored our Media Relations Guide in Mandarin, as well as our Reporting Disability Handbook[8] in Macedonian, or Lesley Abdela, founder of The Shevolution (UK), who wrote for MDI the world's first Media Relations Guide for Roma[9], we have made sure that the very specific media communication needs of NGOs have been met.

Neither this book nor the story of MDI would be complete without mentioning our advisor Eric Heinze, Professor of Law & Humanities at the University of London, who has occasionally triggered intense debate at MDI events with his provocative comments. We are still

---

[8] Jempson, Mike. (2020) DISABILITY: Out in the open. *Media Diversity Institute* https://www.media-diversity.org/resources/disability-out-in-the-open/

[9] Abdela, Lesley. & Symonds, Tim. (2001, June). Media Relations Guide for the Roma. *The European Centre for War Peace and the News Media.* https://www.media-diversity.org/mdi-media-relations-guide-for-roma-2/

learning from his most recent book, The Most Human Right: Why Free Speech is Everything[10], and looking forward to his new one, which should address some of the most controversial issues currently covered by media organizations—the culture wars, wokeism, cancel culture, cultural appropriation, transgender issues.

There are two other people in the journalism field I feel I should mention in this introduction: Aidan White, an ardent believer in journalism as a public good and the author of numerous books, who has always been there when MDI needed him. The other is the late Bettina Petters, the brightest person in the media development world, a fearless negotiator with funders and policymakers, a woman with a huge heart who encouraged me to be professionally self-confident.

IT WOULD BE UNFAIR NOT TO MENTION

Finally, I need to thank people who come from the side of the supporting partners for understanding and assisting our mission. Two of them stand out for their humanity, graciousness and consummate professionalism: Gordana Jankovic, who spent 20 years with the *Open Society Foundation* and brought us to Indonesia and China, and Mary Gunderson, from the US State Department, who has continuously asked the right--although not always easy--questions, and has had an open mind regarding the innovations we have tried to introduce in our work.

[10] Heinze, Eric. (2022). The Most Human Right: Why Free Speech Is Everything. The MIT Press.

THE NEXT 25 YEARS

I could not be happier with what I've learned over these past 25 years. Learned, experienced and shared. I hope that MDI's next quarter century will be less challenging, but I am confident that we are ready to face the future. As Rob Leavitt wrote in this book, MDI's work 'must continue – building on past success and demonstrating the way forward. Continuing to shine a light on the media manipulation that turns difference into division'.

During this period, we have generally had 5-year strategies. However, we have regarded them more as guideposts or goals rather than as being set in stone. That's because most of the time we have survived through project funding while constantly worrying about when we would get the next grant. We received significant core or operational funding for only three of those 25 years. But this is about to change, thanks to a new agreement with one of our supporting partners that went into effect in September of this year. This agreement will provide us with expanded core funding, which will in turn enable us to turn our vision into strategies that will be truly put into practice. It will also help us to expand our fundraising base.

On the organisational level, we have several important tasks. For years, we did not pay too much attention to promoting our work. In an old-fashioned manner, we believed that excelling in what we do was itself the best form of promotion. But we have realised that the reach and impact of our work is limited if others do not know about it. So strengthening our Communications Team will be our first major institutional upgrade.

We need to build up our sister organisations, MDI Western Balkans (Belgrade) and MDI Global (Brussels) and to revive MDI US. We have to diversify the funders of MDI UK, which has lost most of its EC funding in the post-Brexit era. Our practice of employing our former MA students and volunteers has produced great results, providing us with a team of committed, loyal and enthusiastic individuals. Going forward, we plan to increase our efforts to help them develop their careers and professional skills as they transition into employment roles. Strengthening our Programme Development team is part of this package as well. With these changes, we will be able to finally add policymakers to our list of stakeholders so that our voice is heard by key decision-makers.

On a programmatic level, we will continue working in the regions where we currently have programmes – Europe, the Middle East and North Africa, and South East Asia. We also plan to return to regions in which we previously worked, such as West and East Africa and former Soviet countries. We also hope to expand to South America where we have established so many contacts and have seen opportunities to share our expertise and experience with like-minded organisations.

With MDI grounded on a more solid and stable basis, I am confident we can grapple with what lies ahead. As the UN Secretary General has said, a 'tsunami of hate and xenophobia' has swept across the globe, especially in the under-regulated world of social media and, to a lesser extent, conventional news outlets. Populism, nativism, and nationalism have reached the level where expressing racist beliefs has become a matter of pride among far-right extremists and some mainstream conservatives, even as they have hijacked and weaponized liberal terms and constructs like 'freedom of expression'. The public space is dominated by disinformation and misinformation. And the effort to promote 'wokeness' to counter these tendencies has been mocked by the right and also criticized by many liberals as embodying its own form of totalitarianism that undermines core principles of the left.

We still view the media as a bridge between the majority and marginalised groups, a tool for strengthening human rights and reflecting diversity, a forum for dialogue in which prejudices and extremist political agendas can be confronted. We strongly believe that without a fair and inclusive media, democracy itself is at stake. This is our battlefield in the years to come. With like-minded organisations, with great experts and friends, old and new, we are prepared for the challenge.

Lesley Abdela

Lesley Abdela MBE is Senior Partner in UK based Shevolution Consultancy. For decades gender and diversity have been the focus of her work as a journalist, broadcaster, civil society activist, women's rights campaigner, and professional gender and diversity consultant. She has worked on these issues in 50 countries, in Europe, Middle East, Africa, Central and South Asia, and feet on the ground in conflict and post conflict situations including Sri Lanka, Iraq, Afghanistan, Nepal, Sierra Leone, Kosovo, Aceh/ Indonesia, Cyprus, and Bosnia Herzegovina. Clients have included international organisations, Civil Society, media, and private sector companies: MDI, IREX, EC, the British Council, The Inter-Parliamentary Union, UKFCDO. She was Senior Gender Advisor to UN agencies in Nepal. She has developed and delivered hundreds of workshops for institutions and diverse citizens. She holds an Hon D.Litt. Degree on Advancement of Women from Nottingham Trent University.

GENDER AND THE MEDIA: THEN AND NOW

Since 2001 I have had the pleasure of working with the Media Diversity Institute team in different parts of the world. One of our earliest collaborations was a Media Relations Guide for the Roma. My partner Tim Symonds and I were co-authors, Milica Pešić was the editor. This led to further cooperation on media communication workshops in Budapest and Skopje for Roma leaders, guest-speaking at MDI's MA Course in Diversity and the Media in London, workshops on *'Inclusive Media for Inclusive Societies'* for media and civil society organisations in Rabat, Fez, Marrakesh and Oujda in Morocco. My most recent MDI assignment was providing technical support, advice and mentoring to develop a Gender Action Plan for a three-year project in Sri Lanka monitoring and combating online hate speech and disinformation. I worked closely online with enthusiastic, committed young Sri Lankan techies from non-governmental organisation (NGO), *Hashtag Generation,* which is the MDI partner in *"Get the Trolls Out Sri Lanka"* (GTTOSL) project.

Gender and diversity in the media have been the focus of my work for decades. I have worked on these issues in 50 countries, in Europe, Africa, Middle East and Asia, as a journalist, broadcaster, civil society activist, women's rights campaigner, and professional gender and diversity consultant, with feet on the ground in post-conflict situations in Bosnia,

Kosovo, Iraq, Afghanistan, Nepal, Cyprus and Aceh/Indonesia. My articles have been published in the main British broadsheet newspapers and journals, e.g. *The Guardian, The Independent, The Times, Sunday Times, The Observer, The Telegraph, The Economist, New Statesman, The World Today* (a journal from the Royal Institute of Foreign Affairs), and major British women's magazines, as well as international publications such as *The Washington Post, Reader's Digest*, and (on-line) *openDemocracy, The Guardian*'s Comment is Free section, and CNN International.

I have only once been front-page news myself. I had just been selected to stand as a parliamentary candidate for the Liberal Party in the UK 1979 General Election. At that time, single-parent mothers and divorced women were verbally attacked by politicians and some sectors of the media. The frontpage banner headline in *The Hertfordshire Mercury*, the main newspaper in my constituency, declared ***'Liberals Select Divorcee!'***. It felt as though I had been kicked in the stomach. I felt humiliated and shamed. My first instinct was to offer to resign as a parliamentary candidate. But I didn't. I decided to fight back and make the rights of single-parent families one of the two key issues of my election campaign, the other being the environment

Apart from that one headline, the local media, including *The Hertfordshire Mercury* itself, treated me fairly. Although I didn't win the seat, standing for a Parliamentary election was a truly enjoyable experience. The internet and social media did not exist. I got off lightly compared to today with the way online gender-trolling is impacting the physical, emotional and mental well-being of many women in public life and their families.

I would not want to stand for political office as a woman in today's world. On the one hand, the internet has been a miracle in bringing people around the world together to share ideas and promote good causes and democracy. Digital media has served as a powerful tool for women and girls to their efforts to mobilise and bring hidden issues to the attention of media and policymakers. The #MeToo social movement against sexual abuse, sexual harassment, and rape culture trended in at least 85 countries. The campaign prompted survivors from around the world to share their stories and name their perpetrators. The European Parliament convened a session directly in response to the #MeToo campaign, after it gave rise to allegations of abuse in Parliament and in the European Union's offices in Brussels.

On the other hand, it is a global phenomenon that women politicians, women journalists, women's rights campaigners, and women in other sectors of public life receive malicious, misogynist online media abuse, including threats and intimidation, cyberstalking, trolling, cyber-bullying, hate speech, public shaming and doxxing. Women in public life face the same online dangers as men, but in addition they are specifically targeted with abuse and threats simply for being women who choose to take on public roles as human rights activists, journalists or politicians. The situation is heightened and exacerbated by intersectional factors, including racism, religious bigotry, sectarianism, and homophobia, as well as by disinformation.

In 2019, *The Guardian* published an article[1] by Raisa Wickrematunge about a woman named Meena (her name has been changed to protect her identity), whose story exemplifies the pervasive and global nature of online violence towards women in politics. The threats began after Meena decided to run in local government elections in Sri Lanka. In a Facebook post, she was pictured circled in red among a group of people. "We opened some new shops that day, part of a collective project," she told the reporter. "This post implies that I'm the mistress of one of the ministers in the photo."

That was one of the milder insults. Meena was called a sex worker, among other things, and hateful comments were made towards her immediate family. Volunteers helping with her campaign dropped out

[1] Wickrematunge, Raisa. (2019, May 28). Sexism, slander, hatred: Sri Lanka's culture of online abuse. The Guardian. https://www.theguardian.com/global-development/2019/may/28/sexism-slander-hatred-sri-lankas-culture-of-online-abuse

following repeated threats. Stones were thrown at Meena's house, and flyers containing defamatory claims against her were distributed. She went to the police but they took no action in response to her complaints. As with the Facebook posts, there have been no consequences for the perpetrators. "I expected nearly 1,000 votes [in the election]," she said. "Because of the slander and harassment, that number fell by more than half. Now, I'm left with my 333 votes and a file full of printouts of the harassment I received online." Meena's experiences left her needing counselling. "Unless people take action, how are women to move forward?" she asked.

Research published in January 2023 by the Fawcett Society, a United Kingdom gender equality charity, found that 93% of female UK Members of Parliament said online abuse and harassment had a negative impact on them, compared with 76% of men. In an article in *The Guardian* in February 2023, senior reporter Emine Sinmaz gave examples of the brutality of modern-day political life for women in the UK. Caroline Nokes MP, the Conservative chair of the UK Parliament's Women and Equalities Committee, said she had reported death threats to the police. "The worst was from a bloke who said he wanted to rape and torture me until I was dead," she said. Nicola Sturgeon, Scotland's former First Minister, described the current environment for women in politics as "much harsher and more hostile" than at any time in her decades-long career. "Social media provides a vehicle for the most awful abuse, misogyny, sexism and threats of violence for those women who put their heads above the parapet," Sturgeon told the BBC's Kirsty Wark in a documentary. The same day Scotland's First Minister announced her resignation, a 42-year-old man was jailed for sending her an email saying she was going to "face a hanging" for treason. Two weeks earlier, a 70-year-old man was found guilty of threatening to assassinate her.

PERPETRATORS OF HATE SPEECH AND DIVISIVE NARRATIVES OPERATE GLOBALLY ON SOCIAL MEDIA

They use a variety of tools and tactics to contaminate public discourse. Former kickboxer Andrew Tate is a recent high-profile example. Tate rose to fame and notoriety through controversial social media posts where he said that women should "bear responsibility" for having been sexually assaulted. In an interview with another YouTuber, Tate said he was "absolutely a misogynist". Tate's primary audience is impressionable teenage boys, many of whom start to pick up on his sexist statements and views. Tate's influence affects how pre-teen boys see the world — particularly how they perceive women.

He has had a worldwide profile, boasting over 3.5 million followers on Twitter. On TikTok, videos marked as #AndrewTate have been viewed more than 12.7 billion times, although that figure also includes videos made by people criticising the influencer. At the time of writing this, YouTube, Instagram, Facebook and Twitter have banned him, then he was put under house arrest in Romania[2] for suspected human trafficking and organised crime.

THE BALKAN WARS

I had not yet met Milica Pešić at the time of the 1990s Balkan wars. Women journalists in the region Milica comes from were often under deadly threat. In a woman's magazine I wrote, "Vesna Kesic, a Founder of the Centre for War Victims and well-known writer and journalist, and 4 other women journalists were persecuted, received death threats and branded 'witches' by the male-dominated Croatian establishment. Their

[2] Badshah, Nadeem., & agencies. (2023, March 31) Andrew Tate released from detention and moved to house arrest in Romania. *The Guardian*. https://www.theguardian.com/news/2023/mar/31/andrew-tate-released-from-detention-and-moved-to-house-arrest-in-romania

crime? They dared suggest in a newspaper that rape in war might be an attack on women as a gender rather than on a nationality. Vesna said, 'I was shocked at the reaction. I'd thought I was a powerful enough public figure to be safe. War propaganda and strong nationalism in all the countries excluded everyone who doesn't fit the male warrior ideal."'

Women journalists and women human rights campaigners still sometimes receive threats in the Balkans. The life sentence suffered by women and girls raped in war is mostly invisible to the media. The gunfire may have fallen silent but their pain thunders on. Turkish journalist Sherif Turgut lived four years with a Bosnian family in Sarajevo. She said, "The women feel angry. Once they were the centre of world media attention – now they feel they are forgotten." Sherif reported that these women want two things:

1. to see the war criminals who raped and those who ordered the rapes brought before the International Criminal Court at The Hague.

2. to receive training and help to rebuild their lives and earn a living; many are now without husbands.

Men wounded in war are often treated as heroes by the media and by their communities. They are rewarded with respect, pensions, medals and even statues. By contrast, even today in 2023, all around the world women survivors of conflict-related sexual violence (CRSV) - rape, sexual slavery, forced prostitution, forced pregnancy, forced abortion, enforced sterilisation, forced marriage, and other forms of sexual violence - are mostly treated as damaged goods. The lifelong shame, the rejection and stigmatisation they experience from their communities and sometimes even their families, are mostly ignored by the media. In some societies, women who have been raped in war are even considered to have committed a crime. (Men, boys and LGBTQI+ also fall prey to this sort of conduct during war and merit specific separate support and actions.)

Thousands of women and girls across the Balkan region were raped in the conflicts of the 1990s. No-one knows the exact number, in part because many felt too ashamed to report what happened to them.

I was a speaker at an online 2021 conference in which H.E. Atifete Jahjaga, president of the Republic of Kosovo from 2011 to 2016, said, "In Kosovo to this day, thousands of CRSV survivors live in isolation, imprisoned by shame, stigma, discrimination, and fear. They struggle with social ostracism, emotional torment, psychological damage, physical injuries, and in many cases, also diseases. Few women have spoken publicly about their trauma for fear of being ostracised or bringing shame upon their family in a highly traditional society."

WOMEN'S MAGAZINES AND WOMEN'S VOICES

In 1993, Marcelle D'Argy-Smith, then editor of UK *Cosmopolitan*, appointed me as political editor of this best-selling magazine. This was the first time any British women's magazine had appointed a political editor.

Cosmopolitan was the most widely read British women's monthly magazine, with a readership of over 3 million, about a quarter of whom were men. Women's magazines in the UK are a trusted source of information for women, but the male establishment often looked down on these publications. The Serjeant at Arms at the House of Commons refused to give me a Parliament press pass on the grounds that no women's magazine had ever been allotted one.

In addition to my main articles in *Cosmopolitan*, Marcelle D'Argy-Smith assigned me responsibility for writing international news snippets for a regular monthly page titled *Cosmo World*. I later wrote for a similar page titled *Global Issues* in *Women's Journal* magazine. Among the notes I wrote in the 1990s to include on those pages, the following could have been written in 2023:

'Human rights campaigns report the horrors perpetrated in the name of the Mullahs in Iran on women who haven't covered their hair with headscarves in the prescribed manner.'

'Racist and alarmist media coverage of refugees arriving in Dover.'

'In the US the 'Christian Right' soldiers are on the march. George Dean, Founder of the US 50/50 by 2000 campaign, a bi-partisan campaign to get more women elected to the Congress and winner of the US National Women's Political Caucus 'Good Guys Award', told me he was scared by the Christian Right taking over control of the Republican Party, a Party he usually supported: "It will be bad news for women. The Christian Right in America are anti-choice and against giving women equal rights," he said.'

THE 1995 UN BEIJING CONFERENCE GAVE WOMEN'S RIGHTS A BOOST IN THE GLOBAL MEDIA

I was among the 35,000 women (and a few men) from 189 countries who headed to Beijing for the now iconic *Fourth World Conference on Women: Action for Equality, Development and Peace* convened by the United Nations from 4th-15th September.

I attended the conference as a civil society activist and as a journalist filing for Radio Viva in London and writing for *Cosmo*. I still get goose-pimples remembering Hillary Clinton's speech in which she proclaimed, *"If there is one message that echoes forth from this conference, let it be, 'human rights are women's rights and women's rights are human rights'."*

It was at meetings during the UN Beijing conference that I first heard the concept of gender mainstreaming. The conference created *the Beijing Declaration and Platform for Action*[3], the most comprehensive agenda

[3] (2015). Beijing Declaration and Platform for Action, Beijing +5 Political Declaration and Outcome. *UN Women*. https://www.unwomen.org/en/digital-library/publications/2015/01/beijing-declaration

to date on gender equality and women's empowerment. Gender mainstreaming was established as a major global strategy for the promotion of gender equality in the *Beijing Conference Platform for Action.*

A few years later I encountered the terms *intersectionality* and *social inclusion.* These approaches seek to ensure the rights of all groups are taken into account. Looking through the lens of intersectionality is critical for understanding the complexities and inequalities in the lives of women and girls, men and boys.

In 2020, I was the international consultant for *The Gender Charter for Sri Lanka Media,* a joint project of IREX, Sri Lanka Development Journalist Forum and USAID. *The Gender Charter* sets out standards and ethics for media reporting in relation to women and girls. In addition, it covers policies and practices related to gender equality in media-sector workplaces. The contents of the charter were the result of consultations held with a wide range of media practitioners and civil society in Sri Lanka on what they wanted included. I also provided checklists and guidelines on how to consider and apply gender mainstreaming, intersectionality and social inclusion in the media.

'HOME SWEET HOME' - OR IS IT? MEDIA COVERAGE OF DOMESTIC VIOLENCE

The United Nations' *International Day for the Elimination of Violence against Women* is observed each year on 25th November. In November 2008, I was commissioned by *The Guardian* to write an opinion article on the issue. In my piece, I expressed my frustration that even though one or two women were being murdered each week in the UK by a current or former partner, the media rarely covered these individual crimes or named the perpetrators. By comparison, almost every month there was a headliner story in the British media about a youth stabbing.

My article triggered 129 comments from readers, many from men who seemed less than happy I had raised the issue of men's violence against women, even though the story was highlighting the *International Day for the Elimination of Violence Against Women.*

A few victims of domestic violence are men. However, in four out of five cases, the victims of intimate-partner murders are women. Why the difference in media coverage and political outrage? Thirty years ago many people, including editors and journalists, were unaware of the existence or extent of domestic violence, or even felt it was normal and OK for a man to beat his wife or girlfriend. In those days, in the UK, the police were not even supposed to intervene in what they euphemistically termed "a domestic".

Unlike their predecessors, today's editors and journalists can no longer plead ignorance of the topic. In the late 1970s and early 1980s, campaigner Erin Pizzey put the issue of domestic violence into the public domain when she founded Chiswick Women's Aid. Since then, women's organisations such as the Fawcett Society, Southall Black Sisters, Refuge, Women's Aid, and more recently the White Ribbon Campaign, a global movement of men and boys working to end male violence against women and girls, have all drawn attention to this horrific, hidden, silent spring of violence.

WIDOWHOOD

The systematic, widespread and inhumane physical violence and psychological abuse of widows of all ages across the world remains another topic badly neglected by the media. Many widows face economic, social, physical, and psychological violence from their marital families and communities. The COVID-19 pandemic, deadly conflicts, climate change, and humanitarian crises have boosted the numbers of widows. There are a multitude of ways in which widows are mistreated, both offline and increasingly online. In Africa, for example, the widespread online dissemination of the disinformation that sex with young virgins can cure AIDS or prevent HIV infection triggered an increase in the ranks of older, HIV-infected men taking child brides. This has led to a growing number of child-widows condemned to a lifetime of being subjected to mistreatment, ostracisation, forced prostitution, or being trafficked.

PANEL DISCUSSIONS

In the 1990s and the first decade of the 2000s, women in the UK were rarely invited on TV or radio panel discussion current affairs or political programmes or consulted by the press as pundits, authorities or experts. I noticed that when I was invited on panel discussions such as BBC TV *Question Time* and BBC Radio *Any Questions,* the format of the panel generally included three men and, at most, one woman. In one of our campaigns to improve diversity, Tim Symonds and I lobbied TV producers of political and current affairs programmes for gender balance in discussion programmes such as *Question Time, Any Questions* and *Dateline London.* In the latter, foreign correspondents based in London analysed events in the UK through the eyes of outsiders. As part of our campaign, we wrote letters to the programme producers to persuade them to include an equal number of women and men as pundits on their programmes and suggested the names of women they could invite across the range of topics: Politics & Government, Elections, International Affairs, the Economy, Science and Technology, Peace and Security, Environment/Climate Change, Crime and violence, Employment, Sport, Transport, the Arts etc. In addition to our efforts at persuading producers, we wrote articles in the press 'naming and shaming' current affairs TV and radio discussion programmes which featured only or mainly men.

We called on them to improve the gender balance on their shows. In the UK in the past decade, participation by women as pundits in TV and radio discussion programmes and as political programme anchors has changed a great deal for the better - but there is still a way to go. Just under a quarter of expert voices in the news are now women, a rise from 19% five years ago. However, in its *Expert Women Project*, the City University of London's journalism department monitored how the COVID pandemic led to a decrease in the use of women experts on TV. The Project's findings suggest that featuring a male expert is still the norm. Topics deemed to be of interest to men gain more airtime. Male experts are used more often and for longer on stories of interest to men than are female experts on stories of interest to women.

WHO MAKES THE NEWS?

The *2020 Global Media Monitoring Project* (GMMP)[4] found that gender equality as depicted in the news still lags behind gender equality in the actual world. The GMMP predicts that it will take at least 67 more years to close the global average gender equality gap in traditional news media. The GMMP is the largest and longest-running research project on gender in the world's news media. Every five years since 1995, GMMP research has taken the pulse of selected indicators of gender in the news media, including women's presence in relation to men, gender bias and stereotypes in news stories and other content.

Phumzile Mlambo-Ngcuka, UN Under-Secretary-General and Executive Director of UN Women, wrote the foreword to the 2020 GMMP report. She stated, "For the past year, the majority of the global news coverage has been dominated by COVID-19, yet the data shows us that women's voices have been yet again largely absent from the conversation. When women are on average 46 per cent of health specialists in reality, but appeared as such in just 27 per cent of coronavirus stories, inaccurate

[4] (2020). Who Make the News? *Global Media Monitoring Project (GMMP)*. https://whomakesthenews.org/wp-content/uploads/2021/07/GMMP2020.ENG_.FINAL20210713.pdf

gender stereotypes are reinforced. At a time when a 'shadow pandemic' of violence against women and girls raged around the world, the fact that only 6 out of 100 stories were related to sexual harassment, rape and sexual assault against women risks normalising gender-based violence." She finished with a message to the world's media: "By hearing more women's voices in the news as experts and leaders, and by seeing their stories featured centrally in ways that push against simplistic stereotypical gender roles, the media can create the more accurate, inclusive and empowering representation we need as the world rebuilds".

FUTURE CHALLENGES

One emerging trend is ageism compounded with sexism. A 2014 City University research showed that male experts still outnumbered female experts on the main news programmes by a ratio of four to one, but men also had a screen life ten years longer than their female counterparts. UK TV presenter Michael Parkinson rejoiced that he had been able to carry on with his screen career until 73 – "but how many women can do that?"

"We are seeing a pushback on women's rights; we must push back on the pushback," said UN Secretary-General António Guterres in his opening remarks to the Commission on the Status of Women in New York in March 2022. Like many women and men working in the cross-section of civil society sector and the media, I have spent many a year shouting at seats of power. I have recently witnessed women beginning to lose rights they had begun, painfully and slowly, to gain. A recent example involves sexual and reproductive health and rights in the United States. In 1973, the US Supreme Court's landmark abortion decision, Roe v. Wade, made this medical procedure legal across the United States. On 24th June 2022, the U.S. Supreme Court - the nation's final arbiter on what is legal under the US Constitution - overturned Roe v. Wade. The decision dismantled 50 years of legal protection and paved the way for individual states to curtail or outright ban the right to obtain an abortion.

A 2020 report from the Global Philanthropy Project, "*Mapping the funding of the global anti-gender ideology*",[5] defined the anti-gender movement as "a network of actors engaged in campaigns and actions against gender equality and the rights of women, girls and LGBTQI+ people with a specific focus on Sexual and Reproductive Human Rights (SRHR) and access to sex education". The report stated: "An examination of publicly available documents of organisations associated with the anti-gender movement reveals that between 2008-2017: $259 million has been distributed to countries throughout Asia and the Pacific, including Australia; at least $248 million into countries in South America; $238 million into countries in Africa; $174 million into countries in Europe; $94 million into Central America; and $70 million into Russia."

UNITED KINGDOM

I remember as a child seeing notices that read: '*Room to Rent. No blacks, no Irish, no dogs*'. I also remember the cruelty of famous trials in which men were convicted and sentenced to prison for nothing except being homosexual. Until the mid-1970s, women were forced to resign from their jobs in the civil service and as teachers when they got married. It was perfectly legal to declare verbally and in job advertisements that only men could apply.

I am happy to say we have come a long way in the UK since those bad old days. In the past 25 years, Free Media, civil society, political leaders, and thousands of individual women's rights campaigners have helped make progress on issues that have historically been hidden, ignored or considered too hot to handle. We now have a number of mechanisms

[5] Capeci, Jenna., Wilson, Teddy., & Zomorodi, Gitta. (2020, November 12). Meet the Moment: A Call for Progressive Philanthropic Response to the Anti-Gender Movement. *Global Philanthropy Project*. https://search.issuelab.org/resource/meet-the-moment-a-call-for-progressive-philanthropic-response-to-the-anti-gender-movement.html

setting the legal and cultural tone that discrimination is no longer acceptable and that pluralism should be welcomed and celebrated.

Although there is more work needed on implementation under current UK law, it is illegal to discriminate against anyone on the basis of age, race, sex, gender reassignment, disability, religion or belief, sexual orientation, marriage or civil partnership, pregnancy and maternity, when buying or renting property, at work, in education, as a consumer, when using public services, as a member or guest of a private club or association. Social attitudes in the UK on divorce and single-parent mothers and issues such as ethnicity, race, religious tolerance and LGBTQI+ people have liberalised and progressed, LGBTQI+ people can marry. Women and men from diverse ethnicities and religions serve as government ministers, members of parliament, TV presenters, journalists, leaders of local councils, and newspaper editors.

Progress toward gender equality and diversity in the UK is still a work in progress.

MDI IS NEEDED FOR AT LEAST ANOTHER 25 YEARS

There is still a long road ahead to 'achieve gender equality and empower all women and girls' (UN Sustainable Development Goal 5). I hope sharing my memories reminds everyone why MDI's work is needed more than ever in a profoundly disturbed world. Portraying gender in a fair and ethical manner will only occur when it becomes a concern for all media practitioners. This includes digital citizen journalists, bloggers, podcasters, mainstream media journalists, media owners, photographers, news editors, camera operators, programme anchors, cartoonists, TV and radio programme producers and directors, TV/radio debate programme producers, self-regulatory bodies, journalism schools, and unions, fact checkers, and HR managers in media Institutions. Civil society actors contribute to this process through monitoring, advocacy and dialogue with media.

Nadezda Azhgikhina

Nadezda Azhgikhina is a journalist and writer who is Director of PEN Moscow, a Board Member of Article 19 and Member of Russian Chamber for Media Complaints. Azhgikhina was a correspondent, chief of department and columnist for Ogonyok Magazine, as well as a journalist for Russian and International media outlets including Business Tuesday (Russia), and The Nation (USA). Azhgikhina is an editor and author of books and collections of prose and essays on media development, culture and gender, a co-founder of the Association of Women Journalists (Russia 1994-2002), vice-president of European Federation of Journalists in 2013-2019, and a member of the International Federation of Journalists Gender Council in 2001-2016. Azhgikhina is a participant and coordinator of several international projects on freedom of expression, gender equality and culture under the umbrella of UNESCO, UN WOMEN, OSCE and other institutions. Having graduated from Moscow State University with a Ph.D., Azhgikhina lives in Moscow.

A GIRL IN THE SCARLET SAIL

I got my new U.S. visa in Warsaw, Poland, on February 24, 2022.

Getting an American visa has been a nightmare for Russians for years, after the US Embassy in Moscow stopped issuing visas locally because of some diplomatic tension. The only way to get a visa was to go through an expensive agency, which would arrange a visa interview for you in another country. You then had to go to that country, pass the interview, and stay in the country until they issued your visa.

So, I went to Warsaw.

My actual interview took about two minutes. It mainly consisted of exchanging pleasantries with the female visa officer – we chatted about a brighter, better future where you didn't get a migraine from the process of getting a travel visa. It'll get better soon!- we decided.

It didn't.

A week later I got a message that my visa would be ready for pick-up the next morning.

That was the evening of February 23, 2022.

At 9 am on February 24, I was woken up by a phone call from Moscow.

"It's war! Kyiv has been bombed!"

My Polish friend drove me to the visa agency and then to the office of Aeroflot, the Russian airline, to change my ticket so I could get back to Moscow asap.

I was met by a phlegmatic-looking Lithuanian man, Dainius, who insisted that I take the next available flight to Moscow – in 2 hours - and even called the airport, asking them to hold the plane for me. "You've got just enough time to make that plane", he said. He was a godsend.

Back at the hotel, I grabbed my laptop, but as luck would have it, there was no one at reception to get me a cab. I ran to the nearest café. One of the waitresses, although she spoke nothing but Polish, understood my problem, left her clients to fend for themselves, ordered me a cab and walked me over to it, to make sure everything was alright.

Upon seeing us, the driver immediately asked if I spoke Russian – and when I said that I did indeed, he said: "Your commander-in-chief bombed us today. He's a mad man. Poor all of us…."

It turned out that he was from Ukraine.

He got me to the airport in 15 minutes rather than the usual 30.

I'll never forget these people, random people I've never met before, helpful people – and the fact that they didn't see me as an aggressor, but only as a human being in trouble.

Thanks to them, I made my flight – as it turned out, the last direct flight from Warsaw to Moscow. As I sat on the half-empty and silent plane - not even the crew said much during the entire two-hour flight - I kept playing my life over in my head like a movie, my entire life from childhood to some recent international conferences and projects. It felt as if somehow at least half of my personal and professional life had just been unexpectedly reformatted, like a broken file on a laptop that you keep trying to open. As the broken file of my memories slowly loaded, I was overwhelmed by a wave of sensations long since forgotten – the smells and emotions of my teenage years in Moscow – the 1970s. A swirl of faces, sounds, colors, the tiniest details suddenly danced around me, slowly coming into focus. The broken file had almost loaded and in it I saw a world I was sure I'd never see again.

I was flying back to the USSR.

A SOVIET CHILDHOOD

I was born in the USSR, just like my parents, friends, and many other much-loved people in my life. It wasn't a totally boring and gray place, as many of my friends from the West thought it was. It was a strange place, a surreal, crazy and occasionally completely mad place, but it certainly wasn't a country of emotionless clones crowding around the nearest military unit. Of course, from the official side, everything was always under Party control, everyone was unified and united.

But there was another side to how we lived behind the Iron Curtain. We learned to look for exceptions to the rules, for the tiny islands of diversity in the vast ocean of grayness – islands of interesting experiences, different attitudes, atypical priorities. Some of those islands were clandestine, but there were those that managed to gain legally recognized status – like clubs and art schools that existed all over the USSR and were led by enthusiastic teachers who genuinely believed in their students' talents.

My first school was in Moscow, not far from the pompous hotel called "Ukraine" - one of the seven famous Stalin wedding-cake-type high-rises spread around the city. The school was located on a small side street, surrounded by a mix of old buildings with communal apartments[1] and international diplomatic residences. Because of this rather peculiar location for a school, my class included kids from foreign families, children of Soviet bureaucrats, and others who came from a modest, or even poor, background.

You could always spot the foreign kids in our school, because they sold and traded illegal chewing gum and fancy ballpoint pens. They were Mongolian, French, Latin American, Yugoslav. It seems surprising now, but we didn't think about ethnicity back then – it was never a reason for hatred or bullying of any kind. I don't even think I really knew the ethnic origins of all my classmates. Looking back at their last names now, it seems that we had about a dozen different ethnicities in our class of 30 kids.

The only ethnicity we cared about back then was that of the grandparents of one of our classmates. Her grandparents worked at *Romani – The Moscow Gypsy Theater*. *Romani* was a very popular theater, and our class not only got to go to all of their kids' shows, but we were privileged (and cool!) enough to go backstage and meet the actors afterwards. The entire school was jealous of us. The actors' granddaughter was a friend of mine. She lived in the Hotel Ukraine, whose lower floors served as apartments for artists and writers. Her family had a very lavish apartment, with unusual furniture and silver dishes lined up inside a glass armoire. Nobody else in our class lived like that.

Another classmate's grandpa was a religious Jew, who regularly went to the synagogue. When we visited their home, grandpa gave us some matzo and showed us books with weird-looking letters. None of us had ever seen such an alphabet before!

I didn't know it back then, but two guys in my class were Chechen. I only figured it out when we met up as adults.

[1] Large apartments (typically 3 bedrooms or more), where each room was occupied by a family – with a common kitchen and bathroom. Some could include as many as 10 or more families.

The biggest secret we all kept in elementary school was religion. One of our friends had been baptized, despite the fact that his father was a Communist Party member. And one day, my girlfriends and I had gone to services at Novodevichiy Monastery[2]. We were enthralled by the beautiful service and singing; it was so unusual, so clandestine. So that was our huge childhood secret – one baptism and one church service.

I was somewhat different from the other kids, which I came to realize at a young age. Firstly, I had chronic tonsillitis, and as a result I spent a lot of time at home as a child. Secondly, because of my poor health, I never went to Pioneer summer camp, like the other kids. And if that wasn't enough, I was too tall, too thin, I wasn't as well-dressed as the other girls (and especially the girls with diplomat dads), my parents were divorced, I liked reading, I liked writing just for myself and for fun, and I even wanted to become a writer. I didn't really like being a girl – although it was never said out loud in my childhood that women were always second-best, I still felt I would've been better off being a man.

But then came high school. High school was different. It was a special school, where each class had a specific focus – math and physics, biological sciences, or the humanities. I got into the humanities class, and suddenly – I was surrounded by people just like me, people who weren't part of the mainstream.

My parents, just like my new friends' parents, listened to Western radio stations (BBC, Voice of America, Radio Liberty, Deutsche Welle, etc.). We all had home libraries full of pre-revolutionary books, or books that it was forbidden to own. Talking to our parents and their friends taught us how to be critical and how to think for ourselves.

I was still a kid when I suddenly figured out that my dad had spent several years in a prison camp and was only released after Stalin's death. I was shocked! And then I quickly realized that many of my

[2] Although the vast majority of churches and monasteries were shut down and/or demolished during or soon after the Revolution, a small number remained open and held services throughout the Soviet era..

friends' relatives had also been gulag prisoners, and some had even died or been killed in the gulag camps. And then, just as suddenly, I was no longer alone. It was like I became part of this newly discovered minority composed of descendants of prisoners. And among us there were those with a background much more complex than mine. I had a classmate whose one grandpa had been a camp prisoner, and the other grandpa – a gulag officer.

My schoolmates liked Vladimir Vysotsky[3] and the Beatles and blue jeans, which weren't sold in Russian stores. At the same time, we were fond of Silver Age[4] poets, and knew dozens of their poems by heart. We created a world of our own, an alternative to the stuffy and boring world that surrounded us, and we were happy. It was, in a way, a form of immigration within our own society. Later on, many of us joined a subculture or a dissident movement.

I was incredibly lucky – I won a literary contest and was invited to write for *The Scarlet Sail*, the teenage section of the youth newspaper *Komsomolskaya*. I'd never even been inside a newspaper office before!

But the moment I walked it, I felt a kinship with all those other teens, all the young people crammed into a small room full of papers, books, drawings – they were my kind of people. And I wanted nothing more than to stay in that room.

After my first published story, I got about a hundred fan letters from all over the USSR. So, I got to stay in that small room.

And it was in that room that I got my first lessons in journalism and professional ethics and dignity, which have stayed with me ever since.

---

[3] One of the most popular Russian singer-songwriters, comparable perhaps to John Lennon in the West in influence and popularity.

[4] Late 19th - early 20th century.

It was a really strange place, led by liberal-minded journalists who believed in personal dignity and taking responsibility, who dreamt about freedom and were fluent in the Aesopian language[5]. They taught us that our lives and our writing should reflect our personal beliefs and choices, and that one could remain an honest journalist and a decent human being in any situation. In the end, I learned more about Russian and Soviet history, literature, and liberal movements in that crammed room than I did during my years at university.

Many of those who wrote for *The Scarlet Sail* ended up becoming well-known writers, directors, and opinion-makers. Many became leaders of the country's democratization during President Mikhail Gorbachev's perestroika years.

Many live abroad today.

GENDER.
POST-SOCIALIST PATRIARCHAL RENAISSANCE.
ASSOCIATION OF WOMEN JOURNALISTS.

My first article in a mainstream newspaper was published when I was 16. I was really lucky, because as a young journalist I was never faced with sexual harassment or direct discrimination. Of course, all board members at the paper were male, and women, even the most famous and well-respected among them, could only work as writers or maybe chair the "letters-to-the-editor" department.

Yet I still felt the support of both my male and female colleagues – and of course, I simply ignored the stupid comments from everyone else about how a women could only have a career with the help of her husband. I was rather successful, and when in 1995 I married Yuri

[5] A way of writing, common in Soviet literature, which used a large array of literary techniques to mask the actual meaning of the text and avoid censorship. The meaning of an article in Aesopian language would have been quite different, if not the opposite, than it seemed at face value.

Shchekochikhin, an investigative journalist who worked at the liberal weekly *"Literaturnaya Gazeta" ("Literary Newspaper")*, I was actually earning more than he was - which was never an issue for us.

During perestroika, many authors and nearly all liberal media started talking about a woman's "natural destiny" and calling to liberate women from their "labor duties". Looking back, it was almost the opposite of the plight of women in the West – officially, the male and female genders were considered equal in the USSR[6], and back then many women wrote letters to the newspapers about being exhausted from work and wishing they could just stay at home with their families. By Soviet law, men and women alike had to have jobs, so being a housewife was not just impossible – it was illegal. I didn't necessarily agree with these new ideas, but if I was being honest I didn't pay much attention to the topic back then.

The first time I thought about women's rights was when a group of young female writers published a collection of stories about the female experience, including that of sexuality and violence. It was a kind of new female prose manifesto.

And suddenly, all the major critics attacked them in the press. One famous critic went as far as to say that "the very existence of women's prose is impossible, as their soul is just too close to their body." At the time, I was working in *Ogonyok*, a top magazine. I wanted to write something in support of these women, but my editors wouldn't have it – in fact, they agreed with the critic!

Soon afterwards I met Western Slavic scholars and was introduced to gender studies. I met Katrina vanden Huevel, an American editor and publisher and former editor of *The Nation*; Catharine Theimer Nepomnyashchy, a Slavic studies scholar and the first woman to head the Harriman Institute at Columbia University in New York; and Helena Goscilo, a Slavic studies scholar at Ohio State University. We became friends.

[6] Male and female gender equality was made law in the 1918 Constitution of the Russian Soviet Federated Socialist Republic.

I remember telling them that Soviet women didn't face direct discrimination, and that only a handful of idiots said that women should be subordinated to me.

But I learnt quickly that mass media, especially after the fall of the USSR, could turn any stupid idea into a dangerous tool of violence and discrimination. When I wrote an article about unemployment among women called "Unemployment with a female face", I discovered that, with the collapse of the economy, many women lost jobs precisely because of the "natural destiny" propaganda. Male employers decided that "it's better for women to stay home with the kids", despite the fact that, in many cases, the woman was the sole bread-winner and a highly qualified employee.

I began writing about the new women's movement. The fact was, nobody expected it to turn into a movement. Even the intellectuals and journalists who were enthralled by neo-liberal ideas didn't see women's rights as part of the democratization process. Quite the contrary – in November of 1991, a popular liberal newspaper described the first Independent Women's Forum in Dubna, a town near Moscow, as "a harmful gathering of ugly lesbians", demonizing feminism as a threat to normal people and their lifestyles. The "freaky" Forum's slogan? "Democracy without Women is Not a Democracy". Frightening, indeed.

A new ideology, which came to be known as the "post-Soviet patriarchal renaissance" amongst scholars, was quickly becoming a new trend in the 1990s.

In the mainstream media, women were presented only as victims, sex objects, beauty contest winners, pop stars and criminals; in fact, much attention was focused on the reported growth of prostitution. These news organizations - now purportedly part of a "free press" - wholly ignored female professionals and even civil liberties activists.

So, my colleagues and I decided to establish an Association for Women Journalists, with some male colleagues joining us as well. We organized discussions about gender and invited scholars, artists, and our colleagues from abroad for public talks. We started a regular analysis of print media and found that, in 1991, only 1% of mainstream articles were about women, including female criminals and pop stars. We published materials on gender in the media and worked with international organizations such as UNESCO on women's issues. In 1994 we received a grant from the MacArthur Foundation and organized a series of national and international conferences on gender and the media.

In 1993 *Ogonyok* published a collection of my articles about gender issues in Russia. I think I was one of the first people to use the word "gender" in mainstream media. I still remember how, for the longest time, press proof-readers, who had never seen this word before, kept correcting it to "tender" or other words ending in –ender. They were sure it was a typo, because "gender" was a totally unknown word at the time.

That *Ogonyok* issue came out right before the elections, and the magazine asked why women weren't running for the presidency. They published a number of expert comments, including one from the newly established Moscow Center for Gender Studies.

After the issue came out, hundreds of journalists and international experts got in touch with the magazine, so the editor-in-chief decided that we should open up a new department and that I should head it. Even then some of my colleagues found my interest in feminism confusing - after all, I was young, pretty, married, and had a great career. They were absolutely sure that feminism was something only losers were into.

I ran into sexism at my very first editorial board meeting, which began with a colleague uttering: "What a pity, now we won't be able to tell any good jokes at board meetings." I had a good relationship with this colleague, and he respected me as a journalist, but decision-making in the media was still a male-dominated process. Still, I survived.

But I learned that sexism had deep roots in our culture, much deeper than the Soviet system itself. And so, together with my Russian and international colleagues, we set out on a journey to combat sexism. In 1994, my colleague and I became the Russian editors of a Russian-American women's magazine *"We/Myi"*, founded by feminists Katrina vanden Heuvel and Colette Shulman. The magazine was dedicated to reporting on the international women's movement and gender issues all over the world. The Russian edition came out until 2003, though many of our texts were reprinted in other publications for years afterwards.

Our association became the forerunner of a new movement, as many women founded their own media outlets and gender issues became more and more part of a public discussion in academia, civil society, culture and even politics. One could arguably call the late 1990s a golden age of Russian civil society movements, in which women played a key role.

I don't think it would be an exaggeration to say that it was the women who saved Russia during the market collapse and economic crises that hit the country. While the unemployed men suffered existential despair and drank their lives away, unwilling to change careers or do menial work, it was the women who created support groups, who worked as cooks and cleaners, it was the female professors and engineers that spent long hours in street markets, selling Chinese tea and Polish underwear to feed their kids and husbands. Women's groups all over Russia taught their members to learn new skills and arranged for urgent support for those in need. It was a grass-roots movement that truly changed the face of Russian civil society in under a decade's time.

International cooperation started in the early 1990s but became more widespread after the 1995 Beijing UN Conference on Women. Women journalists and writers did their best to cover these developments. Step by step, gender issues became part of the human rights agenda. Lyudmila Alexeyeva, chair of the Moscow Helsinki Group and an icon of the human rights movement, contributed to that a lot.

In 1995, the Women's section of the national independent political daily *Nezavisimaya Gazeta* published my interview with Alexeyeva about women in dissident movements and current Russian politics. We had incredible reader response.

I headed the women's section from 1995 until 2006; sadly, it was the only gender issues platform in Russian mainstream media. We published interviews with Russian female politicians, with foreign political figures and opinion-makers, with European ministers and MPs, with artists, scholars, feminists. Many Russian women's groups and female leaders got their start and first public recognition from our bi-weekly Women's section. At the same time, our Association for Women Journalists began regular training seminars for media professionals, on gender issues in Russia and the former USSR, as well as training for NGOs that focused on communication skills and working with the media.

We were lucky to partner with US and European foundations, including the United Nations Development Program, International Labour Organization, and UNESCO. By 2001, we had conducted several dozen training sessions in more than 30 Russian cities from Kaliningrad to Kamchatka, and also in Georgia, Armenia, Azerbaijan, Uzbekistan, Kirgizstan, Kazakhstan, Tajikistan.

Despite the new restrictions placed on non-governmental organizations in recent years, despite the rise of patriarchal trends in society, it is clear that our efforts since 1990 have not been in vain.

Back in 2002, it was easier to publish a letter written by an openly gay man than, for example, my article about domestic violence. It was put on ice for four months and published only after some shocking figures were made public by the police. It turned out that 14,000 women were killed by their partners and relatives that year. That's more than all the soldiers USSR had lost during the Afghan war.

By contrast, today most Russians understand that domestic violence is a crime and agree that it should be punishable by law. Police officers called for a special law that would enable them to respond appropriately to domestic violence; the law is waiting to be passed. Many TV series include plots in which "good cops" combat domestic violence and gender discrimination. This is a direct result of 30 years of the joint efforts made by women's groups and journalists.

INTERNATIONAL PARTNERSHIP. MEDIA DIVERSITY INSTITUTE AND OTHER PARTNERS.

In 2001 I took part in the International Federation of Journalists Congress in Seoul, where I was invited by the Russian Union of Journalists (RUJ). To tell the truth, back then our association was more well-known internationally that RUJ was. I talked about women journalists in Russia and joined the IFJ's Gender Council. In 2001, after a crisis hit my newspaper, I joined the RUJ and soon became its Secretary General for International Cooperation. I involved our partners in RUJ activities, and we conducted a number of successful projects on safety, combating corruption, union-building, and of course gender. In 2007, at the Moscow IFJ Congress, we organized an international gender event called "Stop Sexism in the Media", with the slogan "Sexism is the last resource of losers".

Later on, I met Milica Pešić in Bali, at the Bali Global Media Forum organized by the Norwegian and Indonesian governments, just after the murder of 12 journalists in a terrorist attack at the *Charlie Hebdo* newspaper office in Paris. I watched her presentation of MDI's work and was greatly impressed with both the organization's approach and activities and Milica's personal dedication and talent as a public speaker. She opened my eyes to a new perspective on professional concerns, and the concept of diversities inspired me. I immediately grabbed some materials from her, and started hosting panel discussions on hate speech based on her statement that we all are racists but we should understand and combat that.

Rather soon Milica became the top expert on a RUJ - Norwegian joint project, which focused very much on diversity, ethnicity and religion in Russian media and offered training to Russian journalists willing to improve their professional skills. She was among the first Western journalists to come to the Northern Caucasus after the Chechen War. We visited a number of cities, and journalists found it not only useful and informative, but many said that working with Milica helped them gain a deeper understanding of current events in Europe as a whole.

I was happy that we continued our cooperation later, with a special MDI-RUJ (Russian Journalists Union) project, which examined how Russian language media reported on Muslims and gender, again bringing hands-on training to mainstream journalists but also offering journalism academics seminars on the development of modules focused on inclusive journalism. I do know that those meetings, discussions and trips contributed a lot to the discussions and debates over gender studies and the media. We were working together on building a new media environment.

Today, the media situation in Russia is very tough. Journalists are faced with pressures and censorship unseen since the Soviet years. Many have left the country, while others just feel frustrated and unable to work properly. Many independent media sources have been blocked online or have vanished completely. But just recently, a number of new initiatives have appeared and many journalists continue to take a stand for decent and honest journalism and understand that we are not yet at the end of our story.

Quite recently the Yabloko party, the only party currently openly calling for peace, organized an open discussion on the future of journalism. Everyone agreed that the Russian experience of resisting pressure and calling for freedom and justice, which is at the core of the Russian cultural tradition and is an important part of the national identity, will once again be a great help in rebuilding the future. It is important to study these qualities and to develop them. As Arseny Roginsky, founder of Memorial said, "Everybody has a small Stalin in his or her heart." Him, Andrey Sakharov, anyone and everyone. What's important is understanding that and making a conscious effort to destroy that part of yourself. This is close to what Milica Pešić said when speaking about racism.

Over a hundred years ago, the great Russian playwright Anton Chekhov, the explorer of the Russian soul, wrote in a letter to his publisher "about this man who, drop by drop, squeezes the slave's blood out of himself." To understand ourselves and our complex of the positive and the negative, and to nurture our internal freedom and squeeze out the slave's blood – this is the only way to arrive at a better future. A future that depends on us and nobody else.

Dr Ed Bracho-Polanco

Dr Ed Bracho-Polanco is an academic scholar, a published author, and a former journalist and media editor. He works as a Senior Lecturer in Communication at University of Westminster, and is Coordinator of the Doctoral Research Development Programme at the Communications and Media Research Institute (CAMRI). He has been working as a consultant in media for various international organizations since 2010. Dr Bracho- Polanco has written for or contributed to various high-profile media outlets and peer-reviewed journals in Europe and Latin America as a scholar, reporter and editor. His research areas of interest include media and democracy, diversity and media, political communication, and sociology of journalism.

DOWN AND OUT IN THE MELTING POT

It must have been during 1995. That I know because I would have been playing the song "Combination Lock" over and over. And I still know that that song was released in 1995 and that I bought the full CD the first week it was in stores. And that I would be playing it out loud from my tiny studio apartment. I loved the band Fugazi. I still do. But no one else did. Not there anyway. Not in that street block of New York City's Lower East Side. Or, as my Nuyorican friends would call it, *Loisaida*.

Isa, Manny, Adal, Ismael... and, I would say, everyone on that whole street where I lived in Loisaida, would hardly listen to anything other than *salsa*, or *bomba*, or *plena*. They might make a concession in listening to a jumpy *cumbia*, although that was "not really Puerto-Rican". But they certainly would not listen to Fugazi's punk rock. They hated it. "White noise *mierda*", my friend Manny would say to me.

Just five blocks away from the street where I lived was the East Village. *Spanglish* was not spoken there, and punk rock was often blasted out of some shops and apartments. That's where I bought Fugazi's record and that's where some reliable punk venues were to be found.

As a non-New Yorker, born in the Hispanic Caribbean, I found it both intriguing and bewildering that a city could vary so much in its demographics, languages, and cultural practices from one street to the next. South of the block where I lived in Manhattan, it was Russian and Ukrainian that one would mostly hear. Further up north, after a ten-minute walk, there was the imaginary border that separated Loisaida from the predominantly white and middle-class Stuyvesant Town. And so it went.

I had grown up hearing people refer to New York City as the quintessential *melting pot*. In fact, many would have said the city was the best urban representation of America's own paradigm of multiculturalism. I am here assuming that a melting pot is that physical space where, at least theoretically, immigrant or minority groups blend or melt together into an almost homogenous society, with its members re-negotiating most of their original cultural forms and values.

It is not a new concept. The French immigrant J. Hector St. John de Crevecoeur, upon arriving in North America in 1782, described how in that part of the world individuals of different nations, ethnicities, and faiths "melted into a new race of men, whose labours and posterity will one day cause great changes in the world". This idea was amplified by poet Ralph Waldo Emerson and his transcendentalist followers in the mid-nineteenth century as a utopian project of sorts that was taking roots in the United States at the time. A "culturally and racially mixed smelting pot", Emerson called the nation.

I found it fascinating that there was even a Broadway play, staged in Manhattan in 1908, titled "The Melting Pot". That year, and during the entire first decade of the twentieth century, at least forty percent of all New Yorkers were foreign-born. Perhaps one could speculate that to generate ideas for the play all Israel Zangwill, its producer, had to do was walk around just half a dozen streets in New York City and observe how the English, Italians, Russians, Irish, Germans, Greeks and others he met were reshaping the cultural tapestry of the place, negotiating cultural forms, apparently integrating through both difference and assimilation.

It comes as no surprise that there are a fair number of references in the play to the *American Dream* having been apparently embraced and lived by New York's immigrants. For example, a character in a crucial scene, says, "America is the great melting pot where all the races of Europe are melting and reforming."

As I walked the streets of the megalopolis, ninety or so years after Zangwill inaugurated his theatrical production, I found myself in a place where people seemed to have been able to *negotiate* their differences and together find cultural channels for diversity. Also, I experienced that such diversity appeared to be adopted as a necessity for there to be a relatively harmonious co-existence.

At a basic empirical level, tensions between certain groups were evident, but so were acceptance and co-creation of cultural products among different communities. It seemed to me that an impressive and varied set of cultures certainly co-existed in the so-called Big Apple. But the notion of an authentic melting pot was, to me, elusive at best. Instead, the *pot* was very much compartmentalised. Pretty much like Macy's, one of the city's flagship stores, with its many separate departments *co-existing* one next to the other in the same building. On the first floor you would have the perfume section, on the second women's clothes, on the third men's, and so on. And there were, alas, some departments that were larger and more visible than others.

Individuals of different cultures, I found, certainly tolerated each other in New York City's districts, living side by side, engaging in polite transactions of all sorts on a daily basis. But they hardly *melted* together *with* one another. I dare say that they struggled to thread together genuine cultural hybridity. I would experience it almost every day: I lived in the Hispanic, salsa-listening, brown-skinned department – the *barrio*. And one single avenue, not too broad, would separate it from the larger, more privileged city compartment, one that was white – or Caucasian, as was the official term used then – and which was part of a dominant faction of North American society. This area of New York, like most of the city, belonged to the groups that tended to dictate the hegemonic narratives and policies of what citizenship, assimilation, social mobility, and diversity were and ought to be.

From the conversations I had with my friends and neighbours in Loisada, it became evident that they hardly agreed with the notion that the city – or indeed the country – was a melting pot. They would, moreover, argue that they felt like members of a peripheral community, visible perhaps as a commodity within a *faux* discourse of inclusivity and equality. The exotic brown Latinos. The sassy *salseras*. The rosary-carrying hustlers. The grandchildren of the Sharks in *West Side Story*... "We are a fringe community, like many in New York, because there is discrimination towards us", Ismael said. "We live by the margins, mostly", another friend echoed.

They conceded that the city did have a veneer of pluralism, of diversity. Yet it was exactly that: a light veneer, a semblance, a superficial brushing. The sense of belonging to a supposed melting pot society, they insisted, was a complex issue. Some of this involved having to do away with some traditions and longstanding cultural forms that were an integral part of their families and community. Like other minority groups in the megalopolis, they felt that they had to adopt much of the mainstream and dominant culture in a dynamic that could be best defined as acculturating rather than as *melting with*.

And the spatial compartmentalization into *barrios*, neighbourhoods or ghettos was only a spatial reflection of this established power dynamic, through which a *specific* type of assimilation was always imposed. Their words echoed those of immigration scholars Susan K. Brown and Frank D. Bean, who both argued that the notion of the melting pot reflects, in essence, an "Anglo-conformist classic assimilation theory". In contrast with what seemed an idealised version of a newly integrated society, as presented in Zangwill's play, the reality of New York City revealed that inclusivity was to be achieved only as dictated by westernised and Anglo-centric discourses. This was a pot of the most eclectic ingredients, but hardly a hybrid, certainly not a fusion, and never a mix. It was more of a set of social and political dynamics aimed at configuring a top-to-bottom monocultural society.

And yet, as much as the barrio represented a specific cultural setting that mirrored the wider complexities and impositions of the melting pot narratives, it was also a place of resistance – one of many in the heart of the megalopolis. Perhaps the manner in which assimilation was imposed – overtly or obliquely – brought forth many practices of resistance from my friends and their community.

No wonder they were not fond of me listening to punk rock – an Anglo white *thing*. Indeed, the salsa and Caribbean beats blasting out of cars and balconies in Loisaida were part of their domestic resistance. So were their Nuyorican words, their loud intonation, and their phrasing. The graffiti and tags that mapped their *turf*. The smell of *fritanga* and beans being cooked. The richness of colours in their apartments' interiors and in their clothes. The motley look of girls and boys. Their banter. Their strut. Their laughter.

At times I would walk from the barrio to the Village or to Soho or to Stuyvesant Town. It would take me fifteen minutes at most. All those sounds, colours, and smells of the barrio would dissipate as I moved along. And once in those other compartments of the city, they became non-existent. Other sounds, colours and smells would take over. Other ways of resistance, perhaps, would make themselves visible, palpable. Or the landscape would be evocative of cultural hegemony, at times in subtle ways but often in an obvious manner.

The last time I visited New York City was in June 2017. The grand narratives of the city being the exemplary melting pot were still prevalent. Possibly every language was and is to be heard in the city, between the East Bronx and Bayside in Queens, Loisaida and Inwood. Spanish and Spanglish seemed to be spoken there more and more. But when I met up with Ismael, Manny, Isa, and Adal again then, they reiterated that, albeit Puerto Ricans and Hispanics had increased in numbers as New York residents, very little had changed in all those years. They were still the *others*, still peripheral, still racialised, still part of the poorer minority. Moreover, they told me they had been forced to leave Loisaida eight years before. "Gentrification everywhere, *bro*... they just came over and took us out of our streets", said Adal. "They bought the whole '*hood*."

The barrio now looked like a theme park for tourists. Its Nuyorican and Hispanic inhabitants were no longer there. The part of the city where I had lived had lost its colours, its shops and *bodegas,* its alternative outlets, its unique sounds that, together, produced different forms of culture and communitarian agency. Now, my friends lived in the suburbs – forcibly, they said. Call it a suburban barrio, far from the grounds where we had lived and where I'd argued, on a given day, that my punk music affinities were not incompatible with my love for salsa – that, in fact, one *melted* together with the other.

Now, in the space that used to be the barrio, alternative cultural and political practices seemed to be more limited than before, and the potential for multicultural transactions that I had envisioned years before, perhaps naively, had disappeared. What could I say to my old friends, now displaced and forced further to the *periphery*? I found less things *melting* in the melting pot, and the melting pot more commodified and compartmentalised than before. As if Macy's stores had further sub-departmentalised their small departments, and made the large ones even larger than before.

The mainstream narrative may be trying to enforce the opposite notion – that the cultural landscape in the Big Apple is more diverse and hybrid than ever. I did not see it when I returned there, I did not feel it. The notion of the melting pot appeared to still be part of a majority-minority delusion, another top-to-bottom discourse of power, silently more restrictive than integrationist, with many of my friends feeling almost like outcasts. Such accentuated divides in language, in race, in ethnicity, in beliefs, and in lifestyles in general, could make for a binary reading – one of *us* and *them*.

On a more domestic note, Adal, Isa, Manny, and Ismael seemed at peace with me still listening to a punk rock tune followed by a Puerto Rican ballad – or vice versa. No dichotomy there. But much more importantly, they are aware that their resistance not only goes on but continues to have a purpose. From the fringes of the so-called melting pot, they still preserve their cultural forms and values, they negotiate with those around them, they still turn the volume on – salsa blasting out of their windows, above their little suburban gardens.

Nick Carter

Nick Carter spent 35 years in regional media, editing award-winning titles and gaining national and international recognition for work supporting community cohesion and inclusive journalism. As editor of the Leicester Mercury he set up the city's multicultural advisory group, including representatives from media, local authorities, police and faith groups. He worked with MDI on projects supporting civil society in Egypt and Morocco and lectured to emerging media in Eastern Europe. He taught a Reporting Faith module on the first MDI/Westminster University Masters course. He ran an economic development company and spent ten years as an NHS commissioner. He is a non-executive director of a company providing GP services to asylum seekers and trustee of a carers' charity.

DOES DE-CENTRED MEDIA HOLD THE SOLUTION TO OUR COHESION CHALLENGE?

This article will attempt to chart my 30-year journey into and through the challenges of media responsibility, with particular reference to issues of diversity, faith and community cohesion.

I approach it in a spirit of optimism for the future – not the easiest of attitudes to maintain in a country where the traditional moderating voice of regional and local media has been substantially lost, leaving the field clear for the discriminatory and often malign influence of most of our mainstream media and the explosion in social media, providing a ready platform from which to amplify the voices of extremism, discrimination and ignorance.

My experience of diversity was predominantly through the lens of regional newspapers in the UK. I ended up as the editor of a large title facing the challenge of serving a city – Leicester - that was being held up as an example of the new diversity of the country. Could we make it work? Could we support that diversity while still running a profitable business?

It was obvious to me from an early stage that as a journalist, whether a reporter or editor-in-chief, I had a clear responsibility for the consequences of what I wrote or published. That was at the heart of my decision-making. Strangely, while other journalists also seemed to accept that responsibility, it appeared to be difficult for some of them to apply it to their everyday work.

I think one of the most important achievements during my journey was to develop an approach that would help any editor engage effectively with the communities they served, act proactively in support of the cohesion of those communities, encourage discussion and debate in order to foster even better community relations and hold up a mirror to society, warts and all, without indulging in knee-jerk, negative journalism. Perhaps even more importantly, we managed to develop a strong business case for doing this, one that did not rely on drama, controversy and exaggeration to generate sales revenue.

The actions we identified were the 'what' in our proposition. The 'how' was a 100,000-plus daily newspaper sale, Monday-Saturday, with around 250,000 people seeing each copy and some 400,000 seeing at least one copy a week. The delivery of that carefully curated package of content, guided by our approach, to a large audience, on a regular basis, gave us a very good chance of making a positive change. Thirty years on, the 'what' remains sound in principle – the 'how' has vanished. We still have the message but the collapse of regional hard-copy sales means we lack that medium to deliver it.

I arrived in Leicester at the start of 1993 to take over the editor's chair of the Leicester Mercury, the largest title in the Northcliffe Newspapers group and one of the top six best-selling regional newspapers in the UK. I had spent the previous six years as editor of the South Wales Evening Post, in Swansea, southwest Wales.

Swansea was a city with a strong sense of identity. It was, however, a city split between the more deprived areas and other neighbourhoods where citizens were generally better off. I wanted to get much more local news into the Post, following the principle that a good newspaper should be holding up a mirror to its communities. To do that, and to get different tones of voice into its pages, we recruited a squad of interested locals who each contributed a weekly column on things happening in their neighbourhood.

It seemed to me that people from the different parts of the city might develop an interest wider than just their neighbourhood. And our research confirmed a significant number of people were reading at least three or four columns in addition to their neighbourhood piece. Even in this small way, we had helped develop a wider sense of a Swansea community.

Attention to local news and a range of voices helped us win two national awards for increased sales during what were difficult days for the industry. It also strengthened my belief that good local journalism had to start with an understanding of the communities in which we were trying to sell.

Leicester, however, was a more complex challenge that would turn out to require an altogether more sophisticated approach.

The Mercury sold across the city of Leicester and the counties of Leicestershire and Rutland – a region with a total population of around one million. Around a third lived in the city, which sits in the middle of the surrounding county. The whole area was predominantly white, until the population changes of the second half of the last century, and was proud to call itself "the heart of rural England".

When I arrived in 1993, the city was already around 35% non-white, following the arrival of a large number of Ugandan Asians, mostly of Gujarati origin and Hindu, displaced by Idi Amin. They arrived during the 1970s and replaced a pre-existing African Caribbean community as the largest non-white group. At that time the Muslim community was comparatively small. It grew during my tenure at the newspaper and now represents the largest single religious grouping.

While other cities with similar histories had experienced varying degrees of tension, Leicester appeared much more harmonious. This was attributed to a number of factors – the new arrivals had been placed in council housing in two main areas of the city, Belgrave and Highfields, and there was comparatively little interaction with other, mainly white, areas. Also, the arriving communities tended to be commercially savvy and very entrepreneurial. Since the 1970s there had been an explosion of small businesses, corner shops and convenience stores. There was thus little evidence that 'locals' had been displaced from work or economically disadvantaged.

Moreover, many of the new arrivals, as they themselves noted, had generational memories of previous displacements that provided a sort of handbook on how to settle into new surroundings. The Church of England also deserves credit for its quick action to set up a Council of Faiths, which provided space for representatives of the different communities to voice concerns and allowed messages of reassurances to be relayed through churches, temples and mosques.

That is not to say there were no tensions at all. In 1972, before the arrivals from East Africa, the city council, worried about how it would cope, advertised in the Ugandan Argus newspaper, warning against coming to Leicester. The aftertaste of that unfortunate action still lingered for many people, even after 20 years. And, of course, the ad campaign had little effect anyway. When people did arrive there were racist incidents, bricks thrown through windows, insults in the streets – the usual nastiness generated by sudden change and the arrival of 'different' people in any community. In 1993, while these incidents were remembered and featured in many of my early conversations with the Asian community and its leaders, there was an appreciation that the situation had very much settled down and Leicester was comparatively harmonious, although its various communities were in many respects leading separate lives.

But the Mercury had a serious problem – despite high sales, its readers were still mainly white. The Asian community, which was the fastest-growing in the area, didn't seem that interested. That was my challenge when asked to take over – without attracting many more Asian readers the Mercury would struggle to find a prosperous future.

This was not a new problem. It had been coming since the 70s and 80s as the demographic make-up of the city evolved. My predecessor as editor had launched an Asia Edition, published Monday-Friday, which replaced up to seven pages from the main city edition, was clearly signposted on the front page, and was available only from selected outlets in those part of the city where the Asian community was concentrated.

I had visited Leicester soon after this edition was launched, as it seemed to represent an even more targeted way of delivering local news than what we were doing at the time in Swansea. I was surprised to find that, far from having a team of journalists producing a significant amount of Asian community news, it was run by just two journalists and much of the content was feature material bought in from the sub-continent. I had my doubts.

During my first couple of years in Leicester we used research to better understand our demographics. The newspaper I took over was beautifully designed and highly profitable – with significant revenue from advertising. But I had misgivings about the amount and mix of local news. As my understanding of our communities grew, I realised the different communities of the city had much more in common than the existence of a separate Asia edition would suggest.

I remember the first big piece of research that changed our thinking. We had brought together elders from the different communities and got them talking about their lives, their experience of Leicester and what interested them. Perhaps we shouldn't have been surprised. There was virtually unanimous agreement that the bus services were poor, the roads needed mending, the city council should be doing more to help them, they were worried about the NHS and about their children – and in particular that their sons-in-law and daughters-in-law were uncaring and disrespectful!

It became clear the way ahead was to produce one newspaper for one city – filled with local news that mattered to the everyday lives of its citizens. A newspaper that would help the cohesion of our communities.

This also signalled the end for the Asia Edition, which had been selling a mere 2,000-odd copies a day. While nervous about losing any sales, we were confident that a more inclusive newspaper would immediately pick up the slack and, with coverage of broader local interest, boost Asian readership. The final straw was a conversation with a successful businessman from the Asian community. He had phoned the Mercury main newsdesk wanting to tell readers about an order won by his firm. He was transferred to the Asia desk. While we were failing to spread good news across the whole city, how could we make progress?

In addition, it had become clear that the five-to-seven pages of local news that were being replaced by content brought in from outside the UK were depriving the Asian community of local news that we knew interested them. By the same token, and this was a key factor for the cohesion of the city, any news of Asian community contributions to the life of Leicester was being denied to the white population because it was effectively 'ghettoised' in a different publication. We shut the edition. Sales in Asian areas picked up.

In chronicling past events, there is a danger that everything can look and sound too easy, too planned, or too clever. That was certainly not the case! My journey with diversity and media was more a matter of growing awareness of the extent of the challenges and complexities and, with the help of my team and many valuable outside contacts in the city, starting to find a way forward. It took at least four years to form a coherent policy aimed at helping the cohesion of Leicester's communities through its newspaper and certainly into the new century before we started seeing results both in readership patterns and acknowledgement from its citizens that Leicester benefitted from its diversity. And, in due course, towards the end of that period we started attracting first national and then international attention for what was seen as an innovative approach to media responsibility.

Sorting out the edition structure was just one step forward. We also needed to review our approach to news content. If we were committed to acknowledging the diversity of the city, we needed to make sure our news-gathering reflected that. Recruitment of ethnic minority journalists had been a challenge for regional media for decades. Journalism just was not seen as an attractive career choice. Of course, things have changed dramatically since and what is left of our regional media is more reflective of our diversity. While always striving to find good recruits from minorities, we also made sure our existing staff were knowledgeable about our communities, their faiths and customs.

Our hard news coverage was good. Little was missed. But the softer news from lunch groups, charities, fund-raising rallies and so forth, the very warp and weft of community life, had trouble getting the attention of a hard-worked, hard-nosed newsdesk. We created a community newsdesk, staffed by a veteran reporter and a non-journalist community activist, that maintained contact with a wide range of groups from all communities and had guaranteed space in the newspaper.

The diversity of the city also needed to be reflected in personal comment, so we introduced the daily First Person column, written by individuals from different communities giving their take on current events. Their perspectives provided an extra dimension for readers on issues involving faith, inequality, and cohesion.

So, did any of this work? It certainly made a difference to selling the Mercury. Our performance year-on-year was consistently the best of the top five or six regional titles over most of my editorship. We even managed to overtake the Birmingham Mail in copies sold – the evening title for Britain's second city.

But had I been able to drive up the proportion of the Asian community reading the Mercury? By 2002, nine years after taking over, and several years after the changes were started, research showed more than 70% of the Asian communities were reading us. We had lost some white readership in that period, particularly in the county areas, and in some part because of the different 'complexion' of the Mercury. I reckoned that was a fair trade for helping to secure at least some of the future.

So far, I have talked about the changes we made to the newspaper after gaining greater understanding of our communities and what interested them. But that was just part, albeit a very important part, of what we were doing.

During 2000, Leicester came under a national and international spotlight after some statistical analyses predicted we would have a minority white population by 2011. As we had come to expect, this was presented as a problem in some national media. We simply reported it as a fact and I wrote a leader column pointing out that it was just numbers and what mattered was our communities, our city, and how we continued to live and work together in harmony.

But the external negativity did spark some more thinking about our role, and in particular how we could become more proactive in assisting community relations and, in what was becoming the buzzword of the period, cohesion.

In the run up to the 2001 General Election it seemed clear to me that the race card might be played nationally. I invited representatives of various bodies and communities to create an informal and independent discussion group that could provide advice to all local media, and, in anticipation of external events, could also provide a united front for the city. Twenty people attended a meeting on March 14, 2001. They included the leader and chief executive of Leicester City Council, the chief executive of Leicester Racial Equality Council, representatives of the police, Leicester Council of Faiths, academics, school principals and governors as well as editors from local BBC and commercial radio and Asian TV in the city.

Their purpose was captured in the minutes of the first meeting: To "discuss threats to the continuing development of a truly multicultural society in Leicester presented by the possible misuse or misrepresentation of race and related issues in any forthcoming General Election campaign," and "to identify what measures, if any, could be taken to counter or lessen the impact of such threats, both in the short and long term".

The first meeting was immediately faced with how to advise the city council on a request from the National Front for a St George's Day march through Leicester. Discussing whether the city council should seek to ban the NF march, which it eventually successfully did, advisory group members felt it was right to take a stand.

The General Election passed without incident, but the group realised it was a unique body and could provide a valuable service to community relations in Leicester – and indeed outside the city. Both the police and city council were keen for it to continue – particularly as a sounding board. One of its most important benefits was that the participation of local media showed we were prepared to be accountable for what we published and broadcast, in a way that was not happening nationally or, indeed, in many regional centres. It was one of the aspects of our approach that raised most discussion with fellow editors in the UK and, later, abroad, whenever I presented the Mercury journey.

One initiative suggested at the group's first meeting – a Leicester Declaration supporting harmonious diversity – was resurrected for the May 2003 local government elections. Leaders of the three main political parties signed a compact based on Commission for Racial Equality guidelines, pledging themselves and their parties to promoting good community relations and to responsible campaigning. The compact was applied several times since 2003 – including at local government elections, when pledges were sought from the political parties on behalf of all their candidates. The Mercury reported all this in detail and our leader columns gave vigorous support.

During 2010, a year after I had left the Mercury, the group developed the concept of a Community Cohesion Charter for the city and county. This committed its signatories to work together for the development of the area as a "thriving and cohesive society of many communities, cultures, faiths, and beliefs". City and county councils carried out formal signing events, followed by other key organisations. Young people developed a youth version.

Sadly, most of the regular discussion groups and formal and informal contacts between communities have fallen into disrepair since the decline of the Mercury, along with the rest of regional media. The recent outbreak of violence in 2022 between sections of the Hindu and Muslims communities came as a real surprise, leaving the city's elected mayor "baffled". Had those old networks still been functioning, we might not have been quite so caught out.

In the early 2000s I was asked to join the Home Office Community Cohesion Practitioner Group, set up in the wake of disturbances in some northern towns, which were believed to have had a racist element. The group produced a series of recommendations for best practice on how media should report on issues affecting diversity. It also generated an advisory booklet – "Reporting Diversity – How journalists can contribute to community cohesion" – written by the Society of Editors and the Media Trust and funded by the Home Office.

It still has relevance, but I would be surprised to find it being used in any regional or national newsroom!

There was also work with the newly created Institute for Community Cohesion, set up by the Home Office and headed by Ted Cantle, a former local government chief executive, who is now chair of a national charity – belongnetwork.com - championing cohesion work.

In 2004 I had a call from Milica Pešić, who was running the Media Diversity Institute. It was not a body I knew about, but a few minutes with Milica put me straight! The approach we had developed in Leicester seemed a perfect fit with the messages that MDI wanted to spread to emerging media in eastern Europe and the Magreb. In 2004 I spoke at an MDI conference in London and presented what I felt were the key principles media needed to follow. They are still entirely relevant today:

- Get involved with their different communities to make sure they fully understand the issues and concerns affecting them.

- Establish effective working relationships and regular contact with key organisations working with and in those communities.

- Play a more proactive role in helping communities move towards a better future.

- Seek to understand to the fullest extent how the content and reporting style of their newspaper, television or radio station impacts on individuals, communities and the overall climate of feeling in their communities.

- Understand it will be tougher for their business, or any business, to make progress in communities where the component groups are fragmented, frightened and apprehensive, than it would be when people share a common desire for a better future and are therefore actively interested and involved in what is happening around them.

- With that understanding, it is also about us getting better at being more proactive in finding opportunities to make a positive difference.

Easy to say, but a real challenge to much of traditional media thinking in the UK at the time – in particular the fear of losing impartiality and thus credibility by getting too involved in supporting communities. Maintaining this balance will always be a challenge, but I believed then, and still believe now, that it just needs a commitment to take a more sophisticated approach and put in the work to maintain credibility, without which no publisher or broadcaster can succeed, while at the same time being proactive in support of our society.

Milica and her team were on a mission and I became an enthusiastic recruit, supporting the work of MDI at conferences across Europe and in North Africa, where the most senior journalists were brought together in the hope they, too, would be proactive in supporting diversity and equality, not just in media but also in how media addressed those issues. I also worked on an MDI project providing advice on running successful media campaigns to emerging civil society groups in Egypt, after the Arab Spring. This was a new experience for me. Our little team, supported by MDI's Egypt office, travelled the country from south to north, meeting bright, brave young people determined to forge a better future and eager to learn any techniques that would help. Whether it was tackling child marriage, gun control, recycling, or domestic abuse, we helped them put together coordinated and practical campaigns to get their message across. Sadly, things changed in Egypt, and I suspect some of their work has been lost.

I was privileged to have been a lecturer at the University of Westminster on a Reporting Faith course, which was part of a Masters degree offered in a ground-breaking partnership between the university and MDI. I think Milica would agree the partnership has been a huge success and the successive years of students offer real hope for the future of responsible and informed journalism. This has to be an important way forward.

I wrote at the start that I approached this task in a spirit of optimism, and there are indeed some reasons to be cheerful. But for anyone working to encourage media responsibility towards diversity, faith and equality, the challenges are coming thick and fast.

I was lucky enough to work in regional newspapers when they provided a moderating alternative to national media. We were more trusted and more widely read. We felt a commitment to our communities and the Mercury was showing how we could be more proactive in support of their diversity.

All that has changed. Sales of regional newspapers have collapsed. They still have an online presence but the number of people buying a carefully curated package of accurate, balanced news and comment is tiny. As Ted Cantle states in his 2022 report, "Cohesion Coming of Age at 21 Years",[1] the significant decline of local newspapers has had negative consequences for cohesion in democratic society – with a 2020 report[2] for the Department of Culture Media and Sport finding a causal relationship between closures and polarised political behaviour.

We now live in a world where audiences have been fragmented and information (and its evil alter ego - disinformation) comes from a multitude of sources, many of them unreliable and with particular agendas and many of them from outside our own society. The person we might have moved away from when they started sounding off in the local pub is now inescapable whenever we venture into social media – an environment where the most extreme views seem to find it easiest to win the largest following.

How can we move forward? Are there green shoots? Regional media is declining, but its reporters are much more representative of our diverse society, as are graduates from university journalism courses.

[1] Cantle, Ted. (2022). Cohesion Coming of Age at 21 Years.

[2] Lave, T et al. (2020). Research into recent dynamics of the press sector in the UK and globally. *Plum Consulting.*

New, independent, 'de-centred' media projects are emerging. What they lack in funding, many make up for in enthusiasm to inform their neighbourhoods and networks. But voices of moderation and balance are isolated and weak in the face of unrestrained social media malice.

This challenge is being recognised in the United States, where groups like the civic media company Courier Newsroom (couriernewsroom.com) are networking to provide credible, fact-based journalism. As one of its publishers, Tara McGowen, said this year: "The most effective counter to the ... disinformation media ecosystem today will be a diverse, distributed network of pro-democracy media platforms + news outlets".

Cantle's update on cohesion highlights the malign impact of social media. The report calls for government investment in cohesion-boosting projects across education, housing and public service providers; wider awareness of responsibility from political parties, and particular attention to social media to ensure anti-democratic narratives can be countered.

Perhaps our hope for the future is to develop the synergy that could exist between cohesion-boosting projects and social media initiatives. That would involve bringing media and cohesion work together again, just like we managed to achieve in Leicester.

Dr Citra Diani

Dr Citra Diani is a journalist, academic and filmmaker with more than 15 years of relevant experience in journalism, academia, and technology. Her writing has been published or cited in Kompas, Tempo, and The Jakarta Post. She is a former Fulbright scholar and a full time, passionate advocate for digital rights and data justice. Citra holds a PhD from the Columbia University graduate school of Journalism, an MA from NYU Media Culture and Communication, and a BSC in Journalism from the University of Indonesia.

THOUGHTS ON MEDIA, DIVERSITY, AND TECHNOLOGY

In 2004, 100 fellow students and I stood all day in Jakarta's muggy weather. We gathered in support of Bambang Harymurti, chief editor of Indonesia's most prominent news magazine, *Tempo*. He had been sentenced to two years in prison for an exposé of a wealthy, politically connected businessman. There were dozens of speeches that day but the spirit was unified. Everyone was there to fight for diversity of perspectives and of politics.

That was an earlier moment in the media politics of my home country, which continues to be a scene of slowly, unevenly ripening freedoms. Until 1997, Indonesia had been ruled brutally by Soeharto, a dictator who controlled the press for personal and political gain for 32 years. More than once, *Tempo* had been shut down for criticizing the regime's policies and tactics. By the time of the demonstration for Harymurti, reporters and editors considered any effort by elite or ruling powers to silence a publication a badge of honor and a signal that journalists and newsrooms were on the right track.

It was still a dangerous Indonesia in 2004, but there was a clarity to how journalists fought against censorship and for diversity and freedom of expression. The battle seemed somewhat simple: journalists resisted any kind of authoritarian suppression of voices. Amplification of a budding social movement was generally good editorial policy. Getting the voices of many groups out there was a singular and simple goal to strive for. Silence is bad, amplification is good.

This was the milieu in which I first adopted freedom of the press as a personal calling and developed a passion for the public's right to equal access to information. My late father, a program manager at TVRI, Indonesia's state-run television channel, had often lamented that he had to "tell lies for the very people who are hurting us." I channeled the spirit of his dinnertime rants, spending my free time affiliating with members of emerging political movements in Indonesia's young democracy.

As someone who has been working on both sides of the world, in Indonesia and in the US, my wholehearted belief that silence is bad and amplification is good has been greatly challenged over the past decade.

When I first worked with the Media Diversity Institute almost 20 years ago, we encouraged Indonesian journalists not to be deterred by any attempt to silence newsroom reporting. I helped MDI provide workshops on security and ways to safely investigate sensitive political and social issues. We covered everything from radical Islamic movements to the rampant corruption that has always plagued Indonesia - and continues to.

When former President Soeharto died on a workshop day, everyone immediately received texts from their workplaces. Suddenly they all had to excuse themselves so they could return to their offices and start covering the events. Before they left, we encouraged them to prioritize their safety. But amplification was good. We wanted to use this event to remind Indonesians of the hardships of Soeharto's repressive regime and the long and arduous struggle for democracy. Accurate news stories could encourage responsive social and political developments in the communities we served, lived in, and cared about. Amplification was good.

These are different times. All around the world, we find ourselves in a media ecosystem turbulent with misinformation and polarizing rhetoric that increasingly pushes extreme points of view. The relationship between silence and amplification is less straightforward than it used to be. It has become much clearer to me that what news media do not cover can be as significant as what they do cover. These days I ponder how silence and amplification figure in the editorial and content moderation practices of current news and social media platforms.

FREEDOM OF DISINFORMATION AND EXTREMISM?

My pondering arises from where the work I do has located me: at an intersection of forces in tension. The free press is a social institution with an enormous responsibility to accurately frame public issues and represent fairly the nature of disputes between individuals and groups, however powerful. Because of their unique role in setting the public agenda, all newsrooms must carefully weigh what they choose to cover and what may run contrary to public interest. With the rise of the Internet over the past 30 years, the press has undergone a dramatic overhaul. As the cost to publish has plummeted, the capacity for nearly anyone to broadcast anywhere has soared.

The roles and responsibilities of news media and platforms are shifting, yet the need remains for cooperation with each other in covering issues that could create public harm. Platforms are battling disinformation propagated by rival mobs of Internet trolls and adversarial governments, both supercharged by financial incentives to spread misinformation.

Some of my work has focused on efforts by Indonesia and the global south to explore ways of expanding access to digital spaces and increasing diversity in those spaces. Since 2019, Indonesia has seen an acceleration in indicators of digital authoritarianism: online censorship, cyber surveillance, and Internet shutdowns. Indonesia is not a unique case of democratic backsliding; much of the world has been in the grip of a democratic recession for the past 15 years. But unlike previous periods, when military or dictatorial national leaders were the primary actors driving the process, in the vanguard of democratic decline today are populist politicians at all levels who enjoy broad support from the people.

More recently, my work with PEN America in the US has brought me closer to the newsroom realities of confronting disinformation and extremism within journalistic traditions that champion free speech and oppose censorship. Everywhere, but in the digital world especially, easier access to information for more people means more exposure to not only diversity of views but also to greater deformation of information, both accidental and malign.

In the past, whether or not topics received broad attention hinged almost entirely on whether journalists were inclined to cover them. Social media has created infinitely more pathways for information to pass through and considerably fewer gatekeepers to vet what comes in. There are still institutional gates, of course, and many of them remain formidable. But journalists are no longer unique in their reach. They now often play catch-up with millions of citizens who are perfectly capable of producing their own news.

These intermingled audiences of citizen-produced and citizen-consumed media, in turn, have the ability to track news and events that aren't being covered by mainstream organizations. They also have the tools they need to raise hell in response. At the same time, powerful and sophisticated new media players have the ability to draw audiences into amplification networks that rapidly spread information, misinformation or disinformation. Many people, unable to do the complex work of assessing online content for veracity and journalistic integrity, can be persuaded by the hyper-partisan media sources trusted among members of their community.

In Indonesia and elsewhere, extreme Islamic perspectives are now more easily shared in the public sphere. This is not to suggest that such extremist positions are new but, rather, that they have become quotidian. Extremist positions have been a part of the political rhetorical repertoire since Soeharto's downfall, but the rapid spread of digital communication and the lack of media-savvy pedagogy have allowed such positions to find a place in mainstream public discourse.

The clearest example of this phenomenon is the mobilization of blasphemy accusations against Basuki (Ahok) Tjahaja Purnama, who sought a second term as Jakarta's governor in 2016-2017. His opponents eventually took him down politically through a mosque- and online media-based campaign suggesting that Muslims who voted for him, a non-Muslim candidate, would be acting against God's will. Islamist websites, such as *PKS Piyungan* and *Arrahmah*, disseminated conservative and sectarian rhetoric promoting the idea of Indonesia formally becoming an Islamic state. As a member of both the Chinese and Christian minorities, Ahok was the subject of frequent racist and anti-Christian comments. Hardliner groups such as the Islamic Defenders Front (FPI) had explicitly opposed Ahok based on his ethnicity and religion since Jokowi chose him as his gubernatorial running mate in 2012.

What started as fringe news was eventually picked up by mainstream media. Ahok's loss at the polls in April 2017 was a significant event in recent Indonesian history: the power of mobilized religion decided an election outcome, which marked a new level of acceptance of Islamist positions in Indonesian society.

In a 2016 speech, Ahok had said it was misleading for politicians to invoke specific verses in the Koran in telling Muslims they should not vote for non-Muslim candidates. *"Ladies and gentlemen"*, he said, *"... you've been lied to by those using [the Qur'an's] Surah al-Maidah verse 51."*

A video of the speech was carefully edited to make it appear that Ahok was saying the Koran itself was misleading voters and then deployed to mobilize orchestrated mass demonstrations calling for the government to charge Ahok with blasphemy. The video went viral, inciting outrage among conservative Muslims. The desired result occurred: Ahok was charged with blasphemy. In a country in which judicial independence frequently yields to public pressure, in May 2017 a South Jakarta court found Ahok "to have legitimately and convincingly conducted a criminal act of blasphemy, and because of that we have imposed two years of imprisonment."

The most alarming aspect of this episode is that it showcases how readily issues can be manipulated and amplified. Digital tools not only enabled the creation of disinformation in the form of the edited video but also facilitated its swift, widespread dissemination.

Digital technology allowed extremist Islamic groups to speedily access a much larger audience than had hitherto been possible, projecting religious intolerance in a newly pervasive manner. The algorithms that underpin these communicative networks also respond in feedback loops that, link by link, amplify toxic views and guide new audiences to them. These online echo chambers strengthen and cement dubious notions, giving them a semblance of legitimacy, which builds a digital environment increasingly separated from reality. Some extremist group leaders in Indonesia, as in the US, are highly educated and carefully couch their hateful beliefs in language that gives them an aura of reasonableness and legitimacy.

JOURNALISM AND STRATEGIC SILENCE

Decisions about what to cover - and what to monitor but not publish - are part of a calculation that a growing cadre of reporters tracking extremism has to make all the time. Many journalists have deep concerns about the impact of publicizing polluted information and just as many express deep concern about the impact of not publicizing such information. Journalists are worried that they are doing the public a disservice by not publicizing the existence of a certain political discourse, such as white extremism. But at the same time, they are also worried that even framing the issue as disinformation can potentially inflame it.

In both the US and Indonesia, journalism perpetuates public ambivalence by attempts to cover "both sides," finding equivalencies between extreme and more commonplace and commonly understood ideas or actions. The effect is to create nudges toward normalizing extremism. Placing fringe positions on equal footing with one or another selected aspect of more mainstream positions helps legitimize hateful and dangerous claims. In Indonesia, too many journalists entertained a false parallel that allowed Islamic extremism to breeze into the public square, not as an authoritarian abomination but simply as the moral and political equivalent of being a religious Muslim.

In early 2018, the Wahid Foundation released the results of a survey on intolerance among Muslim women in Indonesia. The survey found that the principal targets of intolerance were religious and political minorities, as well as lesbian, gay, bisexual, and transgender (LGBT) communities. In Indonesia, Islamic classifications of decency and statutes involving pornography practically define what is considered proper and improper.

In the past decade, the types and number of groups vulnerable to prosecution for online religious speech have grown, and cases alleging blasphemy on digital platforms have increased. What was a very rare political case prior to 1998 is now common. Indonesia's Legal Aid Foundation (YLBHI) reported 67 cases of alleged blasphemy in 2020 alone.

In the US, covering right-wing extremists as one among the many diverse voices democracy produces - perhaps presented as the voice of a respected "silent majority" of "working people" - is a dangerous practice insofar as such coverage can easily disguise anti-democratic ideologies and intentions.

The presumption that all speech must be heard, regardless of what effects that speech might end up having on people who hear it, aligns with the "libertarian, content-neutral ethos" that legal and technology scholar Nabiha Syed characterizes as the prevalent way speech online is framed. In addition, more news outlets now appear to promote the notion that radical beliefs aren't a fringe phenomenon but represent only one among a variety of groups. However, just because beliefs are no longer considered "fringe" elements in public discourse doesn't mean they should be normalized. Unfortunately, particularly when it comes to reporting on hate speech, newsrooms tend to begin and end with the question of whether or not someone has a right to say something, not whether or not they should have.

Joan Donovan and Danah Boyd of Data and Society, a New York based think tank, argue for "quarantining" hate speech through "strategic silence," which notably includes reporters not covering it at all. Strategic silence is defined as a deliberate and conscious effort *not* to communicate certain information, an alien concept for most journalists committed to the public's right to know. Some outlets, including *The New York Times*, have found themselves on the defensive after readers reacted negatively to individual opinion pieces they felt went too far in normalizing ideas that are either false or close cousins to hate speech. This happened when the *Times* published a June 2020 op-ed by a Republican Senator, calling for the government to invoke the Insurrection Act to have the military put down protesters responding to the killing of George Floyd.

That kind of amplification can be a step toward normalizing an extreme act as a lawful act and, at the same time, result in targeting a person or a group as lawless. It is even more troubling when the people targeted are already harassed, belong to vulnerable populations, or even represent large groups that significant numbers of people despise.

The line between coverage and amplification has thinned. In 2022, Indonesian scholar and activist Ade Armando was assaulted by an Islamic mob while covering a demonstration. Conservative Islamic media published a lie - that the police started shooting after Armando's beating to justify the riot that happened. Soon after, when the press debunked the fringe media's lie, it actually inflamed the lie to spread further as mainstream media picked up and thus amplified mis- and disinformation purveyed at the outer fringes of the Internet.

In the US, as soon as journalists started to report that a figure from a 2005 comic, Pepe the Frog, had become a symbol of white supremacy, searches and shares of the Pepe image propelled it into the mainstream. Press coverage of Alex Jones's fabrication that the 2012 Sandy Hook Elementary School shooting in Newtown, Connecticut, was faked helped the lie to spread widely. Even when reporting takes an explicitly critical stance, news coverage of extremist messages can help make those messages, and their messengers, much more visible.

Amplification and sensationalistic journalism also simplify complicated conversations. A 2020 report by Remotivi, an NGO focusing on journalistic practice, analyzed mainstream media coverage of attacks on members of Ahmadiyah, a minority strain of Islam. Indonesia has seen an increase in selective prosecutions of citizens or organizations whose online religious communications dominant Muslim groups deem offensive. The Remotivi report shows that attention-driven journalism fails to capture the complicated nuances of religious oppression in Indonesia, which extends beyond legal statutes. For instance, media reporting can bring social consequences, such as public shaming or social isolation, which are sometimes more powerful punishments than official sanction.

In the US, journalists have expressed concern that debates about systemic racial injustice and everyday instances of white supremacy in 2020 were being supplanted by sensationalist, neon-flashing-light press coverage of individual neo-Nazis. In other instances, some people have observed that generally peaceful protests covered by the press featured decontextualized nighttime images of fire and smoke that led to violence and chaos being associated with largely peaceful protests.

Amplification also risks desensitizing people to harmful views. The language of violence encountered every day through reporting has desensitized many journalists to such an extent that they sometimes fail to register violent threats, even when these threats are directed at them personally or their newsroom more broadly.

Bigoted and dehumanizing messages emanating from extremist corners of the Internet are impossible, and maybe even unethical, to ignore. So the unsolved brain-teaser for journalists is how to report on issues that matter without amplifying misinformation or normalizing extremist ideas.

IS IT POSSIBLE TO BALANCE 'SILENCE' AND 'AMPLIFICATION'?

To me, the idea of not covering extreme movements and extreme ideas doesn't seem like an option, given how prevalent they are. The risk with disinformation is not necessarily that it will overtake real news but that its constant presence will drown public discourse, and then democratic deliberation itself might drown in noise and doubt. Without standards for what counts as journalism, societies lose the basic materials for participatory democracy. Journalism practice relies on editorial discretion in determining how best to serve the public good: for instance, weighing the benefits of reporting something by whether and how it might affect policy, hold the powerful accountable, or bring marginalized voices into public discussion in a shared space with other voices. The benefits have to outweigh the potential harms.

Joy Francis

Joy Francis is co-founder and executive director of Words of Colour, co-founder of Digital Women UK and the award-winning Synergi Collaborative Centre. The former print and broadcast journalist is a curator, producer, cultural strategist and longstanding activist for racial equality and cultural inclusion in literature, publishing and the media. She collaborated with the Media Diversity Institute to launch its Diversity and the Media MA at the University of Westminster in 2012. In 2016 she was appointed as the media liaison lead for the Hillsborough Inquests and in 2017 for the Camber Sands Inquests by award-winning civil rights law firm Birnberg Peirce. Joy was elected to the Royal Society of Literature as an Honorary Fellow in 2022.

WHEN CHANGE ISN'T ENOUGH

When I was introduced to Media Diversity Institute (MDI) founder Milica Pešić in 2000 by Freedom Forum Europe director John Owen, the print and broadcast media were facing growing scrutiny over their lack of commitment to racial diversity.

It was also the year when I and four other black and brown journalists - Paul Macey, Veena Josh, Henry Bonsu and David Gyimah, officially launched The Creative Collective, a media and organisational development consultancy for this very reason.

We were galvanised to collaborate by the main finding of the Macpherson Report (1999) into the racist murder of Stephen Lawrence on the 22nd of April 1993: that the Metropolitan Police was 'unwittingly' institutionally racist.

We were also perplexed at the absence of any media censure over its own racial bias, which was painfully evident with the initial gaslighting of Lawrence's murder. Garnering minimal coverage in the local press[1], the public was deprived of the chance to emotionally connect with a

[1] Burrell, Ian., & Peachey, Paul. (2012, January 4) How the press ignored the Lawrence story – then used it to change Britain. *The Independent.* https://www.independent.co.uk/news/media/press/how-the-press-ignored-the-lawrence-story-then-used-it-to-change-britain-6284645.html

life cut short through a heinous act. Instead, black people were once again left with the message our lives didn't matter.

As practising journalists of colour, most of us worked in overwhelmingly white, middle class newsrooms. We wanted to challenge the single [white] narrative and unspoken status quo at the heart of mainstream media reporting. We didn't want to collude in our misrepresentation. Lawrence could have been my brother or cousin. It hurt and was triggering. Racism was our lived experience. We wanted, and deserved, meaningful change.

Meeting Pešić was a breath of fresh air. We instantly bonded over our respective missions to challenge media outlets (and media literacy) to be more inclusive. Pešić and I were both women, both journalists and both minorities in Britain: Pešić, a Serbian immigrant; me, a London-born citizen of Jamaican parentage.

Both of us had helped create fledgling organisations. MDI was two years old, focused on freedom of expression, reporting diversity in the media, media democratisation and amplifying the voices of civic organisations.

The Creative Collective was months old, yet we were determined to challenge the media's inability to fairly report the global majority experience. Facilitating third sector organisations to develop their own media platforms and be the lead narrators in their stories was an essential component of that vision. MDI's focus was international. Ours was UK-wide.

Connecting with Pešić was both timely and apt as that year the Cultural Diversity Network (CDN) launched[2] with 11 broadcast-focused organisations, including Channel 4, to address race, class, disability, religion and belief, gender and ageism inequities.

---

[2] Campbell, Lisa. (2010, April 15) Oona King, Channel 4. *Broadcast.* https://www.broadcastnow.co.uk/channel-4/oona-king-channel-4/5012771.article

The CDN Diversity Pledge, supported by 200 production companies, provided a process of accountability where signatories agreed to "take measurable steps to improve diversity". If an independent production company didn't sign up to the pledge, broadcasters were given the agency to refuse to commission them.

Meanwhile, tumbleweed rolled uninterrupted down Fleet Street as minimal progress was being made by newspapers to address the lack of diversity in their newsrooms. At the time, data on the number of journalists of colour, the roles they held and where they were geographically based wasn't being collected or published. Ethnic monitoring and exit interviews, anecdotally, weren't commonplace, nor was engaging with the growing public debate and dissatisfaction over the lack of media diversity.

A common belief doing the rounds in industry circles was that there weren't enough talented journalists of colour to be recruited. A view that was reinforced through our interviews with black and brown journalists who had left print journalism for publishing and broadcasting. Conversations that were later mirrored in discussions held with some national newspaper editors.

This unaccountability motivated me and my Creative Collective co-founders to act. After forming an alliance with Freedom Forum Europe and John Owen, I was invited to a week-long field trip to be an 'Observer' on Freedom Forum Washington's Chips Quinn Memorial Fund for Minority Scholars in Journalism[3]. I spoke to and interviewed East Asian, South Asian, African American, Hispanic American and indigenous journalism scholars.

Without exception, each scholar was surprised and excited that I was from England. "I didn't know there were black people in Britain" was a

[3] Chips Quinn Scholars Program for Diversity in Journalism. *Freedom Forum.* https://www.freedomforum.org/chips-quinn-scholars-program-for-diversity-in-journalism/

common refrain. To many, I was from an unheard species called Black British journalist. My heart sank. The CBI, British Council and the British media clearly weren't doing a great job reflecting the true diversity of Britain.

My presence reinforced the now universal mantra that representation matters, especially as virtually all of the Chips Quinn tutors, many of them Pulitzer Prize winning journalists and editors, were white. A reality that was publicly acknowledged by the organisers and journalists themselves as evidence of the newspaper industry's legacy of whiteness which the programme was seeking to redress.

At the end of the trip, I was invited to meet the Freedom Forum board. After a lively conversation with Chips Quinn's founder John C. Quinn, I was unexpectedly offered $10,000 seed funding for The Creative Collective to launch an adapted version of its successful programme, which had already put 500 budding journalists through newspaper internships.

Convinced that British newspapers were a "tough nut to crack" on diversity, and unlikely to fund an internship, the only stipulation was that we secure three newspapers to match fund bursaries for three to six-month internships.

Once back on English soil, we worked to secure support for the programme. Channel 4 News lead anchor Jon Snow, New York Times political correspondent Jonathan P Hicks and Guardian correspondent Gary Younge didn't take much persuading. The National Union of Journalists and London College of Printing agreed to be partners.

We visited journalism schools around the country and spoke to journalism tutors and students of colour to understand the challenges they faced as once they qualified, many didn't transition into the print media. The few who did weren't being retained.

Every single national and regional newspaper in England was invited to be part of The Creative Collective National Print Media Internship scheme. The overwhelming majority ignored us. One national newspaper, that shall remain nameless, returned the full information pack back to us. The initial signs weren't promising.

Our launch on Monday 15th January 2021 got press traction nationally and regionally, including in The Guardian[4] and Press Gazette. We beat our target of three newspapers by securing The Times, Nottingham Evening Post, Manchester Evening News, Bradford Telegraph and Argus and The Big Issue. It was also timely as the week before, BBC director general Greg Dyke agreed with a BBC Radio Scotland presenter's description of his corporation as "hideously white"[5].

Bradford Telegraph & Argus Editor Perry Austin-Clarke[6] signed up because he wanted his newspaper's staff to be more representative of the local community. "We're not looking for more journalists from the ethnic minority communities so that they can cover only ethnic minority affairs. It's long been our policy that all our journalists are here to serve all our readers, whatever their ethnic background."

The Financial Times[7], Supply Management and Scunthorpe Telegraph joined in year two. All the newspapers and publications stayed with us, and we secured additional funding through sponsors from the NGO and public sectors. In three years and three rounds, over 22 journalism students were recruited to the programme as some newspapers took on two interns at a time.

---

[4] Hodgson, Jessica. (2001, January 15). Journalists' scheme targets ethnic minorities. *The Guardian.* https://www.theguardian.com/media/2001/jan/15/pressandpublishing

[5] Hill, Amelia. (2001, January 7). Dyke: BBC is hideously white. *The Guardian.* https://www.theguardian.com/media/2001/jan/07/uknews.theobserver1

[6] (2001, May 14). A level playing field in the newsroom. Telegraph & Argus. https://www.thetelegraphandargus.co.uk/news/8042289.a-level-playing-field-in-the-newsroom/

[7] Reeves, Ian. (2002, March 21). FT joins The Creative Collective programme. *Press Gazette.* https://pressgazette.co.uk/archive-content/ft-joins-the-creative-collective-programme/

After every internship, the majority of the interns were offered full time positions. Those who accepted worked at The Times, The Big Issue, Financial Times, Manchester Evening News and Nottingham Evening Post.

Over 60% of the interns went on to have a career in the media, both here and abroad, from Al Jazeera, The Mirror and Marie Claire South Africa to Community Care magazine and BBC Radio and TV. The scheme was cited as a model of good practice in the Society of Editors Diversity in the Newsroom report (2004)[8].

Goldsmiths, University of London, in partnership with The Financial Times, established a diversity bursary fund for BAME students to enable them to complete their studies. The internship scheme was selected as a top 30 media diversity initiative[9] by the European Commission in 2009, and from 2006-2008 we adapted the model for Transport for London's press office[10], which became a rolling programme.

While running the internship programme and fielding positive (and negative) responses from the print media and right-wing opponents, I was still a practising journalist. Within a year of being established, The Creative Collective showed what was possible with a small team, an even smaller budget and a growing ecosystem of collaborators, bolstered by a targeted media and recruitment campaign.

It was ironic that I had to secure American money to run a national print media internship programme for journalists of colour in Britain. It was

[8] (2004, October). Diversity in the Newsroom: Employment of Minority Ethnic Journalists in Newspapers. *Society of Editors*. https://www.societyofeditors.org/wp-content/uploads/2018/10/Diversity-in-the-Newsroom-Report-PDF.pdf

[9] (2009, March). Media4Diversity: Taking the Pulse of Diversity in the Media. A Study on Media and Diversity in EU Member States and 3 EEA countries. *European Commission*. https://www.coe.int/t/dg4/cultureheritage/mars/Source/Resources/References/Media4diversity_en.pdf

[10] Transport for London. (2007, March 12). *Interns join Transport for London press office.* [Press release]. https://tfl.gov.uk/info-for/media/press-releases/2007/march/interns-join-transport-for-london-press-office

also telling that our programme targeted journalism students of colour who had already beat the odds to be part of the 1% on newspaper and periodical journalism programmes, only not to transition into a newspaper career, which they paid to study for.

Instead of attracting journalists of colour, large swathes of the print media did very little to become transparent. Many journalism jobs weren't widely advertised as they are now. Unpaid internships were rife, affordable only to those with money. Professionally, newspapers were viewed as an unattractive and culturally unsafe option for people of colour. Word of mouth about discriminatory experiences in the newsroom was enough to stop students of colour from applying for the sake of their wellbeing.

By 2002, I chose to run The Creative Collective full time. I knew that change wouldn't happen quickly enough while working inside the industry. The newsroom was a microcosm of wider society, which meant I had to be in the world, with more independence. Part of that pivot was a desire to work directly with the communities under fire, including Muslim communities who were a growing target for inflammatory coverage and Islamophobia in the wake of the 9/11 attacks against the US in 2001.

I kept my hand in the game as a contracted freelance broadcast and print journalist and journalism lecturer. One of the pieces I wrote for The Guardian reflected on the impact of two high profile race discrimination[11] cases brought against the BBC.

One of the complainants, World Service broadcaster Sharan Sadhu, spoke of the "colonial culture" and boys club. Coming a year after Greg Dyke's "hideously white" admission, it signalled loud and clear that "recruiting ethnic minority staff without attempting to nurture and accommodate racial and cultural differences doesn't work".

[11] Francis, Joy. (2002, May 13). BBC still showing its 'hideously white' face. *The Guardian.* https://www.theguardian.com/media/2002/may/13/mondaymediasection.raceintheuk

While researching the piece, a black female journalist who had freelanced for the BBC for more than three years said: "There is this unspoken reality that, although I look different from you, I must act, think and speak the same as you, which is then promoted as diversity."

An Asian female BBC producer I spoke to said that her role changed, without consultation, to an "ethnic brief", which wasn't in her job description. She was expected to bring in black and ethnic minority stories and was criticised for not doing enough.

The Journalists at Work Survey 2002 by the Journalism Training Forum[12], and a follow up report in 2012, commissioned by the National Council for the Training of Journalists[13] cut through the lack of transparency for the first time.

They found that the levels of ethnic diversity remained 'troublingly low', in an industry where over half of those employed worked in London and the South East – the most ethnically and culturally diverse regions in the country.

Unsurprisingly, the surveys also revealed how unpaid internships were commonplace, making the profession an occupation where social class impacted on the likelihood of entering the industry.

During this time, I was delivering media training and consultancy through The Creative Collective for third sector organisations and NGOs, including the Refugee Council, MDI and Article 19. Working with journalists and editors in former communist countries in the Balkans on understanding intersectionality, the impact of hate speech, the exclusion of Roma people and recruiting women journalists was an eye-opener.

---

[12] (2002, July). Journalists at Work Their views on training, recruitment and conditions: An independent survey by the Journalism Training Forum. *Journalism Training Forum.* https://www.screenskills.com/media/1396/journalists_at_work_2002.pdf

[13] Spilsbury, Mark. (2018, October). Journalists at Work. Their views on training, recruitment and conditions. *National Council for the Training of Journalists.* https://www.nctj.com/wp-content/uploads/2021/08/JaW-Report-2018-web.pdf

I was unfailingly the only black person in the room. Any fear of having to confront unwelcomed or inappropriate racial tropes was quickly dashed. Unlike my experience in Britain, being black was viewed as an asset. My Black British journalist credentials and navigation of racism and discrimination carried weight. My lived experience was of genuine interest, and I didn't have to 'justify' my presence or thought leadership. What I did have to face was nuanced sexism.

Looking like I was in my mid-20s when I was in my late-30s, there was a tendency to show more deference to the older white male media trainers. When the relevant participants were challenged on this point over social drinks at the end of the programme, lively and honest debates ensued about gender politics in their respective countries.

The experience of working in countries where I didn't see any people of colour, apart from the occasional billboard featuring supermodel Naomi Campbell, allowed me to experience my blackness and woman-ness through a different lens, which was liberating.

Of course, I was operating in a privileged space with highly educated journalists and activists who prided themselves on their intellectual and philosophical acumen. I couldn't say the same while in equivalent spaces in Britain. I remember walking through various overwhelmingly white newsrooms in Fleet Street while doing a recce for our internship programme. Not only did I feel like an outsider, I felt my blackness being assessed through a colonially-imprinted lens. I had to ground myself in my value, buoyed by my knowledge, cultural self confidence and activist spirit.

My understanding of why reporting diversity is vital was expanded through my work with MDI. I was exposed to other cultures in their country of origin, often at risk of government oppression. Creating workshops and facilitating civic leaders, human rights organisations, NGOs, doctors and academics in countries like Morocco, Albania,

Hungary and Algeria to be media confident was humbling, exciting and life-changing.

Whether it was providing tailored consultancy to a civic organisation's staff and volunteers over three consecutive days, facilitating a five-day programme on how to run a media campaign, developing digital communications strategies on destigmatising HIV or challenging misreporting while being interviewed on live TV, the participants were fully engaged.

They brought their real-life experiences, passions and traumas to the table. They relished the role play and the opportunity to meet and interview real journalists while having the media demystified. They trusted me with their stories, worldviews, and points of difference, all within a structured and compassionate space. At the end, they left with an action plan and a personalised roadmap for change.

Little did I know that my collaborative relationship with MDI would hit another level of impact. In 2011 I was invited to create a Reporting Migration, Race and Ethnicity Module for MDI's new Diversity and the Media MA[14], the first of its kind. Hosted by the University of Westminster, the module provided a critical and practical assessment of journalistic practice and the cultural production and representation of race, ethnicity and migrancy in contemporary media, with a particular focus on print media.

During the months spent drafting the module, the Leveson Inquiry[15] - the largest public inquiry in British history - was gathering evidence on media abuse and phone hacking. By the time the MA was launched

[14] (2020, December 14) MA PROGRAMME: DIVERSITY AND THE MEDIA. *Media Diversity Institute.* https://www.media-diversity.org/ma-programme-diversity-and-the-media/

[15] Leveson, Lord Justice. (2012, November 29). Leveson Inquiry - Report into the culture, practices and ethics of the press. *Department for Culture, Media and Sport, UK.* https://www.gov.uk/government/publications/leveson-inquiry-report-into-the-culture-practices-and-ethics-of-the-press

in 2012, the inquiry was under fire for not robustly investigating discrimination and racism[16] after campaigning from civic organisations, public figures and journalists of colour.

When the inquiry reported in November 2012, Lord Leveson stated that "when assessed as a whole, the evidence of discriminatory, sensational or unbalanced reporting in relation to ethnic minorities, immigrants and/or asylum seekers, is concerning".

Leveson added that there were enough examples of "careless or reckless reporting" to conclude that discriminatory, sensational or unbalanced reporting in relation to ethnic minorities, immigrants and/ or asylum seekers is a feature of journalistic practice in parts of the press, rather than an aberration.

Dr Nafeez Mosaddeq Ahmed, in Race and Reform: Islam and Muslims and the British Media[17], 2012, said: "Research shows that not only do a third of the British population admit to racism but institutional racism is still pervasive in British social institutions from education to the judiciary. Despite regulation, codes of conduct and robust internal procedures, ethnic minorities are still underrepresented in the mainstream media. A picture that has barely improved over 10 years."

Against this backdrop, the MA was not only timely but ahead of the curve. The curriculum reflected the intersections of gender, disability, faith and racial identity and sexual orientation, and supplied a newsroom, practice-based environment for the status quo and media norms to be challenged.

---

[16] Ekeh, Chizom. (2012, Sep 27). Racism and the British press. *Operation Black Vote.* https://www.obv.org.uk/news-blogs/racism-and-british-press

[17] Ahmed, Dr. Nafeez Mosaddeq. (2012, July). Race and Reform. Islam and Muslims in the British Media. A Submission to the Leveson Inquiry. *Unitas Communications.* https://www.discoverleveson.com/evidence/Submission_by_Dr_Nafeez_Ahmed_on_behalf_of_Unitas_Communications/8052/media

A key element of the MA, which attracted a diverse range of students (from the UK, Serbia, Egypt, Malaysia, China and Brazil), was to inspire them to transfer the learning to their coverage of ethnic minorities, migration, race and racism in their respective countries. Two of my cohort went onto secure distinctions in their Masters, and 11 years later, the MA is thriving.

My relationship with MDI didn't end there. I became an MDI trustee in 2016 and have been part of its journey to becoming a significant influence globally, encouraging accurate and nuanced reporting on race, religion, ethnicity, class, age, disability, gender and sexual identity in numerous countries from China to the US.

Since my first interaction with MDI, the language on media diversity has changed, assisted by the proliferation of social media which continues to break stories as an alternative media platform for the global majority.

There is a considered shift away from using the acronym BAME to a multiplicity of hybrid self-definitions, as shown in this piece, including the terms black and minoritised or racialised communities. They all have a place.

Creative Diversity is the new buzz word. Inclusion is uttered as often, if not more, than diversity. The Covid pandemic's disproportionate impact on communities of colour, George Floyd's murder on 25th May 2020 and the BLM global protests inspired many organisations to declare their intention to become anti-racist organisations. The proof, though, is in the pudding.

We are now talking more openly about structural, systemic and inter-personal racism while racial justice and racial healing are part of the under-reported narrative of recovery and reparations as Grenfell and the Windrush Scandal remain unresolved.

Now faced with the fallout of Brexit and the cost of living crisis, we have a government and a national newspaper cluster that are predominantly centre right or right wing in tone. There is a sense that they have bought into Prime Minister David Cameron's view in 2011 that "state multiculturalism" had failed[18].

We have a Home Secretary Suella Braverman that sees deporting migrants to Rwanda as her professional dream[19]. News Corp's chief Rupert Murdoch has been outed for secret phone hacking settlements, including to Prince William in 2020[20], the very scandal the Leveson Inquiry shed light on back in 2011.

Where light isn't being systematically shed is on the media's progress on diversity and inclusion. The Creative Diversity Network[21] and its introduction of Diamond, a single online system used by the BBC, ITV, Channel 4, Paramount, UKTV and Sky to obtain consistent diversity data on programmes they commission, releases its findings annually.

That aside, it feels as if most newspapers and some broadcast outlets are lagging behind. This perception was reinforced in June 2020 when 50 journalists of colour accused UK newsrooms of repeatedly failing to improve diversity in the industry[22]. The Independent columnist Yasmin Alibhai-Brown said that "brilliant" young journalists are being missed

---

[18] (2011, February 5). State multiculturalism has failed, says David Cameron. *BBC News.* https://www.bbc.co.uk/news/uk-politics-12371994

[19] (2022, October 5). Suella Braverman, UK minister, slammed for saying deporting refugees to Rwanda is her 'dream'. *The New Arab.* https://www.newarab.com/news/suella-braverman-says-uk-rwanda-deportations-are-her-dream

[20] Waterson, Jim. (2023, April 25). Murdoch firm 'paid secret phone-hacking settlement to Prince William'. *The Guardian.* https://www.theguardian.com/uk-news/2023/apr/25/prince-william-murdoch-phone-hacking-claims-court-filings-prince-harry

[21] Creative Diversity Network. https://creativediversitynetwork.com/

[22] Tobitt, Charlotte. (2020, June 24). Fifty ethnic minority journalists urge faster action on diversity in newsrooms. *Press Gazette.* https://pressgazette.co.uk/news/fifty-ethnic-minority-journalists-urge-faster-action-on-diversity-in-newsrooms/

because of nepotism, laziness and ignorance from the people "making judgements about who should be there". They called on the Society of Editors (SoE) to do more.

Unfortunately, a year later, the SoE's executive director Ian Murray issued an uncleared statement rejecting the Duchess of Sussex's claim that parts of the media were racist[23]. This led 168 journalists, writers and broadcasters of colour to write an open letter claiming that Murray's statement proved the SoE was "an institution and an industry in denial".

The current stalemate at the BBC over its plans to significantly curtail its black radio shows after a sustained campaign in the black press, has raised fears that any diversity gains are being rolled back.

These unsettling developments remind me of a still relevant quote by media and culture academic Dr Anamik Saha from 2017[24], on the idea of media industry equality being advanced by sector diversity initiatives.

"The inclusion of ethnic minorities within the industry's dominant whiteness does not necessarily produce a more racially harmonious industrial condition. Black and minority ethnic creatives are often denied autonomy, editorial control, and must exist within an unaltered institutional climate where they remain subjected to various and habitual forms of racism. This suggests that more off-screen diversity does not necessarily produce 'better representation' on screen or neatly unsettle industry norms."

My conclusion is unequivocal. Our work is never done. Thirty years after qualifying as a journalist, and 23 years after meeting MDI's founder

[23] Bland, Archie. (2021, March 10). Society of Editors in turmoil over its statement on Meghan. *The Guardian.* https://www.theguardian.com/media/2021/mar/09/society-of-editors-claim-uk-media-not-racist-laughable

[24] Saha, Anamik. (2017). Race and the Cultural Industries. *Cambridge: Polity Press.*

Milica Pešić, I continue to pursue my mission for unheard stories to be told, now as part of Words of Colour[25], a purpose-driven immersive change agency I co-founded in 2006.

Using the principles of inclusive journalism, storytelling and racial justice, we aim to build sustainable models and ecosystems in different spaces, from universities and theatres to research bodies and publishers, and to develop writers, creatives and entrepreneurs of colour to be change agents.

My MDI journey may have ended in the autumn of 2022, when I stepped down as a trustee to make way for new voices to shape its promising future. But my learning continues.

[25] *Words of Colour*. https://wordsofcolour.co.uk/

Dr Naila Hamdy

Dr Naila Hamdy is associate dean for the School of Global Affairs and Public Policy at the American University in Cairo. She has authored numerous articles in international journals, book chapters, edited volumes and other contributions, covering the fields of journalism, global communication, and political engagement.

A media commentator, a public speaker and distinguished visiting professor, she has also been frequently invited to lecture at numerous universities worldwide.

She is a member of the board and a former president of the Arab-U.S. Association for Communication Educators (AUSACE) and a member of the board of the Broadcast Educators Association (BEA) representing the international division.

Photo credit: Ahmed Montaser

ENSURING DIVERSITY IN EGYPTIAN MEDIA

Egypt, a very populous nation of over 100 million and one of the most influential cultural powerhouses in the Arab region, has an extremely diverse population, although this is a subject rarely highlighted in public narratives.

Yes, Egypt is diverse in its makeup: it has people of different skin colors, different subcultures, different religions, and different genders. This is why representation in the media is vital. People need to see themselves in films, television dramas, and popular music; they need to see themselves in news and current events talk shows. When reviewing the history of Egyptian media and the past 25 years of my work as an academic in this field, it has been a challenge to find representation of minority groups and marginalized persons.

Media diversity flourishes in an environment that promotes the free flow of information and ideas in society, allowing media to provide a voice to, and satisfy the needs of, all of a nation's citizens. My understanding of diversity is that it is complex and should include diversity of source, diversity of outlet, and diversity of content. This degree of diversity is essentially a product of free expression in a democratic atmosphere.

So let us study that aspect in the context of Egypt.

To begin with, media in Egypt is and has always been controlled by the state, with ownership concentrated between government, sanctioned political parties, and state-approved private organizations. Obviously, this is not the ideal ecosystem for representation of diverse communities, since ownership affects content and public narratives are typically prescribed. But then again, it is not a totally bleak picture; there are some encouraging signs and good examples of diversifying representation.

Up until the mid-1990s, the Egyptian public only had access to state-owned and political parties' newspapers, along with sedate state-owned broadcasting services and a highly censored film and music industry. Playing the role of a parent, the government preferred to keep the public uninformed about many domestic and international events and misinformed about others, and even handpicked their entertainment. State censors had a tight grip on content: they chose which information was to be printed or broadcast and which point of view and what entertainment material was appropriate for public consumption. Other types of media - namely independent public service and community media - were banned. Conditions for diverse media did not exist.

It wasn't until the public had access to satellite television stations and the internet that the government allowed a much wider selection of media outlets. This occurred during the first decade of the 21st century - ironically, during the reign of the former authoritarian president Hosni Mubarak. But the easing of media restrictions was less likely due to any genuine desire on Mubarak's part than to other factors, such as the recognition that new communication technologies allowed everyone unlimited access to international media content and possible US pressure following 9/11 to boost liberalization and reform.

This was a revolutionary moment. In fact, Egyptians referred to the open skies as "the satellite revolution" and the digital transformation as "the internet revolution". Several private newspapers, such as *Al-Masry*

Al-Youm and *Al-Shorouk*, were launched. Private television stations such as the *Mehwar* and ON TV channels were born. These news organizations published and aired material on topics never discussed or talked about publicly before. Their work ranged from investigative journalism stories on corruption to talk shows addressing previously hidden social ills.

A marked openness in film themes also became apparent. Government censors relaxed their guidelines. In addition, the exposure to the outside world that came through abundant satellite stations and access to the internet gave ordinary citizens a voice online. The winds of change were sweeping away numerous media restrictions.

With that being said, it was not until after the 2011 Egyptian uprisings and the fall of former president Mubarak that media had the freest, most chaotic, most eclectic, and most heterogeneous age that I can recall in Egypt's recent history. Unfortunately, the bubble has burst. In the past few years, ownership patterns and media content have changed once again.

After a vibrant scene of somewhat diverse ownership, and the beginning of openness to new forms of media, the brief instant led to a period of acquisitions. That, in turn, has led to more concentrated ownership. Today one private company, United Media Services, owns nearly all private media in the country. This company has acquired or launched new media outlets and media services, including production and distribution companies and platforms. Not surprisingly, the same company has also acquired public relations and advertising agencies. It is known to be owned by handpicked businesspersons close to the ruling regime and is often referred to in conversation as a front for the military intelligence services.

Thus, as I write this essay, the media environment has become constrained in unprecedented ways, with virtually all media messages serving the interests of a small number of owners. Even popular internet-based Egyptian sites fall under the same pressures, and those that venture outside of the guided narrative are simply blocked by authorities.

And as if this were not enough, there has also been a purposeful tightening of the noose around the press.

The turning point took place when armed members of the National Security agency stormed the offices of the Press syndicate, a labor union, for the first time since its establishment in 1941. They attacked the journalists there and detained two who had dared to challenge a controversial political decision. Overall, we have recently witnessed a greater rise in draconian disciplinary and criminal accountability measures against journalists, efforts to control content, and underhanded threats against media professionals than the country has seen in decades, all under the pretext of protecting national interests.

Diversity will suffer in such a situation, since the representation of marginalized groups would be politically sensitive and undesirable. So, for those journalists and media professionals who still dare to work, self-censorship is the only method of survival.

But not all is bleak.

In the case of Egypt, I believe that, even with the absence of freedoms, the state can take action to enable a freer media environment and to at least provide opportunity for Egyptian citizens, who are equal according to the constitution, to be heard and to enjoy positive representations in the media.

In this context, diversity, meaning the differences among human beings, is mostly limited to religion, gender, social class, geographical location, ethnicity, and physical abilities. In some cases, the media does present these diversities in unbiased narratives that will reach and strike a chord with the audience. The concept of diversity is relatively new in Egypt but there are many instances of conscious efforts made to improve representation of the under-represented.

In Egypt, one of the main minority groups is the Copts, the Egyptian Christians, who make up an estimated 7 to 15 percent of the population, according to official sources. The exact figure is debated, supposedly unknown, and never published by the government.

Since it is impossible to know the exact number - the country's census records certainly contain the answer - it is very likely that the reason for concealing it relates to the perceived political sensitivity of the issue. It is possible to make this assumption because Egyptian identification cards list a person's religion. Therefore, an exact number must exist. Public knowledge of this number would also certainly impact media representation. In addition, a smaller number of religious minorities from other Christian denominations also exist, but are nearly completely omitted from the media.

The underlying truth is that media attention to minorities is related to the type of political leadership at a given moment. At the current time, with the heightened support of the president, Abdel Fatah El-Sisi, for the Copts of Egypt, the media has covered more Coptic affairs, included more of their voices and treated their concerns with more respect than in earlier periods.

Nevertheless, most of the news coverage and media presentations are related to religious ceremonies and visits of government officials to Coptic institutions. In contrast, incidents of violence against Copts, which have been occurring for decades, do not get enough play. The rationale for not fully covering these crimes is the belief that to do so is portraying Egypt in a negative light, which in itself is prohibited.

It is undeniable that the film industry, which is arguably one of the country's most impactful creative forces, has grappled with the inclusion and portrayal of Copts. If you go through a list of Egyptian films that represent Copts, you will find that in the politically liberal '30s, '40s, and '50s they appear as equal to Muslims. In the '60s, the salient political theme changed to "unity among Egyptians," and thus diversity was not emphasized at all. The films of the '70s, '80s, and '90s mostly depicted Copts as victims of Islamic extremists who refuse to accept non-Muslims.

Real change coincided with the relatively freer media environment of the Mubarak era. Among the realistic representations of Copts in films was *I Love Cinema*, directed by Osama Fawzy in 2004, which focused on the life of a Coptic family and reminded audiences of the realities of Egypt's pluralistic society. A series of equally powerful films representing the same community soon followed. Several of these films met with harsh criticism, especially from the Coptic clergy, who consider representations focused on the challenges of daily life rather than religious belief and practices to be demeaning and therefore offensive.

Women, by contrast, are not a numerical minority, but despite that they have often been represented poorly in the media. Nonetheless, state support of gender equality over the years, especially in the last three decades, has led to considerable improvements in the depiction of women.

There is also no doubt that the development of new media in the '90s, as noted by the media scholar Naomi Sakr, occurred simultaneously with the increase of women's groups and associations. Arab media was changing, she said. And she was right. It did. Perhaps the improvements have not gone as far as they might have, but there has still been significant progress. Egypt is a country with a strong commitment to development, and Goal 5 of the UN Sustainable Development Goals addresses gender equality and the empowerment of women and girls. This in turn has led to state action to ensure equality in media representation.

For instance, the government-backed National Council for Women monitors media and calls out examples of stereotyping and sexualized representation. One moment that comes to mind was the 2019 release of the song "Salmonella" by the artist Tamim Younis. The song's lyrics describe how a man, after a woman turns down his marriage proposal, begins to threaten her, insult her, and defames her publicly. The song caused controversy because many feared it would encourage violence against women; others, including Younis himself, defended it as an effort to make fun of insecure and violent men and disagreed that it undermined women.

The government-backed council denounced the song as sexist and as encouraging bullying and violence against women. The council contacted Google for removal of what it viewed as inappropriate material.

Since this is government-backed feminism, the outcomes have at times been effective. In addition, the president of the country has been exceptionally supportive of women, further enabling their empowerment.

That doesn't mean that this support always translates to suitable representation of women in the media. Many Egyptian films continue to portray women as the lesser gender - weaker, dumber, and helpless. Some of the most popular films have normalized sexual harassment, which is rampant in Egypt. That being said, many films and television dramas have also given women full voice.

Cairo 678, a 2010 feature film directed by Mohamed Diab, addressed the issue of women's exposure to sexual harassment on a daily basis and how to take action against it. More recently, during the holy month Ramadan of 2022, when filmmakers, actors, and scriptwriters race to produce and highlight their best work, one series stood out: *Faten Amal Harbi*, written by the eminent journalist and writer Ibrahim Eissa, directed by Mohamed El-Adl, and starring Nelly Karim. This series about the antiquated personal status laws portrays the lead actress as a strong woman, a dedicated mother and provider for her family, trapped in a legal battle over her divorce. These are just two among many examples of productions with meaningful representation and social impact.

The 2021 award-winning film *Feathers*, directed by Omar El Zohairy, offers a brutal analysis of patriarchy. The lead character in this avant-garde production is a downtrodden, meek woman whose attitude slowly changes as she discovers some self-respect. Despite the skill with which the woman's transformation in consciousness is portrayed, the film received much criticism for going too far even by members of the supposedly liberal movie industry, several of whom stormed out of a film festival showing as a sign of protest.

Advertising as a supporting medium also plays an important role in promoting inclusivity and diversity. In the early 2000s, I served on a thesis committee for a student who had studied the portrayal of women in Egyptian TV ads. Not surprisingly, the literature review showed that men were portrayed in professional settings or outdoors, while women were mostly portrayed at home using products for cleaning, cooking and other household activities. Even in these domestic portrayals of women, men generally provided the voice-overs as the authorities on whatever products were being sold. This form of predictable stereotyping continues.

As for news media, I would say from an anecdotal perspective that the increase in women in parliament, government, and formal professions, has led as a natural consequence to improvements in the representation of women. Yet rarely is there a focus on some of the issues that are of particular concern to women, such as sexual harassment, forced marriage, marital abuse, discriminatory laws, and deprivation of inheritance.

And the majority of women, especially poorer ones or those who live in rural communities, are often omitted all together.

Oddly enough, although veiled women are the majority in Egypt, they are much rarer in news and the entertainment media. Perhaps social media is the space that has been freest for women who choose to dress conservatively. Deemed not modern enough to be seen on any of the local channels, whether owned by the private sector or the state, they are nearly invisible on the airwaves. Today, on most TV stations that display the slogan logo "The New Republic" in reference to a newly envisioned modern Egypt, you will notice that the females, particularly those who present the news or programs, have a certain appearance: young, pretty, long hair, wearing very sharp professional suits or dresses - an image disconnected from the reality of the lives of many if not most viewers.

Living in Egypt means you cannot escape noticing the sharp divisions between social classes. Social class representation suffers on countless levels. The working class and farmers are associated with negative stereotypes, such as that they are poorly educated country buffoons or unrefined laborers deserving to be humiliated for their social position. Oddly enough, rich people are also negatively stereotyped, in their case as corrupt, deviants and immoral.

Only members of the middle class escape this negativity, mostly because they do not experience the inhumane living conditions of the poor, nor do they have the wealth that allows them to behave as decadently as the rich.

Social classism is obvious in Egyptian media, with two distinct types of content. Highbrow productions, such as films that intellectually stimulate their audiences and Western media, appeal to the cosmopolitan and often well-traveled upper class. The lower and middle classes consume local media that better represent them, their lives, their values and aspirations.

This has always been the case. Now that Netflix Arabia and other non-Egyptian companies have begun to produce locally adapted US series, it is clear that a show like the Egyptian version of *Suits*, for example, has no frame of reference for the majority of the public. Set in a law firm, this legal drama featuring an A list of actors, remains heavily inspired by the original version, which is very far from the experience of most people, including those who work in Egypt's legal profession.

Social classism is obvious even where you might not expect it, such as on food shows. For the longest time, Egyptian TV shows featured Westernized-looking women who made chocolate-covered American cupcakes on the air. It was not until the unusual turmoil and changes that occurred immediately after the 2011 protests, and the launch of the short-lived Channel 25, that the network owner Mohamed Gohar plucked Ghalia, his sister's domestic helper, to star in a cooking show. Making dishes that poorer people knew and could afford was unheard of, and Ghalia quickly won hearts with her charismatic simplicity. She became an unlikely but refreshing symbol of social justice.

Perhaps music is where this schism is the most visible. The emergence of *mahragant* (festival) Egyptian street music from underground to mainstream was a product of the 2011 revolution. The social and political changes at the time became a catalyst for this development, and *mahragant* has proved to be exceptionally popular among youth. The lyrics reflect the life, loves, and everyday struggles of the slum-area poor in Egypt. Songs include obscenities and are viewed as vulgar and inappropriate by more conservative older people and government censors. As recently as 2016, *mahragant* music was banned from the radio. Even more recently, the popular singers Hassan Shakoush and Omar Kamal were temporarily banned from the music syndicate that controls much of the industry for their references to drinking alcohol and smoking hashish in the song "*Bent El-Geran*" (Girl Next Door). Soon afterwards, all *mahragant* music was banned in Egypt, although this rule was later rescinded.

Closely related to social classism in the media is the representation of residents of certain geographical locations, especially Upper Egyptians - inhabitants of the south region of Egypt - and the distinct ethnic groups of Bedouins and Nubians. Upper Egyptians are often misrepresented in films and drama, framed as stupid and old-fashioned, leading residents of Cairo to hold prejudicial stereotypes about them. Egypt is Cairo-centric due to the city's vast population and job opportunities, and residents still have warped perceptions of those who live elsewhere. Ethnic groups are also misrepresented or not represented at all.

Often, we see Nubians portrayed as doormen or waiters. I cannot recall an instance in which a Nubian was presented as a professor or doctor. Racist comments are often made on air about Nubians, mocking their darker skin. The infamous lawyer and former parliamentarian Mortada Mansour called a football player a "doorman" during an interview, implying that he was less deserving of respect. As for the Bedouins, and specifically those of the South Sinai region, the predominant stereotype is that of an outlaw, the "other", the non-Egyptian, and more recently the terrorist. Little of the real life and identity of Bedouins is shown in Egyptian media. One exception was the portrayal of the loyal Bedouin in the 2019 patriotic war film *The Passage*.

After the events of 2011, media content underwent a major change. One unusual example was the advertising created for mobile telephone companies. Several ads revolved around diversity and unity, depicting an Egypt full of many types of people. A glance at the Vodafone Egypt website shows the company's focus on diversity and inclusion, among both its customer base and policy initiatives. This may not be a grassroots-Egyptian idea, since this is probably a global Vodafone policy, yet the effort to localize the notion is certainly notable. The ads were so popular and widely seen that they must have had some impact on the Egyptian public.

When reviewing the representation of genders earlier in this essay, I purposefully identified gender as male and female simply because these are the two socially constructed genders and most commonly accepted to be the norm with all their associated roles and behaviors. Homosexuality is not criminalized in Egypt, but that does not mean that it goes unpunished either. LBGTIQ+ people have little support from the public and are frequently charged with debauchery. News coverage of LBGTIQ+ arrests has been exceptionally negative and often dehumanizing.

The most prominent example is the case of the Cairo 52 in the 1990s, which began with a raid on a gay party on a boat. The raid resulted in the arrest of 52 men, nearly half of whom received severe prison sentences. A more recent incident, the "Rainbow Flag Case," involved the arrest of several young LBGTIQ+ activists for waving a rainbow flag at a 2017 concert of the Lebanese indie band *Mashrou' Leila*. The band's lead singer is openly gay and advocates for LBGTIQ+ rights. Media coverage of the story and subsequent arrests, particularly in state news outlets, was ruthless. The media-generated moral panic destroyed any chance of support or legitimacy for what is viewed as deviant behavior and the promotion of harmful ideas arising from Western influences in a nation that regards itself as upholding high morals. The situation led the Supreme Media Regulatory Council to issue an order to ban the appearance of homosexuals or promotion of homosexuality on Egyptian media.

Yet cinema and television programs, as stated earlier, have a higher ceiling of freedom on taboo topics. Depictions of cross-dressing and homosexuality have always existed with some frequency in the media of Egypt. Nonetheless, most of these depictions are negative, in line with the country's religious values, whether Muslim or Christian. On occasion, more liberal depictions have appeared on our screens, escaping official censorship but never the criticism of the more conservative segments of society. Filmmakers like Youssef Chahin in the 1978 *Alexandria Why?* and Yousri Nasrallahin's 1993 film *Mercedes* have depicted gay characters and homosexual experiences. *The Yacoubian Building*, a 2006 film directed by Marwan Hamed, realistically portrays a gay character who has a relationship with a police conscript from rural Egypt.

However, Egypt as a nation prefers to reinforce its heterosexual identity. *The Yacoubian Building* stirred much controversy in parliament at the time, while parliamentarians debated whether such a depiction promoted immorality and an undesirable homosexual identity. Not much has changed on that front. Egypt continues to view the depiction of homosexuality as incompatible with the image of a strong and principled state. And so the argument continues. When Netflix aired its 2021 Arabic version of *Perfect Strangers*, it sparked public debate on both traditional and social media about whether homosexuality should be tolerated.

Media can improve social acceptance by helping to normalize differences in people. The public can better accept persons with disabilities and even find many to admire or relate to when they are portrayed positively and inclusively in the media. In the case of Egypt, and similar to the coverage of Copts and women, only a top-down directive will improve the depiction of the disabled. President El-Sisi has shown great concern for citizens with special needs; he has started a special foundation and has personally adopted this cause.

According to the Egyptian government, the population includes around 11 to 14 million differently abled persons, and they have mostly been ignored by media in the past. In contrast, the president meets with the disabled and invites them to the World Youth Forum, an Egyptian government-sponsored summit that gathers youth from different cultures and nationalities. He attends events related to the International Day for the Differently Abled, and has called on the media to include the lives of disabled citizens and highlight their successes. These efforts appear to have made a difference, at least from my personal observation.

In conclusion, despite the lack of freedom that is a prerequisite for full media diversity, it is possible to achieve some of the desired goals by having the state impose direct obligations on news and entertainment organizations. Just as the Egyptian parliament has a quota for women, Copts, and other minorities or marginalized groups for the purpose of allowing them fair representation, the same principle can be applied to media diversity. A wide range of voices in media can be ensured by the media regulation authorities.

Dr Zahera Harb

Dr Zahera Harb is International Journalism Studies Cluster lead at City, University of London. She has published widely on Journalism and Politics in the Arab countries. Her publications include an edited collection titled *Reporting the Middle East: The Practice of News in the 21st Century* (IB Tauris 2017). She is co-editor of *Middle East Journal of Culture and Communication* and associate editor of the internationally renowned academic journal *Journalism Practice*. She is currently board member trustee of Dart Centre Europe for Journalism and Trauma, Marie Colvin Journalists' Network and member of Arab Reporters for Investigative Journalism (ARIJ) board of directors. She also sits on the board of the UK Press Recognition Panel (PRP). Zahera previously served as member to the UK broadcast regulator Ofcom content board and board member/trustee of the Ethical Journalism Network. Before moving to the UK, Zahera worked, for over a decade, as a broadcast Journalist in her native country Lebanon, for local and International news organisations.

DE-WESTERNISATION OF JOURNALISM STUDIES ENHANCES SECTOR'S DIVERSITY AND INCLUSION

Twenty years ago, I realised that my journey into British academia would be full of challenges. It was that moment when my first-year undergraduate students, found it strange I was not able to relate to their British popular culture references. I was still at the early stages of my PhD journey, when I got a part time job as a graduate teaching assistant. Teaching these upper and middle class, privileged, young students proved to be tricky.

They were not very familiar with tutors from different cultural backgrounds who speak English with a foreign accent. I remember one occasion, after I earned a full-time lecturer post at a highly reputable university in England, when concerns were raised about a white British student missing several classes in a row. Upon being asked about why he had been missing so many classes, he gave this answer; "I do not understand the tutor's accent".

Do not jump to conclusions! He was not referring to me - he was speaking of my Canadian colleague, a native English speaker with a noticeable Canadian accent.

This incident made me aware that students at major universities in England are not the best at understanding what diversity means and what it brings to the educational system, especially in the field of media and journalism studies.

Research has indicated that female lecturers, especially those from an ethnic minority background, get lower evaluation scores from students than their white male colleagues. Still, many English universities have not factored that into their staff evaluation system.

According to the UK government,[1] around 73% of entering undergraduates in 2019/2020 were white Caucasians. The other 27% were divided between Asians, blacks, mixed race, and other. This percentage is barely changing. The Higher Education Statistics Agency reported in 2020 (HESA)[2], that only 2% of the overall academics in British universities are black. Other ethnic minorities do not score higher than that. In 2021, I discovered that among the 941 academics listed on my current employer's website, only five - including me - are of Arab ethnicity. That makes us the minority among the minority.

We are the other. In 2011, I was the first non-British, non-European - the first person whose ethnic and cultural background was "other" - to be hired by my current department. However, since then, we have grown slightly in numbers and presence. As black and ethnic minority academics in journalism, we mirror the poor state of diversity in the media industry in the country at large.

Diversity in the UK media industry has been a topic of discussion and concern for several decades. A 2019 study by ScreenSkills[3] in

[1] (2022, June 9). First year entrants onto undergraduate study. *UK government.* https://www.ethnicity-facts-figures.service.gov.uk/education-skills-and-training/higher-education/first-year-entrants-onto-undergraduate-degrees/latest

[2] Adams, Richard. (2020, February 27). Fewer than 1% of UK university professors are black, figures show. *The Guardian.* https://www.theguardian.com/education/2020/feb/27/fewer-than-1-of-uk-university-professors-are-black-figures-show

[3] (2019, May 21). New research reveals detailed look at the UK screen industries workforce. (press release). *ScreenSkills.* https://www.screenskills.com/press-releases/new-research-reveals-detailed-look-at-the-uk-screen-industries-workforce/

collaboration with British Film Institute (BFI), indicated that less than 10% of those working in the UK's TV and film industry are from black and ethnic minority backgrounds. No significant change has occurred since then. The industry is perceived as exclusive with a culture that is difficult for those from diverse backgrounds to penetrate.

I come from Lebanon, the small Arab country on the Mediterranean coast, where I worked for many years as a broadcast journalist. By the time I resigned from my job in Beirut and left for the UK to pursue my postgraduate studies in Journalism and Political Communication, I had already established a successful career and become a household name in Lebanon as a broadcaster.

It was not long into my studies that I realised that all my journalism experience and that of my Lebanese colleagues needed to be contextualised within western scholarship traditions if to be taken seriously. None of my research arguments about local journalism practice would be viewed as authoritative or significant unless they were grounded in the framework of Western theories, concepts and experiences.

I am grateful to my PhD supervisors, who believed that my argument and arguments introduced by the unique experience of one non-western nation, could be indeed a significant addition to International Journalism scholarship. I have discovered throughout my years working in academia in the UK that it is down to individual scholars' openness to engage with ideas emerging from outside western doctrines that we are able to read significant scholarship that speaks of other realities.

My PhD, later adapted and published as a book, explored the world of journalists who cover atrocities caused by foreign military invasions. I wrote previously[4] about an interview producer who was interested in

[4] Harb, Zahera. (2022, March 9). "Ukraine war: Is impartiality always key to quality journalism?" *AlJazeera.com*, https://www.aljazeera.com/opinions/2022/3/9/is-absolute-impartiality-always-a-necessity-in-journalism

having me as a guest for a household name show at an established British broadcaster. When she heard about how I am arguing a different approach to understanding objectivity in journalism, she dismissed the whole argument. She seemed unwilling to open up to ideas of objectivity seen as factual and not neutral. Ideas that are not influenced by western experiences and doctrines. My book was never featured on that show. When the Ukraine war fell upon us the narrative of coverage shifted to match what I argued years before.

Diversity is about engaging with knowledge and scholarship influenced by experiences outside the western hemisphere. The late Palestinian-American thinker and literature professor Edward Said speaks of dominant knowledge as that produced by those who have the power and means not just to produce it but also to disseminate it.

We are working at changing that. Many academics from diverse backgrounds, including those of us at the journalism department at City, University of London, are working on de-westernising our curriculum. We want it to reflect non-western scholarship as much as it reflects western theses. De-Westernization represents a revision of the power relations in global academic knowledge production and dissemination.

Scholars from the Global South have struggled for decades for international recognition of their voices and intellectual contributions to a global academic community. A de-westernization movement has emerged in journalism and media studies, as seen in the rise of global comparative studies and in the growing numbers of non-western scholars being invited to present their work at international conferences previously dominated by western intellectuals.

Another movement has also been gaining momentum–the de-colonisation of journalism and media studies. ***De-westernisation*** asks to revisit the power relations in global academic knowledge production and dissemination and ***De-colonisation*** challenges the uncritical adoption of research epistemologies and methods favoured by former colonial powers in efforts to solve local problems, since these approaches fail to consider the complexities of non-Western societies and communities.

As a journalist from Lebanon, I have been steeped in journalism and media scholarship from the US and Britain. My PhD project engaged with reflective ethnography analysing if our practices as Lebanese journalists in covering Israeli assaults on our country align with the academic literature on propaganda published in the west. Propaganda (in its negative connotation), is what we were often accused of. I also engaged with the question of news objectivity in our coverage of those assaults and the human tragedies they inflicted.

Being trained as a journalist in Holland and the UK, I viewed objectivity as the cornerstone of my understanding of my own practice. It was also in the accounts of my colleagues whom I interviewed for my research. When one professor asked me if we were taught about objectivity in journalism school in Beirut, I was reminded that objectivity is actually an Anglo-American construct. At that point, I realised that the journalism objectivity they claim in the Anglo-American journalism culture might be somehow different to ours. I started investigating new understanding for both notions: propaganda and objectivity.

For propaganda I had to dig deeper than the modern negative understanding of the term, which took me to the propaganda campaigns of the suffragette movement in 1866 and the church campaigns as early as 1600s and also to the campaigns that propagated Islam in far East Asia through trade (the Silk Road). I studied our coverage within the context of these campaigns and introduced the new understanding of "Liberation propaganda" (see Harb 2011)[5] and as Tele Liban former TV chairman Fouad Naim coined it "the propaganda of the truth".

[5] Harb, Zahera. (2011). Channels of Resistance in Lebanon, Liberation Propaganda, Hezbollah and the Media, *IB Tauris, London*.

To understand our objectivity, I had to question my Lebanese colleagues' understanding of what does objectivity mean to them and how they had applied it to their coverage? After questioning their understanding and digging deeper into the matter, I concluded that objectivity to them meant being factual but not being neutral.

My research took on a new notion of objectivity introduced by two Egyptian scholars Muhammad Nawawi and Adel Iskander in their book *Al-Jazeera* (2002), which explored the Arabic channel's coverage of the Afghanistan war in 2001, the international sanctions against Iraq in the 90s and the Israeli Palestinian Conflict. They termed it as "contextual objectivity". I found the term fit closely with what we as Lebanese journalists understood of objectivity.

Back in the day, very few accepted the term, contextual objectivity, within the Anglo-American academic community. Later on, other studies started emerging questioning the notion of objectivity and its connotation of ultimate neutrality.

The problematic push back against the term came from the industry and practitioners, which brings me to the example and point made above. To De-Westernise journalism studies we need to de-westernise journalism as a profession from fixed ontologies of what it means to produce quality journalism. Journalism values of balance and impartiality, for example, have proven to be disputable even within western context.

In 2018, The BBC admitted applying[6] "false balance" in its reporting on climate crisis. Their attempt to strike balance in the coverage meant balancing scientific analysis and data with commentary from global warming deniers. Fran Unsworth, the former BBC head of news at the time, sent out a statement advising BBC journalists to consider "false balance" when reporting on climate issues.

[6] Carrington, Damian. (2018, September 7). BBC admits 'we get climate change coverage wrong too often'. *The Guardian.* https://www.theguardian.com/environment/2018/sep/07/bbc-we-get-climate-change-coverage-wrong-too-often

In recent years, discussion about Impartiality and its understanding came to light with the case of Naga Munchetty[7]. The BBC had to reverse its decision to sanction the BBC Breakfast show presenter for breaching the guidelines on impartiality rule. This came after Munchetty expressed on air a personal response to the former US president, Donald Trump's statement that four American congresswomen of colour should "go back... to the infested places from which they came". This triggered a legitimate question among many UK journalists and civil societies organisation, whether impartiality is to also be sought when it comes to racism and if journalists should be censored, under the auspices of impartiality and refrain from calling racism by its name.

A team of international scholars, led by Thomas Hanitzsch[8], Worlds of Journalisms Study (2011) has been a good step to understand how journalists perceive journalism and their role in different parts of the world. In it the authors concluded that journalists across different countries believe that objectivity is a universal value and not only an Anglo American one. And I agree with that. Journalists I interviewed across two Arab countries, Lebanon and Egypt, affirm the same, but what objectivity do they mean. Their understanding of the term is what matters.

De Westernising journalism and journalism studies, is to give space to those different and maybe difficult ideas to emerge and introduce new epistemologies that fit local communities.

---

[7] Waterson, Jim. (2019, September 30). Naga Munchetty: BBC reverses decision to censure presenter. *The Guardian.* https://www.theguardian.com/media/2019/sep/30/naga-munchetty-bbc-reverses-decision-to-censure-presenter

[8] Hanitzsch, Thomas., Hanusch, Folker., Mellado, Claudia., Anikina, Maria., Berganza, Rosa., Cangoz, Incilay., Coman, Mihai., Hamada, Basyouni., Hernández, María Elena., Karadjov, Christopher D., Moreira, Sonia Virginia., Mwesige, Peter G., Plaisance, Patrick Lee., Reich, Zvi., Seethaler, Josef., Skewes, Elizabeth A., Vardiansyah Noor, Dani. & Yuen, Edgar Kee Wang. (2011). MAPPING JOURNALISM CULTURES ACROSS NATIONS. *Journalism Studies,* 12:3, 273-293 AND Hanitzsch, Thomas. & Mellado, Claudia. (2011). What Shapes the News around the World? How Journalists in Eighteen Countries Perceive Influences on Their Work. *International Journal of Press/Politics* 16(3) 404–426.

Going back to Edward Said's thesis, the power of producing knowledge is in the hands of those who have the means to pay for the production of knowledge.

In my role as associate editor and co-editor for academic journals, I process many articles that come from low-income countries. Some feature excellent research, yet they rarely get cited. Citation follows mostly buzz words generated mainly in American scholarship and are followed across. An article written by a white American male scholar focused on a single case study or single newsroom will get more attention and citations than an article that explores journalism and disinformation in a country in the southern hemisphere. An article on news practices in the United States is often universally generalised. The US is not seen as a region within the media research community, whereas all other national centred research is seen as research that is region focused and is situated within regional scholarship. The Anglo-American scholarship is universal and the rest is regional.

To de-westernise Journalism studies we need to de-westernise the structure and approach that we all follow in the world of academic publishing. I can speak of articles rejected by reviewers who clearly based their decisions on prejudice and a sense of intellectual superiority, if not to assume more obnoxious reasons.

The global academic world needs to give more space to research coming from the so-called "Global South" conducted by researchers in the "Global South". We need to support those researchers' position within global academia. We would still be restricted to those writing in English, but it can be a start. Their research could also generate universal outcomes. We need to allow space for research that does not necessarily conform to Western trends and doctrine. We need to allow researchers to explore ideas that address and focus on their own local contexts. It has become vital to give space to the power of arguments and not to the power of western epistemologies.

We need to accept that there is a world of philosophy and philosophers beyond the English language domain that allows researchers to make sense of what is happening around them in their own journalism culture and that there is something to learn from those research endeavours.

Diversity means acceptance of others from cultural and educational backgrounds different from your own. Diversity means to acknowledge and recognize that those "other" cultures have as much legitimacy and as much to offer the world as yours.

Dr Eric Heinze

Dr Eric Heinze (Maitrise *distinction*, Paris; J.D. *cum laude*, Harvard; PhD *cum laude*, Leiden) is Professor of Law and Humanities at Queen Mary University of London, and has recently served as General Rapporteur on the Criminalization of Hate Speech for the International Academy of Comparative Law. Heinze's books on free speech include *The Most Human Right: Why Free Speech is Everything* (The MIT Press, 2022) and *Hate Speech and Democratic Citizenship* (Oxford University Press, 2016), along with over 100 major articles. He has been a Fulbright Fellow (Utrecht), DAAD fellow (Berlin), and Chateaubriand Fellow (Paris), as well as holding grants from the Nuffield Foundation and from Harvard University. He was Project Leader for the four-nation EU consortium Memory Laws in European and Comparative Perspectives (2016-19).

MEDIA DIVERSITY AND THE PERILS OF PANIC

A few years ago, a fellow academic told me about a surprise homophobic moment in her workplace. It happened while she was teaching an undergraduate tutorial, and the assigned topic was gay marriage.

A student raised his hand to speak out against it, declaring that homosexuality violates religious and moral values. Caught off guard, my friend fired back with a predictable stock of politically correct boilerplate: Britain is a multicultural society, we all need to think carefully before making these types of statements, it is important to consider the feelings of other class members. In short, she stopped the discussion.

On these sorts of issues my friend usually takes broadly left-of-centre views. She had taught the course for several years with no hitches, so, being caught off guard, she panicked. She later felt comfortable enough to tell me this story because I have always been "out" and had published a fair amount on gender and sexuality. I seemed like someone she could confide in.

Imagine her shock when I told her she had handled the class all wrong. I told her that she should not have cut the discussion short. She should have let it continue.

TABOO TOPICS

What? Allow a student to blurt out homophobia? In a university classroom? In London, a city proud of its values of openness and pluralism?

For lack of any subtler way of answering these questions, I will summarise my response as follows: Yes. That is precisely what she should have done. She should have allowed the student to spout homophobia. Of course, this was not the response that I, a gay male working in British academia, was supposed to have.

"Just let the student carry on speaking," I explained. "That way you hand the problem back to the class and let them work it out on their own. Just ask the other students what *they* think." Otherwise the dissident student was not having gay rights explained to him, but was merely being shamed into accepting them.

My friend was not convinced: "But then what do I do if they just sit there without saying anything?" Of course, group silence may mean many things. It may mean that the students understand the complexities of an issue, which would be a good first step. One of the biggest mistakes we can make in these situations is to equate silent audiences with stupid ones.

But far more likely from my experience, the students may *not* sit silent. They may talk. In fact, they may talk a great deal. They may come to surprisingly good resolutions without the lecturer ever having to intervene.

Another option would have been to break the students into groups and have them work on the following problem: *In a democracy, if some people, indeed even a majority of people, find an otherwise harmless practice immoral, does this mean that the law should give effect to their views by banning such conduct?* Surely this is one of those vintage undergraduate debating points. You can easily fill an hour with these types of discussions, which sometimes fire up even the most bored of students.

The most effective way to teach gay rights is to take the risk of allowing students to come to realisations on their own, not to impose dogmas. Tolerance-by-decree and truth-by-fiat are illusions. They are false friends to groups that have experienced social exclusion.

THE STREISAND EFFECT

But even if this free speech principle can work within the four walls of the university classroom, does it work in the same way through the anarchy of today's mass media? Can it resolve the controversies stirring around that ominous watchword of our early 21st century – "cancel culture"?

Even if my colleague had allowed the discussion of gay marriage to go forward, a lecturer is usually in charge of the classroom and can actively guide the discussion in ways often absent in the world of electronic media. So my classroom analogy might seem naïve. Perhaps it places too much faith in an ideal advocated in 1859 by John Stuart Mill. In his famous tract *On Liberty,* Mill had argued that the freedom to air even wrong ideas would allow them to be put to the test and openly defeated by better ideas. This concept is sometimes called the "marketplace of ideas," even if Mill never actually used that phrase.

Admittedly, there are plenty of problems with this marketplace ideal. For example, while responding to my friend with some confidence, I was certainly in no position to offer guarantees that the students would leave the classroom with better ideas in their minds than those with which they had entered.

Indeed, what if my friend had encouraged the discussion to continue, only for the homophobic student to end up prevailing, which might well have happened if he had been a sufficiently skilled debater? More importantly, this is not just a classroom risk. The risk seems greater *outside* the classroom in the wild west of today's online media, where—in the words of another grandee, Jonathan Swift—"Falsehood flies, and the Truth comes limping after it."

That concern has sparked even more panic around what in recent years have become ubiquitous controversies, namely, about trans rights. Many trans advocates refuse to engage in any kind of organised debate about their rights. They insist that they cannot engage in a fair or rational debate with rivals who deny their very humanity, insofar as gender identity remains integral to individual personhood and dignity. They add that once they can be dehumanised in this way, it is a very short step to their facing immediate violence. Given the small numbers of trans people, this concern is understandable.

Yet here again: I dissent – though I certainly appreciate the plight of trans people. What we need to recall is that many groups, such as women or members of racial, ethnic, religious or national minorities that are often vastly outnumbered by the majority, have had to fight for essential rights. These fights have at times prompted open debates that have seemed futile or humiliating for militants at the vanguard.

By definition, if a group is fighting for fundamental rights that have already long been enjoyed by the more privileged strata in society, then in some sense those group members too are fighting against an assumption of their inferiority. To state the point simply: An assumption of lesser humanity is not what blocks the debate, rather it is what the debate is all about.

The sooner we realise this, the more candid and productive the debate will be. Yes, there is still plenty of room for further progress but, at least in the West, no one can doubt that conditions for many traditionally excluded groups have considerably improved since, say, the mid-20th century—at least if we look at statistics on education, employment, and other basic life contexts.

In other words, Mill's ideal is not as naïve as it might at first seem, even if things do not always run as smoothly or in the linear way that he sometimes seems to suggest. It is a process that runs in fits and starts. Perhaps for every three steps forward we fall two steps back, but that is still a step achieved, which is more than we get when discussions are halted entirely.

Even when censoring hurtful speech seems morally right in some circumstances, it is often far from clear that this tactic achieves its supposed aims, and frequently backfires. Countless controversial speakers, like shock journalist Milo Yiannopoulos or the far-right agitator Richard Spencer, both in the US, have gained vastly greater fame, not less, through others' efforts to silence them.

This is sometimes called the "Streisand effect." After an internet user posted aerial photos of the legend's home, she took legal action for them to be removed. Well, guess what happened? Suddenly, information that had at first sparked only moderate interest become the hottest item on the net.

MEDIA - OPEN AND CLOSED

And then a funny coincidence occurred only recently. This time it was in one of my own classes, and that stubborn topic popped up once again: equal rights for gays. One of my students put forward the time-honoured claim: If everyone were gay, then humanity would die out!

Should I have felt piqued? Incensed? Raging mad?

I confess it was more a sense of nostalgia that hit me. By the time my student days were behind me, I never thought I would come across that old chestnut again. But the first thought to hit me was: "No need to panic. Just let him talk." The dumbest thing I could have done would be to shame him in front of the group by hinting that he was hateful or ignorant. Nor did I think he was either of those things. He was an undergraduate in a phase of asking questions, which is better than going through life *without* asking them.

Instead, my response was that I felt grateful to him for opening up a discussion that still needs to take place in many places around the world. Nothing bores me more than a roomful of students who dutifully agree out of fear of disagreeing.

The first thing that happened was that half the room groaned at the student's remark. In fact, a student who teaches Islamic jurisprudence to young people in his spare time was the first to roll his eyes in disbelief.

Still, I did not want our speaker to feel censored. "What you're saying is very interesting," I responded. "So if I understand correctly, your view is that a limit can legitimately be placed on individual freedom *if* humanity would become extinct as a result in everyone indulging *only* in that freedom. Correct?"

His face lit up. I had made his point sound intellectually elevated. I continued: "And therefore if everyone only engaged in homosexual conduct, then humanity would die out, so a government can legitimately place limits on such conduct. Correct?" I confess at this point I was sounding just a wee bit patronising.

Yet by now he was nodding triumphantly, seeing in me an unexpected ally. I carried on: "So for example, it would be legitimate to ban sugar, because if all people only ever ate sugar then humanity would die out. Correct?"

He stopped nodding. "In fact, even broccoli would kill us if all of us ate nothing else. So it would be legitimate for governments to ban broccoli, given that humanity would die out if everyone ate only broccoli?"

By this time he had got my point. He even chuckled and greeted me sunnily a week later in the corridor. In other words, I never needed to silence him, let alone to embarrass him. Of course, I took a risk, since this outcome was never certain. The student, who had been raised in a country where state-sponsored anti-gay propaganda is common and often vicious, might simply have tuned me out, or might have grasped at straws for any other anti-gay arguments he could concoct.

AND THEN CAME MDI

These kinds of risks, be they in the classroom or in the mass media, never come with guarantees of success, and will sometimes backfire. But they are worth taking.

I have long believed that diversity in the media, no less than in the seminar room, means expanding voices and perspectives, and arming people with rational arguments instead of clamping down on provocative ideas. This was why my ongoing collaborations with the Media Diversity Institute always seemed like an obvious match.

When I travelled along with other MDI members to a Brussels meeting on cyberhate in 2016, I very much appreciated the fact that Milica Pešić actively encouraged me to challenge the common knee-jerk instinct to devise penalties. I preferred MDI's attempts to promote pro-active strategies of education and awareness rather than overly relying on penalties, which, as we see every day, can never be applied in consistent or even particularly coherent ways. The organization's Get the Trolls Out! project was - and still is - certainly an innovative step in this direction, particularly aimed at young people who will have grown up with electronic media from infancy.

It was a joy for me to continue exploring these channels through MDI's countless other activities. In 2020, after Donald Trump had been kicked off Twitter and Facebook, and as his re-election campaign was heating up, MDI's brilliant intern, Mikhail Yakovlev, contacted me for a long interview about the emerging far-right *Parler* platform. The year after, Mikhail interviewed me for MDI website on the related theme of "cancel culture" in democratic society.

In 2022, MDI's involvement in MEDIADELCOM, a research project focused on deliberative communication, allowed me once again to engage in a deeply probing discussion, this time with the Estonian media expert Dr Urmas Loit. In a podcast, Dr Loit and I examined controversies surrounding hateful expression and cancel culture within the context of deliberative democracy – once again seeking means that would be not only more politically legitimate but also more pragmatically effective than imposing bans. The Swedish expert Professor Lars Nord added to that podcast a commentary of his own.

That same year, MDI affiliate Hannah Ajala was kind enough to host me on her Twitter Space for a conversation entitled "Does the diversity movement have a glass ceiling?" We discussed the fact that in many countries the most basic non-discrimination norms continue to be violated, for example with respect to women and LGBTQ+ minorities – and unsurprisingly in such places freedoms of speech tend to be severely restricted, both officially and informally.

I could add many more items to this list. But for now, I aim only to illustrate how my contacts with MDI have enriched my own research, teaching, and writing on the complexities of free speech, and I shall look forward to many more years of cooperation.

Anne-Marie Impe

Anne-Marie Impe is a journalist and essayist. She has written several handbooks for journalists: *How can we cover migration in an ethical and relevant way?* (EFJ, 2023); *Reporting on violence against Women and Girls* (UNESCO, 2019), and is the author of *Human rights in my Municipality* (Amnesty International, 2018). She has been the editor-in-chief of a quarterly magazine, *Enjeux internationaux*, and taught journalism at the IHECS Brussels School. Before this, she worked for 13 years in Senegal with a communication for development project in a slum and as a contributor for international radio stations and magazines (*BBC, RFI, DW, Jeune Afrique Economie*).

DIVERSITY: A UNIVERSAL HERITAGE THAT CHALLENGES THE MEDIA

My first contact with Milica Pešić and the Media Diversity Institute was in 2005. Two years earlier, Jean-Paul Marthoz and I had founded the *Enjeux internationaux* magazine. This quarterly, independent of any party, pressure group or Church, aimed to provide readers with the keys to decoding major international issues while trying to avoid succumbing to the temptation of simplification and peremptory statements. The aim was to offer quality information in order to "*shed light on the complexity of reality*" and to enable readers to "*better understand global issues in order to better act as citizens of the world*".

The magazine's wish was to "*become an incubator of ideas, a place for reflection, debate and analysis, where opposing points of view could collide until they provoked innovative outbursts*", as I wrote in the first issue in my role as editor-in-chief. Our goal was to practice slow journalism, to tackle subjects that other media did not cover and to present forward-looking reporting by spotting, under the turbulence of everyday events, the underlying currents that might foreshadow the future. To do this, it seemed important, as I added in my editorial, to "*give the floor to authors from all over the world to propose cross-readings of the same reality (South/North, researchers/field workers, journalists/academics)*". Some of the best minds – about 150 authors representing more than 50 nationalities – gave us the honour of writing for our magazine on relevant themes. The pluralism of voices and the dialogue of cultures were thus clearly part of the DNA of the quarterly from its inception.

RESPONSIBLE JOURNALISM

The ninth issue of *Enjeux internationaux* was devoted entirely to cultural diversity. So who better to call on for an article on diversity in journalism than Milica Pešić, the executive director of the Media Diversity Institute? In "Describing the world as it is", Pešić noted the following: "*Diversity is a reality. Whether we are talking about race, ethnicity, religion, age, gender, physical ability, political opinion, socio-economic status or sexual orientation, some or all of these characteristics together make up a human being or a group. The society in which we live is plural.*"

Yet, she added, "*the media rarely reflect the diversity of the societies in which they operate*". She described the efforts of some news organisations, such as the BBC, to "*correct this distortion between demographic and media realities*" and increase the representation of ethnic minorities in programmes as well as in the newsroom. But she also warned that it is not appropriate to assign these journalists solely to cover their own communities. Recalling the extent to which certain media had fueled deadly hatred in various conflicts around the world, she concluded that "*diversity journalism (...) is first and foremost a journalism of responsibility*".

I thoroughly appreciated Milica Pešić's article and sense that we were on the same wavelength. Yet she and I did not meet in person until some years later, in 2018, at the Perugia International Journalism Festival, where she moderated a compelling and informative roundtable on the rise of the far right and the press coverage of this phenomenon.

"ZINNEKE" AND PROUD OF IT

If diversity issues have always been close to my heart, it is probably because of my personal background. I am, in fact, what we call a "zinneke" in Brussels, a term originally referring to a dog that is a mix of two or more breeds. A mongrel, in other words! But this word, which was initially perceived as insulting, has since evolved. It is now more often used to suggest an openness to the multiculturalism and cosmopolitanism that characterise Brussels. So much so that, since 2000, there has been a "Zinneke Parade", a large biennial event with an often surrealist tone, which celebrates the multiculturality of Brussels.

My father was Flemish, my mother Walloon. And my brothers, my sister and I were "zinnekes" who spent our entire childhood and adolescence in Brussels, happy with our ethnic and cultural mix. At the time of my parents' marriage, there were still many inter-community unions between Flemings and Walloons; linguistic quarrels between the communities were mainly conducted by politicians. In 1962, an internal linguistic border was established in Belgium. It geographically divided the country into two territories, one Dutch-speaking in the north, the other French-speaking in the south, with Brussels, the capital, remaining bilingual. It was a consequence of growing community tensions in the Kingdom, but it also contributed to increasing identity-based quarrels on both sides, until an ever-growing number of institutions that had previously been national and united – academic, scientific, museum, health and, of course, political – were split apart.

Today, right-wing and far-right pro-independence parties dominate the political landscape in Flanders more than ever before, while left-wing parties, Socialists and far-leftists prevail in Wallonia. Legislative elections scheduled for 2024 could easily deepen the divide between the North and the South and make the country even more ungovernable. After the 2019 parliamentary elections, the country had been without a federal government for 16 months because the various quarreling parties couldn't form a coalition government. Will we see the break-up of Belgium this time? The political declarations we are hearing in advance of the elections are hardly reassuring.

WHAT COMMUNICATION FOR WHAT DEVELOPMENT?

To a large extent, these incessant sandbox quarrels pushed me to fly away to other, less suffocating environments, as soon as I finished my journalism studies in 1979. I was seeking to learn about other cultures, other ways of living and thinking. I landed in Senegal. I quickly found work with a development project in a shantytown on the outskirts of Dakar, initiated by the Senegalese Ministry of Social Development and the international non-governmental organisation Enda Tiers-Monde.

My job was to use grassroots communication for community development. It was a team effort, with Senegalese facilitators promoting and maximising the participation of the slum dwellers in improving their living conditions, environment and health. An exodus from rural areas had led many of them to settle in this suburban neighbourhood in an unregulated manner on plots of land that were frequently flooded during the rainy season. The shantytown was not connected to the sewage system so all the waste flowed into the sandy streets. Children played in the muck, which exposed them to a range of infectious diseases carried in the sewage. There was no running water either: people relied on public fountains.

The means of communication that we used as tools to raise awareness about environmental sanitation and improving the health of all were varied, but always designed with the slum dwellers: posters, models, exhibitions of photos made by the young people or puppet plays put on with different groups of women in the neighbourhood. The communication initiative that I remember most vividly was the recording of an audio message in Wolof, one of Senegal's national languages, aimed at alerting fathers and mothers to the dangers that stagnant water posed to their children's health.

This "communication-action" approach made an impression on me in several ways. Firstly, because the recording proposed concrete solutions that could be implemented by the inhabitants of the neighbourhood, namely the digging of individual and collective sumps for waste water. Secondly, because we obtained the collaboration of a local imam, who was convinced of the merits of the project and offered to broadcast the recording via the loudspeakers of one of the mosques. And finally, because following this broadcast, which was critical for the success of the project, most of the fathers dug a sump and the problem of wastewater was solved in large areas of the slum.

To be honest, the health argument was not the only one to convince them: before this effort, the faithful often used to arrive at the mosque to pray with the bottoms of their long basin boubou, a traditional dress, soiled by foul water from their walk in the streets. For many, this situation had become intolerable. An interesting synergy was created, based on a conjunction of interests, from which there are many lessons to be learned in terms of grassroots communication for development.

JOURNALISM CONNECTED... TO THE AIR ON THE STREET

It was also in this context that I fully understood the importance for journalists to be connected to reality and to know the life of the people they were covering. I worked part-time in the slum and part-time as a freelance journalist for a dozen media outlets, including several radio stations (the *BBC*, *RFI*'s cooperation service, *DW* and Swiss German radio), magazines (including *Jeune Afrique Economie* and *Croissance des Jeunes Nations*), the Belgian daily *La Cité*, the *Inter Press Service* news agency, etc. It is clear that this immersion gave me a certain knowledge of the field and insight into the living conditions of the most disadvantaged. Because of that, I did not interview a politician or an economic actor in the same way as other journalists who just flew in and out briefly. My experiences also influenced my choice of topics and the angle from which I approached them.

In 2023, journalists leave the office much less than they did 20 or 30 years ago, assuming that the Internet will provide them with the information they need. This is partly true. But working in an ivory tower necessarily disconnects you from reality. As the legendary US Hutchins Commission on freedom of the press stated in 1947, journalism is supposed to give a true picture of the world and events. "*Journalists are not responsible for the world as it is, but for the conformity of the image they give of it*," recalled the Belgian journalist Albert du Roy in 1992. It is difficult to meet this requirement without leaving one's desk! As Jean Dominique, a famous Haitian reporter, reminded us, "*To be a good journalist, you have to smell the air on the street.*"

I stayed in Dakar for thirteen years. Enough time to discover and appreciate the country, its people, but also its arts and literature. Senegalese literature has some excellent writers, such as poet Léopold Sédar Senghor, who was also the first president of the Republic of Senegal and the first African to be elected to the French Academy; Mariama Bâ, author of the novel *So Long a Letter*, a major work for understanding the condition of women, which caused a great stir when it was published in 1979; or Cheikh Hamidou Kane, whose remarkable novel, *Ambiguous Adventure*, should be read by anyone interested in diversity. His book very accurately portrays the dilemma of the Diallobé chief and his elder sister, the Grande Royale: should they send their children to the whites' school or keep them in the village and continue to educate them according to the Koranic and customary traditions? "*If I tell them to go to the new school, they will go en masse. But as they learn, they will also forget. Will what they learn be worth what they forget?*" wonders the chief. The school "*will kill in them what we love and preserve with care today*", worries the Grande Royale. Both characters pepper their inner journey with many subtle reflections.

I was lucky enough to carry out reports or missions in 34 of the 55 countries in Africa. After my return to Belgium, I also had the opportunity to travel in Asia and Latin America. One of the beneficial effects of encountering other cultures is to better understand one's own, to question, through comparison and perspective, what we had previously taken for granted. One day, when I arrived at work, a Senegalese colleague asked me if I was all right. "*Not really*", I replied, explaining that my nine-month-old son was ill and that, even though he was of course not alone at home, I was worried. She looked at me dumbfounded and said, "*What the hell are you doing here? Go home and look after him!*" A clash of values: she considered my primary role to be that of a mother, whereas I thought my duty was to go to work and not leave everything to my colleagues. An interesting exchange of views ensued about the priorities of each of us, strongly influenced by the culture in which we had been brought up; but we also discussed the possibility of modifying, by personal choice, the cultural software programmed at the outset.

MAKING OTHER VOICES HEARD

Reflecting what I have experienced during my stays and travels, various forms of diversity have always been very present in my articles and radio programmes, in which I try, whenever possible, to give a voice to those who usually do not have one.

Making visible those whom society marginalises, rejects or discriminates against is a challenge, as the mainstream media take little interest in their daily lives. That's why I have often worked with community media. In this context, I wrote several articles on street children and castes in Senegal. In collaboration with *No-Télé*, a local community television station in Tournai, Belgium, and DAHW, the German association for leprosy assistance, I produced a 20-minute television report, the title of which was itself a manifesto: *Les lépreux, des hommes comme les autres* (Lepers, people like any other).

The common thread of my journalistic commitment has always been this: to make other voices heard, in particular those of the most vulnerable, those left behind, the outcasts, and to show that other societal choices are possible. In fact, I have always worked on issues that challenge and put into perspective the conventional or majority opinion and different forms of domination or oppression, be they economic, political, ethnic, religious, gender, ageist or ableist. Isn't this role of countering power one of the essential missions of public interest journalism, which is essential to guaranteeing the proper functioning of democracy? In any case, this is what I opted for, without hesitation, when I was a student of journalism.

CRIMES AGAINST HALF OF HUMANITY

The main feature of the last issue of *Enjeux internationaux* was devoted to women. The title bore a militant overtone that was not in the magazine's usual style, but which seemed to us to impose itself: "*Women, this half of humanity that is murdered, raped, forcibly married, repudiated, excised, beaten, burned, disfigured with acid, stoned, harassed or discriminated against. And who has had enough.*" It was when she discovered this issue of the magazine that Mirta Lourenço, then Chief of Section for Media Development and Society at UNESCO, suggested I write a manual for journalists on media coverage of violence against women. It is called *Reporting on Violence against Women and Girls*, was published in French in 2019 and translated into six other languages: English, Chinese, Russian, Arabic, Spanish and Kyrgyz. It is available free of charge online in these languages on the UNESCO website.

Organised in ten chapters, each dealing with a different form of violence against women, the manual provides dozens of very concrete tips to help journalists improve their coverage of this delicate subject. Among these, I will mention three that seem essential to me. Firstly, journalists should ensure that words are chosen carefully and not use language that minimises, trivialises, waters down or even conceals violence. Secondly, they should avoid making women victims twice: once because of the violence they have suffered and again because of degrading or discriminatory media coverage that essentially blames the victim while downplaying the conduct of the aggressor. Finally, they should explain the systemic nature of the phenomenon: violence against women is not one incident, it is not about isolated acts or private intra-family disputes. No. These human rights abuses are recurrent, structural acts that originate in an ancestral patriarchal system that has established relationships of power and domination between men and women.

In the wake of this publication for UNESCO, the Association of Professional Journalists of French-speaking Belgium (AJP) asked me to write a practical guide on the same subject. It is entitled *How to report on violence against women? 10 recommendations for journalists* and is available on the website of the association. The AJP promotes a policy of inclusion and diversity not only within newsrooms, but also in editorial content, with the creation of Expertalia.be. This interesting database for journalists lists and presents, on the one hand, women experts in different fields, whether or not they come from a diverse background, and, on the other hand, male experts but only those who come from ethnic minorities. The aim is to increase the presence of people from diverse backgrounds, both in terms of gender and origin, in media content. Another way of promoting diversity of content and encouraging less sexist treatment of news is to appoint a "gender editor", following the example of the *New York Times*, in 2017, when the Weinstein affair had just broken out. In France, *Mediapart* followed suit in 2020 by appointing an "editorial manager for gender issues". And in Belgium, RTBF, the Belgian French-speaking public service broadcaster, created a position of "diversity and equality manager".

THE TABOO OF ELDER ABUSE

Another form of discrimination I was interested in was ageism. This was long before the Covid 19 pandemic revealed to the general public the conditions in which elderly people lived in residential and care homes. My mother was looking for a nursing home to live in. I accompanied her on her visits and was shocked to discover how the human rights and dignity of the elderly were being violated in some institutions. During the 2010s, there was little coverage of the elderly in the media. So I decided to investigate the fate of the elderly in nursing homes.

But the sector is complex. In order to get to know it better and to deal with it with all the rigour and precision required, I trained to become a nursing home director. The training lasted one year and took place in the evenings and on Saturdays, which allowed me to continue my work as a journalist. I have always believed that journalists have a duty to know and must "*understand in order to make others understand*", as the French writer and journalist Françoise Giroud used to say. After graduating, I published a series of articles on institutional abuse, the glaring shortage of staff, the high and not always appropriate consumption of medication in many institutions... I also participated in an investigation called *Nursing homes in the blind spot. The human rights of the elderly during the Covid-19 pandemic in Belgium*, carried out by the Belgian section of Amnesty International. My most recent reports were published in November 2022, by the daily *Le Soir*. They dealt with the use of restraint in nursing homes – that is, immobilising persons by tying them to their armchair, by locking them in bed with rails or by making them take tranquilizers, antidepressants and antipsychotics.

In order to see for myself how elderly people with Alzheimer's and other forms of cognitive impairment were treated, I took advantage of the holidays, a period when the shortage of nursing staff is particularly acute, to offer my services as a volunteer. And as I had a degree as a nursing home director, I was welcomed with open arms. While in some institutions the welfare and dignity of the elderly is respected, this is far from being the case everywhere. And in the facility I investigated, run by a private commercial group, the condition of the elderly with Alzheimer's-type diseases was terrible. Those who had no family would never get taken outside; as there was no garden, they were confined to their room or a common area without ever again breathing in the open air. I am not talking about confinement due to COVID, but about the ordinary daily life of these people that prevailed before and continued after the pandemic.

THE HIGHLY IDEOLOGICAL COVERAGE OF MIGRATION

At the request of the European Federation of Journalists (EFJ), I returned to Senegal in March 2022 to conduct a training course for local journalists on how to cover migration. This is a particularly sensitive subject and is handled in a very ideological, often Manichean way by many news organisations, who offer a positive or negative perspective without any nuance. Some media fuel their circulation by exploiting the xenophobic feelings of a part of the population. I gave the participants an example of a Belgian daily newspaper which, on page 1, ran the headline: *"The 2,000 bone tests have spoken. 70% of migrants are 'false' minors!"* On page 2, the same newspaper drove the point home: "*1500 migrants lied about their age*". However, on page 3, another article mentioned that these bone tests were not reliable: "*This test is not accurate at all*", the headline read.

This was a perfect example of sensationalist journalistic treatment that reinforced fears and prejudices. By stigmatising migrants (70% are liars!), the article contributed to society's rejection of them and to the rise of racism. I also showed the workshop participants that the Senegalese media also engaged in the stigmatisation of migrants, with this headline from a local daily newspaper: "*Begging: Dakar, the foreign invasion*".

As Catherine Wihtol de Wenden, Director of Research at the France's National Council of scientific research (CNRS) and a leading specialist in migration, notes: "*...the media play an essential role in the formation of collective imaginations*". This point highlights the importance of the approach known as the "journalism of responsibility," which MDI director Milica Pešić mentioned in her article for our magazine *Enjeux internationaux*. This key professional obligation is clearly recalled in Article 9 of the World Charter of Ethics for Journalists, adopted at the 30th Congress of the International Federation of Journalists (IFJ) in Tunis, in 2019: *"Journalists shall ensure that the dissemination of information or opinion does not contribute to hatred or prejudice and shall do their utmost to avoid facilitating the spread of discrimination on grounds such as geographical, social or ethnic origin, race, gender, sexual orientation, language, religion, disability, political and other opinions".*

Shada Islam

Shada Islam is a Brussels-based EU analyst and commentator on EU foreign, security, trade and development policy and EU-Asia relations as well as on diversity, equity and inclusion. After nine years as Director for Geopolitics at Friends of Europe, she now runs her own global strategy company, New Horizons Project. Shada is also Senior Advisor at several think tanks, including the European Policy Centre. She is Visiting Professor at the College of Europe (Natolin Campus) and contributes to several international publications including EUObserver, the Guardian and East Asia Forum. In 2017, Politico identified her as one of Brussels' 20 most influential women. She is the recipient of the prestigious "career award 2023" from the European Journalist Association in Catalonia for her work on building an inclusive Union of Equality.

WHERE ARE YOU REALLY FROM?

It was nothing special, just a run-of-the mill encounter at a pre-Christmas reception attended by European Union policymakers, foreign diplomats and others in the so-called "Brussels Bubble". As a friend introduced me to the EU representative of an international organization, she mentioned that I was a European "expert" on EU stuff. There was a quick exchange of name cards. The woman looked at my name and then at me. She was clearly puzzled for a bit, but then had a Eureka moment.

"Ah, I see you are from somewhere over there!" she said. "Is it Iran, Afghanistan, Pakistan, maybe Syria or Lebanon? Where are you really from?"

There was an awkward silence. The person who had introduced us turned bright red. I started to say something but decided against it.

No harm in the question, many will say: it is innocuous enough. Harmless. The woman was just being curious. Why be so thin-skinned, so sensitive? These arguments are familiar, and I have been asked where I am "really" from on countless occasions. I am usually quite easy-going about providing a short answer, usually quite politely. Mostly, it doesn't matter. The questioner and the question are soon forgotten.

This time, however, I could not get the exchange out of my head. The question stuck with me as I celebrated Christmas with my wonderful big, blended, mix-and-match, multi-cultural family. It stayed with me as I left Brussels right after Christmas to visit my mother in Karachi after three years of Covid-induced separation. By the time the Turkish Airlines flight landed at Quaid I Azam airport, I knew I had to tackle the issue head on. Why had the question upset me so much?

Unlike Ngozi Fulani, founder of a British domestic abuse charity, who was repeatedly asked where she was *really* from at a royal event in London in 2022, the query had certainly not "traumatized"[1] me. But this time, unlike any time in the past, the seemingly harmless query had triggered a complex mix of emotions: anger, irritation and sadness - all at the same time.

I needed to clear my head and clarify - for myself as well as for others? - just why asking "where are you really from?" could be hurtful to so many people. So I did what all journalists do: I wrote an op-ed[2] about the experience, highlighting how the question had "pigeonholed, classified, and categorised me". It also had simplified me, and turned me into a one-dimensional version of myself, denying my ability to move seamlessly between cultures, histories and geographies in a very complex world. The response was largely positive and supportive, with friends and others writing in with their own anecdotes. Of course, there was also plenty of hate mail and unpleasant comments. "Why are you always so critical these days?" asked one friend. Another insisted she had never seen me as a non-white person because "you could pass for Spanish or Italian".

---

[1] Atcheson, Sheree. (2022, December 2) Where Are You Really From? Not-So-Subtle Racism In A Nutshell. *Forbes* https://www.forbes.com/sites/shereeatcheson/2022/12/02/where-are-you-really-from-not-so-subtle-racism-in-a-nutshell/?sh=1edcf7c56b80

[2] Islam, Shada. (2023, January 17) Six reasons why 'where are you really from?' is racist. *EU Observer.* https://euobserver.com/opinion/156611

Why all the fuss? After years of working, living and loving in #Brussels So White[3], why on earth was I venturing into the choppy and uncharted waters of defining EU identity? Why, after years of being a successful journalist and think-tanker, was I making people feel so uncomfortable? Why, when we were faced with a real war in Europe, was I so bent on engaging in a damaging, polarizing culture war? As a white male friend asked me: Why are you so woke?

Why indeed? I've been reporting, writing and speaking for a long, long time about the very visible need for more diversity and inclusion - and less discrimination - within EU institutions and in the Brussels ecosystem of lobby groups, consultancies, think tanks and media. It has never been easy. People in and around the EU do not like conversations on race, color, religion and ethnicity. When these conversations do take place, they are excruciatingly uncomfortable.

This time, however, the question I'd been asked felt different, more aggressive, more deliberate. More disappointing. After the Black Lives Matter movement gained international momentum, the EU had promised to fight structural racism. I had assumed--obviously wrongly--that EU policymakers and people who worked in and around the EU had become more aware of their biases as well as the role of microaggressions and myriad discriminatory actions and policies.

Clearly, not much had changed. I was running out of patience. Worse than that, I was also running out of hope.

On some days, it certainly feels like those who want to live in a real Union of Equality – a Europe where people of different races, religions and cultures feel safe and at home – are fighting a losing battle for EU-wide diversity, equity and inclusion. Around us, across Europe, the opposite

[3] (2017, December) #BrusselsSoWhite. *Politico*. https://www.politico.eu/special-report/diversity/

appears to be happening: racism, discrimination and Islamophobia are on the rise as the Far Right's toxic rhetoric, ideas and actions seep into mainstream discourse, further spreading hate across societies.

Racial and ethnic minorities – Europeans of color - make up about 10% of the EU population. Yet reports by the EU's Fundamental Rights Agency have underlined that 45% of people of North African descent living in Europe, 41% of Roma and 39% of people of Sub-Saharan African descent report having faced discrimination in the EU. Among Jews, 11% feel discriminated against, and Muslims experience prejudice in a broad range of settings, particularly when looking for work and while on the job, as well as when seeking to access public and private services.

In 2022, in the midst of the Russian invasion of Ukraine, the contrast became clear between the warm European welcome offered to refugees from Ukraine and the EU's criminalization of both those fleeing wars in Africa and Asia and those trying to help them. Brown and Black students in Ukraine seeking to leave the war zone were pushed back by Ukrainian and Polish border guards. Yet for many EU policymakers, journalists and others in the Euro Bubble, such discussions remain quasi-taboo, conducted – if at all - in whispers.

So I asked myself over and over again: Given this generalized state of denial on racism and discrimination across the EU, wasn't it time to give up the struggle for diversity and inclusion, to drop this fanciful idea that people who are non-white, non-Caucasian, non-Christian can really and truly be accepted as European? Are the Far Right - and increasingly Europe's mainstream politicians - correct to view us as eternal foreigners, permanent and unwanted outsiders in a white, Christian Europe? Will "real Europeans" ever accept that people who look different, pray differently and speak multiple languages, including non-European ones, also have the right to call Europe "home"?

Some argue that "Europeanness" is intrinsically tied to whiteness and Christianity. As such, non-white people can never be "European". As historian Shane Weller shows in *The Idea of Europe: A Critical History,* a persistent belief in European superiority runs throughout European history. For as long as Europeans have thought of themselves as such, they have also considered themselves better than the rest of the world. Additionally, Europe's search for unity — or identity — has been constructed in opposition to an external Other.

And that Other is Black, Brown and Muslim. As the legal scholar Sahar Aziz notes in her book, *The Racial Muslim: When Racism Quashes Religious Freedom*, race and religion intersect to racialize and disempower Muslims in both the US and Europe. That is also my experience and why I believe that fighting Islamophobia must be part of the wider anti-racism agenda.

So what we are up against is deep-seated structural racism. Yet, for many Europeans, racism is seen as a problem limited to a few nasty apples. Casual Islamophobia is brushed off as "natural" and acceptable, nothing to get angry or upset about.

It is because racism is seen as a problem solely of bad individuals that many Europeans quickly identify Hungarian Prime Minister Viktor Orbán as *the* most openly racist European politician. There is no doubt that he peddles a particularly toxic blend of xenophobia, antisemitism and ethnonationalism. But bigots like Orbán are only part of the problem, which is systemic and structural.

Racism is thriving across Europe because racist and xenophobic discourses and dog whistles to populists and far-right extremists have become deeply embedded in Europe's mainstream politics, policies and institutions. They are also infecting the EU's foreign and security policy; EU Foreign Policy Chief Josep Borrell recently compared Europe to a garden, a presumably civilized place, and the rest of the world to a jungle that could invade the garden at any moment.

The headwinds facing advocates of a more inclusive and less racist Europe are strong and unrelenting. But it is impossible to abandon an effort one believes in so passionately. Although countries like Pakistan, where I was born and lived on and off until I was eighteen, have a reputation for being intolerant, the reality of my childhood years was very different. I went to a Christian school, my nanny was Hindu, my closest friend was a Buddhist from Burma, and the other children I played with came from different ethnic groups, spoke different languages, and belonged to different religions. We celebrated Christmas and I took part in Diwali festivals. As I grew up, I also learned from my father that I should always speak up when I believed people were being unfair or unjust. When things get difficult, don't be afraid to raise your voice, he told me.

Diversity was also part of my life in Belgium. I studied at the very multi-cultural and progressive Universite Libre de Bruxelles. I had friends from across Europe, Latin America, Africa and the Middle East.

When I graduated and found a job working for a newsletter on the EU, entering the world of the union's tradition-bound institutions was strange. Most journalists were white and almost 90 percent were male. Fresh out of university, Brown and quite young, I stuck out like a sore thumb. But I was gutsy and curious.

So I asked disruptive questions, including on why EU institutions were so lacking in ethnic and racial diversity. For years, my questions were shrugged off as a distraction, or I received the glib response that EU recruitment policies were "color blind" and that nothing could be done to change the existing situation. Europeans of color didn't quite have the "qualities" required to join the EU I was told by one very self-satisfied spokesman. Another argument I heard repeatedly was that the EU lived by its motto of "unity in diversity" because the bloc's member states represented an array of people, histories, cultures and geographies. No one listened when I said, yes, but the representatives and officials are all white.

Inclusive policies were also not the norm in Brussels-based consultancies, lobbying groups, think tanks and media organizations, where conversations on equality focused on ways to empower, promote and recruit women but sidestepped other forms of diversity. With Europeans of color largely absent in EU press rooms, it was rare that officials had to answer questions on race, religion or color-based discrimination.

It took some time before the winds of change began to blow softly even through the white bastions of EU power.

EU policymakers and many others in Brussels had a rude awakening when #Black Lives Matter protests erupted across Europe following the death of George Floyd, the African American killed by police in Minneapolis in June 2020. The first EU reaction to the killing was awkward and clumsy, with some officials adamant that ethnic minorities in Europe did not face discrimination or police violence on the same scale as African Americans.

Those (false) claims were not surprising. They reflected the simple reality that there are very few Black or Brown staff members in EU institutions, whether major ones like the European Commission, the EU Council and the European Parliament or smaller and more obscure specialized agencies. With very few people of color in EU institutions or in cafes, restaurants and shops in its neighborhood, even a quick walk around the quarter suggests that most inhabitants of the "Brussels so White" bubble have little or limited interaction with Europe's ethnic communities, or "second-" or "third-generation migrants", the preferred EU label.

I also learned very quickly that black or brown people seen in EU corridors were either cleaners or members of the security staff. If they were attending parliamentary meetings, they were usually Asian, Arab, African or Latin American diplomats. To many, I was always a "foreign journalist", sometimes mistaken for a "lady from an Asian Embassy".

As underlined by former British European Parliament member Magid Magid, non-white Europeans are so rare in EU circles that they can be viewed as unwanted intruders.

Still, to my delight (and some surprise), the Black Lives Matter movement spurred the EU and some national governments into belated action. Suddenly waking up to issues that had been around forever, European Commission President Ursula von der Leyen hastily promised to create an “anti-racist Europe” and acknowledged the importance of countering institutionalized racism and the need for more diversity in EU institutions.

An unprecedented “anti-racism action plan” was adopted and a first-ever “anti-racism coordinator” was appointed to help implement it. “Diversity Advisors” working at the Commission and the European External Action Service, the EU’s diplomatic arm, who had previously worked on promoting women through EU ranks, were now also tasked with overseeing the recruitment of ethnic minority staff. A new “anti-Muslim hatred” coordinator was finally selected, joining the one on fighting antisemitism, who had been in the post since 2015.

The EU’s baby steps to recognize structural racism and try to eliminate it were slow and painful and really only started after the #Black Lives Matter movement. My own “awakening” had occurred much earlier. It was also painful but it was sudden, happening brusquely, from one day to the next. That day was September 11, 2001, when Middle Eastern terrorists attacked the Pentagon and the World Trade Center. Overnight, Muslims across the world found their lives disrupted and forever altered.

I was no exception. Before 9/11, as a busy reporter working for several Asian and European media, my battle for diversity and against racism and discrimination had been intellectual and rational, not personal. Married at that time to a Spaniard, and busy juggling journalism with raising a son and daughter in a progressive, privileged and liberal environment, I had rarely faced open racism or discrimination. I had climbed through the ranks as a journalist, trying to meet deadlines, interview the most interesting people and get the best stories I could, but I had never bothered much about religion. We spent wonderful summers in Spain with my former husband's not very Catholic family and equally wonderful winters in Pakistan with my open-minded and open-hearted parents.

The 9/11 terror attacks changed all that in the blink of an eye. Suddenly, I was in the fray, as my surname and skin color cast me among "those people" - reviled members of the Muslim community, who were collectively guilty of the terrible crime committed against the West. I had suddenly migrated from being one of "us" to becoming a part of "them", "the Other", repeatedly asked to explain how "my" religion could encourage such vile acts. Why, why, why?

So the arguments, loud and often abusive, began. Everyone became an expert on Islam. I became used to acquaintances and strangers – and even some friends - offering unsolicited and often offensive advice and opinions on my faith. Islamophobic comments became - and still are - part and parcel of Brussels' dinner party chatter. There were also constant small irritants. When I called my osteopath for an appointment, her new assistant asked warily: "You aren't a fanatic, are you?" I stopped using my surname to make restaurant reservations. I kept telling people to stop asking me about the Koran, because I was an expert on the EU, not on Islam.

To be fair, there was no change in the behavior of close friends and most colleagues, and there was also a professional upside. Many, including the media outlets I worked for, were genuinely curious about this very visible "clash of civilizations" between Islam and the West and wanted to know what, if anything, could be done to prevent it. I received invitations to travel and report on trips to Muslim countries by EU officials such as Chris Patten and Javier Solana, respectively the former external relations commissioner and the former high representative for foreign and security policy. Both of them sought to distance Europe from US President George W Bush's post- 9/11 call for a "crusade"[4] against terrorists, which many in Europe feared could spark conflicts between Christians and Muslims, sowing fresh winds of hatred and mistrust.

I certainly did not become religious, but I read up on Wahhabism and Salafism, on Al Qaeda and the Taliban, whose version of Islam was so far removed from the mystical Sufi interpretation of the religion that had formed the backdrop to my childhood in Pakistan. In addition to reporting on the EU, I also started writing about Islamophobia, calling out those who conflated Islam with terrorism, reporting about European Muslims and the violence and discrimination they faced. I wanted to understand the drivers of Europe's anti-Muslim hatred and sought to spotlight Islamophobia's diverse and damaging manifestations.

I also began writing more personal stories, editorials and op-eds about the need for cooperation across cultures and religions, for more inclusive EU policies and more diversity in EU policymaking. If people could just stop shouting, provoking and insulting each other, I thought, the world would be a better place and we could end or at least reduce? division and hatred.

As I wrote in the Brussels weekly, *The Bulletin*, on September 20, 2011: "In these dangerous times, EU governments – with their close historical and cultural ties to the Muslim world – have a crucial role to play in keeping the channels of communication open with their Arab and Muslim neighbours and in ensuring that the voices of moderation are heard above the clamour of fanatics."

[4] Waldman, Peter & Pope, Hugh. (2001, September 21) 'Crusade' Reference Reinforces Fears War on Terrorism Is Against Muslims. *The Wall Street Journal.* https://www.wsj.com/articles/SB1001020294332922160

It wasn't to be. Those voices of moderation I was so desperate to hear were drowned out even further after the Danish newspaper *Jyllands-Posten* published twelve caricatures of Prophet Mohammed in September 2005, prompting an all-time high in Islamophobic sentiments across Europe and Muslim anger at the West. In many unfortunate ways, we are still stuck in that vicious circle.

As a journalist, I struggled to change that dynamic. I worked with Aidan White of the International Federation of Journalists and the late Bettina Peters to launch an Ethical Journal Initiative[5], a tool box for reporters seeking to provide more reasoned and less sensational coverage of the ups and downs of a rapidly changing world.

We noted that in Europe, many newspapers remained wedded to an old-fashioned and outdated concept of a continent where "immigrants and foreigners" are still viewed as exotic outsiders who have brought dangerous ideas and customs into Europe. And we pointed out that such toxic narratives were being peddled in the face of mounting evidence that more, not less, migration of people is needed in order to make up for labor shortages and maintain standards of living in a region where populations are ageing and the birth rate is static.

We urged newsrooms to become more inclusive and diverse, to recruit more people from Europe's ethnic minorities. We said the media was stoking the fires of intolerance and racism instead of raising awareness, helping fight prejudice, and engendering inter-community understanding. When I look around me today at Europe's media landscape, our assessment remains true. Changes may have been made by some media groups, but they are minor.

I'm often asked why I care so much. Well, as they say, the personal is political. Truth be told, I am passionate about Europe, sometimes –

[5] Islam, Shada., Peters, Bettina., & White, Adrian. (n.d.) Ethical Journalism Initiative. Quality Media for Diversity and Pluralism. *European Institute of the Mediterranean.* https://www.iemed.org/publication/ethical-journalism-initiative-quality-media-for-diversity-and-pluralism/

admittedly - naively so. I was – I still am - mesmerized by Europe's story of reconciliation between enemies, the coming together of countries to make sure there were no more wars, the premise of building a European community where everyone was equal – a Union of Equality - and which would be a force for global good.

Europe's vision spoke to me. Growing up, I had become tired and frustrated with South Asia's politics of hate, the constant fear of war, the trading of insults – and too often, of bullets. I had lived through two India-Pakistan conflicts, seen the devastation cause by Pakistan's military during the 1971 war that led to the creation of Bangladesh. My mother often spoke about the violence and carnage that took place during the Partition in 1947, how she had wept as a young girl when her Hindu friends had been forced to leave Lahore for India.

Despite prevailing perceptions, many of the estimated 25 million European Muslims share my attachment to the EU ideal. And like me they suffer each time Islamophobia invariably reaches fever pitch after any Islamist-inspired terrorist act in Europe or elsewhere in the world. Anxiety over Muslims as the "enemy within" goes much deeper than post-terrorism trauma. Anxious debates on the place of Islam in Europe, and claims that European Muslims represent an impossible-to-integrate "other" and are foot soldiers in an ongoing existential confrontation between Europe and Islam, have dogged Muslims across the continent for decades.

There is a dangerous new shrillness to the conversation and a frightening sharpness to the allegations. The situation requires urgent attention and correction, both at the national level but also by the European Union. A combustible mix of geopolitical brinkmanship, unease over migration flows and fears of increased Islamist-related terrorism are adding to existing anti-Muslim sentiment. French President Emmanuel Macron may have denied allegations of fostering racism against Muslims ahead of presidential elections held in 2022, but Amnesty International had to warn French authorities to stop contributing to a "portrayal of all Muslims as suspects" and to end the "stereotypical, stigmatizing and discriminatory comments targeting Muslims and refugees".

Watching these signs of disconnect between many European governments and their Muslim citizens has been disturbing. The relationship is visibly dysfunctional and in dire need of a reset.

As a first important step, the myth of Muslims in Europe as eternal outsiders, with a culture and customs that make them forever "untrue" Europeans, must be challenged. This means not conflating the tiny minority of Islamist extremists with the massive majority that abhors such views. It means accepting not only Islam's historical role and influence in Europe but also recognizing, as German Chancellor Angela Merkel did in 2018, that Islam is a part of modern Germany – and of Europe.

Crucially, improving the situation also requires an end to the outsourcing of Europe-Muslim relations to foreign leaders of Muslim majority states. The acrimonious war of words between EU leaders and Recip Tayyip Erdogan of Turkey or EU leaders' interviews with Arab news channel or plans to appoint an envoy for the Muslim world or inter-faith discussions are beside the point. Worse still, they are counterproductive. These foreign leaders know little of the real problems facing European Muslims. Also, EU leaders who talk to their foreign counterparts over the heads of their own Muslim citizens are not only being insulting, they are reinforcing perceptions of European Muslims as exotic and alien non-citizens.

Women in particular are in the firing line. A recent project[6] I worked on with MDI focused on the discrimination and violence faced by Muslim women, especially those who wear the Hijab, who have to fight the perception that they are either victims in need of help or a public threat.

[6] *Muslim women and communities Against Gender Islamophobia in soCiety.* https://magic.iemed.org/

And yet my own experience shows that the large majority of Europeans who follow Islam live fulfilling and productive lives as law-abiding and tax-paying European citizens. Many are involved in local politics. Across Europe, Muslim entrepreneurs are revitalizing impoverished urban neighborhoods, creating jobs and prompting innovation in business. They excel in sports as well as art and culture. These stories may be less sensational than those of misfits and criminals but they also need to be told.

The Open Society Institute has noted that European Muslims and non-Muslims share the same concerns, needs and experiences, including the quest for a "better quality of education, improved housing, cleaner streets and [the tackling of] anti-social behavior and crime". Notwithstanding populist and racist rhetoric, an overwhelming majority of Muslims in France and Germany describe themselves as loyal to their country and see no contradiction between French/German and Muslim values. "There is no evidence supporting the common contention that Muslims are living in a separate, parallel society," according to Germany's Bertelsmann Foundation.

My own journey is proof that the struggle against Islamophobia is part of the wider struggle against racism and discrimination. Campaigning for an anti-racist Europe also means fighting Islamophobia. As such, combating prejudice and bias against Islam must be an inherent part of Europe's broader equality agenda. Hatred and discrimination against Muslims are a stain on Europe, its values, its internal cohesion and global reputation.

Europe's hopes of exercising more geopolitical influence and making more friends in the Global South are stymied by its Islamophobic discourse and actions, its discriminatory policies towards Europeans of color, and its harsh treatment of racialized migrants and asylum seekers. EU governments' reluctance to dive into uncomfortable questions, such as Europe's legacy of colonialism and participation in the Atlantic slave trade, also stand in the way of a more powerful global Europe.

I have often pointed out that while the great European wars and the Holocaust are frequently commemorated, a strange silence has reigned over the ugly reality of Europe's imperial and colonial history. Many European states arguably see the EU's establishment in 1957 as a 'virgin birth' which erased any collective responsibility for EU states' colonial pasts.

Some of this is changing slowly, but there is no miracle solution or quick fix, no one policy that can change years of willful neglect. However, the situation is not all gloomy everywhere. The good news is that even as national politicians step up the anti-Muslim rhetoric, local officials, especially city mayors, have adopted a different and more welcoming approach. Additionally, COVID-19 has spotlighted the strong presence of Muslims in many frontline services across the continent.

Even some national leaders are trying to make amends. Belgium, France, Germany and the Netherlands have all – in their own way – tried to voice regret over the harshness of their colonial rule. European museums are working to repatriate at least some of their (mainly stolen) colonial-era artefacts. Amsterdam's Rijksmuseum has held an exhibition on the Netherlands' participation in the trade of enslaved people. And Dutch Prime Minister Mark Rutte has finally acknowledged that it is time that the Christmas tradition of Black Piet, a white person with blackface who plays one of Santa's little helpers, died out.

More, much more, needs to be done at the EU and national levels. At the EU, there will have to be a mix of immediate actions—such as promoting awareness of dehumanizing language and unconscious biases, less discriminatory EU recruitment policies, collection of data on ethnicity, improved police training, and stricter enforcement of the EU's own anti-racism laws and regulations. These efforts will have to go hand in hand with determined longer-term policies and measures to change deeply-anchored and long-standing prejudices, stereotypes and cultural norms.

EU leaders and institutions must play their part in discouraging outdated, largely one-dimensional definitions of 'European identity', in favor of a recognition that 'hyphenated' citizens and residents, with fluid, changing and multiple identities, are also true Europeans. More diversity in media is needed to keep politicians on their toes and to ensure political accountability.

In the end, it's very simple: Europe needs to live up to its rhetoric on values and equity and to respect the human rights of all Europeans, regardless of their race, religion and color. Europe's future, prosperity and societal cohesion depend on becoming more inclusive and accepting – nay, celebrating – its diversity. As Europeans, we belong here. Europe is our home too.

Željko Ivanović

Željko Ivanović is a journalist and human rights activist from Montenegro. He was a founder and one of the editors of the first Montenegrin political magazine *Krug* (1990) that promoted values of open society, democracy, and liberalism while nationalism was advancing in a dissolving Yugoslavia. With a group of colleagues, Ivanović also founded the first independent daily newspaper Vijesti. Between 2008 and 2010, he started both the Vijesti TV channel and the online news portal. Vijesti Media Group is the largest and the most influential media organisation in Montenegro today. In 2022, he received the prestigious Transatlantic Leadership Network (TLN) Freedom of the Media award for outstanding Commentary and Criticism.

WHY?

I was always curious...I asked my momma, I said, 'Momma, how come everything is white?' I said, why is Jesus white with blonde hair and blue eyes? Why is the Lord's Supper all white men? Angels are white, the Pope, Mary... I said, 'Mother, when we die, do we go to heaven?' She said, 'Naturally we go to heaven.' I said, 'Well, what happened to all the black angels? They took the pictures?' I said, "Oh, I know. If the white folks is in Heaven too, then the black angels were in the kitchen, preparing the milk and honey. "Momma, I don't want no milk and honey, I like steaks." ... I always wondered why Miss America was always white. All the beautiful brown women in America, beautiful sun tans, beautiful shapes, all types of complexions, but she was always white. And Miss World was always white, and Miss Universe was always white. And then they got some stuff called White House cigars, White Swan soap, King White soap, White Cloud tissue paper, White Rain hair rinse, White Tornado floor wax, everything was white. And the angel fruit cake was the white cake and the devil food cake was the chocolate cake. I said, "Momma, why is everything white?" And the President lived in the White House. And Mary had a little lamb with fleece as white as snow, and Snow White, and everything was white. Santa Claus was white and everything bad was black. The little ugly duckling was the black duck, and the black cat was bad luck, and if I threaten you, I'm going to blackmail you. I said, "Momma, why don't they call it 'whitemail'? I was always curious. And I always wondered why..."

Muhammad Ali, the chatterer from Louisville, the greatest boxer of all times, but also one of the greatest champions of human equality and racial justice, said the above in one breath, on the BBC, in the autumn of 1971. Earlier that year--on March 8th--the historic Ali-Frazier match had taken place, just three days before my ninth birthday. It was in connection with Ali, or Clay as us kids called him, that I asked my mother that day – why?

We were preparing ourselves for a long night, for staying up until the early hours of the morning to watch the match televised live from Madison Square Garden in New York City. Everyone was excited and we started talking with our next-door neighbours, who had to come over because they didn't yet own a TV, about who was rooting for whom. As far as I was concerned, there was no dilemma – I was for Clay, of course. Because of his dancing feet, his skill, his charm, you had to love him.

I was still too young to know or understand the significance of his commitment outside the world of sports. His opposition to the war in Vietnam, his change of religion as a form of protest, and his unwavering fight for the rights of African Americans--at a time when they were still called Negroes. My mother's angry response to my glorification of Ali was: *Quiet! Bite your tongue! You don't know anything, Frazier is our man...* I wouldn't let it go, I kept talking about his boxing skills, predicting a stunning victory for my idol, but since my mother kept going on about Frazier, I finally asked her – why? Why are you rooting for Frazier when Clay is so wonderful...Red in the face, she came up to me, took me gently by the ear and whispered: *Frazier didn't become a Turk...*

I didn't know what it meant at the time, to 'become a Turk', and I didn't understand why she had to whisper it in my ear. I decided that she did it to punish me, in tweaking that ear.

A few years later - I was twelve, the situation was different, but the message was the same, and the problem, again, was about being different - I understood what it meant 'to become a Turk'. I understood why three or four years earlier my mother had whispered those words in my ear in connection with Frazier. Now it had to do with the first time I fell in love.

The girl from my neighbourhood was named Drita. She was Albanian, and a Catholic, not "one of us" Orthodox Christians. All I cared about was that she had a beautiful name, long black hair falling down onto her shoulders, the faintest of freckles sprinkled across her face, and unforgettable eyes, deep and as green as the Morača River that flowed through Podgorica, our town. Again, my mother chose the wrong side. She started off by saying Drita isn't for you, she's a year older than you, finishing up with her ace argument: She's not one of us! Again, I asked my mother – why? She replied coldly: She's a Malisor[1]...

I was a big boy now and this time I didn't need any explanation about what my mother wanted to say. I remembered that evening in 1971 when she was rooting for Frazier. Now I already knew that 'to become a Turk' meant to convert to Islam, and she had whispered it into my ear because sitting with us in the apartment, watching the match on TV, were our next-door neighbours, the Šabotićes. Muslims. My mother had coffee every morning with Tuna Sabotić, and often made crepes or fritters for all "our children", as she and Tuna used to refer to us. That continued until we moved away to a different neighbourhood.

I still don't understand it to this day, and I didn't want to ask lest it make me even more miserable. Why was a different religion for her a heresy in my upbringing at home but not in daily communications with others outside the house? If she had the best possible relations with her neighbours and colleagues at work, with no sign of prejudice, why did

[1] An Albanian from the mountainous area of Malesi (the Montenegrin-Albanian border).

she feel it necessary to plant the seed of racism and stereotypes in her own child? I think that, like any mother, she was figuring out how best to protect her child. And tradition, full of various conspiracy theories, was more important to her than her own personal experience.

Stereotypes that she picked up in her village during childhood convinced her that children had to be protected from anything different. Because when hard, troubling times come, that's when you see that "blood is thicker than water." Regardless of whether it is about religion, nation, skin colour or names. For my mother, the Šabotićes were simply neighbours, which was why she doted on them. She simply didn't think of them as Muslims. Because Muslims were different, they were unfamiliar enemies from history schoolbooks and the stories of her parents and ancestors.

Then it came time to go to university. Fortunately, since I was ready to leave home, journalism wasn't taught in Montenegro, so I went to Belgrade. That was in 1981. Tito had just died; right away the bureaucracy he had left behind to govern started showing signs of ineptitude and being out of its depth. The big country where I was born, the Socialist Federal Republic of Yugoslavia, started to wobble. And it was again through sport that I had a new, strange experience—and this one convinced me that the struggle for acceptance of diversity and difference was actually my lifelong calling.

Again, as with Ali, I asked why, and again, as with my mother, my university friends gave me a similar answer. In this case, it was the finals of the Yugoslavia Cup in football, and I was with four Belgrade friends at the north stand of the iconic Marakana stadium in Belgrade. But, again, the most interesting part happened before the game itself. The official announcer told the crowd of 80,000 fans that there would be a pre-game event, what I would call an ideological performance: parachutists would jump out of a helicopter above the stadium and land in the middle of the pitch, each bearing the flag of one of the country's constituent republics. The spectators rose to their feet, the parachutists were announced one by one, along with the flag they were carrying, applause reverberated throughout the stadium--until the announcer said that the next parachutist to land in the middle of the pitch would be carrying the flag of the Republic of Croatia.

As with the previous parachutists, I started to applaud, but it was lost in the deafening sound of catcalling and booing that filled the stadium! I was taken aback. I didn't understand what was happening. I asked my university friend Marko, to whom I was closest – why? Why was this parachutist different from the others? Marko laughed and said: Who are you for?! "For Red Star", I replied tersely. "And you?" The answer was: just so long as it's not the "Bili" or "Modri'! [Red Star is a Serbian football team; Bili and Modri, which mean "white" and "dark blue" respectively, are Croatian teams.]

I didn't get it. Except that, as with Muhammad Ali, the problem was again in the colour. So, it wasn't just black that was wrong; white and dark blue could darken the mind as well. Again, I saw the imprint of human fear and stereotypes on the colours, the unwillingness to accept the different and diverse.

And when the majority of people in a society hold onto stereotypes, when they respond more to conspiracy theories than to scientific discoveries or indisputable rational arguments, when religion and nations, rather than values and shared opinions, determine whom they feel close to, then you have a sheep pen, not a state. Then sheep rather than citizens live in the place. And then we have an overriding need for a shepherd or a leader.

That is how an anonymous communist apparatchik called Slobodan Milošević became the Leader in the late 1980s. And that is how the citizenry became quickly intoxicated with nationalism, blinded by hate speech against anything that was different, against religions and nations that were different, against diverse opinions, until the moment came when guns and tanks were handed out.

This was in October 1991. My wife Dragana had just given birth to our son Filip, and it was around then I received my call-up papers. My fellow Montenegrins, my neighbours, relatives, the vast majority of them, were already under arms in the shameful march on and aggression against Konavle and Dubrovnik. I somehow remembered a story from my student days. A university friend, a student from Palestine, told me how Yasser Arafat had to sleep in a different place every evening to keep safe from his enemies. I was looking at a similar choice – to save my dignity and follow my belief that the war was not just. Even if it meant risking my life.

The propaganda was so unrelenting that one day my mother was convinced that she would lose her son. She had already lost her brother, father and five uncles in World War II. They had all joined the partisans. One autumn day that year of 1991, somebody named Babić, from the Defence Ministry, came to the Assembly of Montenegro and told everybody watching the historic session on television that any deserter who refused his call-up papers would be arrested and summarily executed.

Although I was in hiding, Dragana and Filip were still living at our apartment. I had just dropped by to see them, grab a sandwich and go to the new hiding place that my wife and I had found for that evening. The phone rang. Dragana was nursing Filip, so I had to take the call, worried that the voice at the other end might belong to some military commander chasing down renegades and deserters. I picked up the receiver and first waited to hear the voice so I would know who it was. Instead of a voice, I heard weeping...And sobbing...Žeka... Žeka...It was my mother. That was a relief. What is it, why are you crying, I asked, although I knew why, of course. They'll execute you if you don't respond to the call-up, the minister just said so, she said.

Beside myself with fury at the situation, I slammed down the receiver and broke off the call. I picked up the sandwich, kissed my wife and child goodbye, and left. For my new hide-out, of course. Again, I had let my mother down by choosing what she thought was the wrong side, the way she used to think I had chosen the wrong girlfriend. That night, as I tried to get some sleep at our friends, the Radovićes – he had been the best man at our wedding - I silently asked minister Babić, his commanders, Milošević, Bulatović and Đukanović – why? Why was the Croat, who only yesterday had been our neighbour and brother, now an Ustasha[2]? Why did he have to be robbed, humiliated, displaced, even killed? Why were our Muslim and Albanian neighbours our enemies too? Why did they become Balijas and Shiptars overnight?[3] Why war, the biggest in Europe since World War II, rather than parting ways with a smile and a glass of champagne, like the Czechs and Slovaks?

It was because of the war that I went into journalism. To fight against all forms of violence and promote all forms of freedom. That was why, in the early 1990s, a group of colleagues and I launched the magazine Krug (Circle), which later turned into the weekly Monitor. This was the first news organization in Montenegrin history that was not under government control, and it has spread the ideas of diversity and civil rights for all these decades.

However, as with any great, true mission, a high price was paid for championing free and independent media. Just as Clay had to lose his freedom, change his religion, and spend the rest of his life asking why, so we promoted the value and importance of diverse opinions and free thought, perhaps unaware that in so doing we were risking our lives--even after one of us was murdered.

---

[2] Croatian fascist movement that ruled the Independent State of Croatia during World War II.

[3] Derogatory names for Bosnian Muslims and ethnic Albanians.

It was May 28, 2004. My colleague and friend Duško Jovanović, the editor-in-chief of the rival daily Dan, had been shot dead the previous evening. Shortly after midnight, after the paper had gone to press, he walked out of his office building, crossed the street, and got into his car. While he was putting on his seatbelt before starting the engine, he was sprayed with bullets from a moving car - a Golf. Just like in an American gangster movie set in the 1930s. After a sleepless night, I was sitting in a café with the editor-in-chief of our paper, Vijesti, for which I was the director. We were both speechless in the wake of the killing, barely able to string a few words together, and again I said – why? Why was Duško murdered, but also, why wasn't I? Who decided, and how did they decide, that an editor-in-chief and founder of a newspaper had to be killed? And why Duško but not Željko?

A few hours later, my son Filip, who was thirteen at the time, answered my question. When I came home around five in the afternoon, Filip opened the door, took one look at me and, his chin trembling, on the verge of tears, he hugged me tight and whispered: It's a good thing, Dada, that you're not an editor-in-chief! Of course, it wasn't an answer to my earlier 'why', it was simply a reflection of the pain and worry of a child. Avoiding the thought that it could have been his father killed the previous night, he had found comfort in the idea that editors-in-chief, not publishers, are responsible for media criticism of the authorities and powers-that-be. So, his director Dad was safe.

Until then, I had thought that Montenegro wasn't Russia, even though I knew that Milo Đukanović, the Montenegrin President, was the same as Putin. Less than a year before Jovanović's murder, another journalist and editor whom I personally knew was killed. His name was Yuri Shchekochikhin. We'd met and spent a few unforgettable days together in Herceg Novi, on the Montenegrin coast, where Milica Pešić and MDI had organized what is to this day the biggest media conference Montenegro can remember.

He worked for Novaya Gazeta, the only independent media in Putin's Russia. I admired this man who spoke so passionately about investigative stories connected to corruption in the Russian Duma and the clandestine operations of the FSB (Federal Security Service), dismissing concerns from many colleagues about his safety. Many years later, after I was physically assaulted myself, I realised that Yuri had thought the same way I did that evening – why would the regime, however unscrupulous, beat up or kill a journalist just for doing his or her job? In the autumn of 2004, after returning from Beslan—the scene of a deadly school hostage-taking siege that Putin's regime was trying to minimise--Yuri was poisoned. Probably on the plane taking him back to Moscow. He died twelve days later at hospital. The Russian Office of the Prosecutor never agreed to Novaya Gazeta's request for an investigation into the death.

Some ten years later, in homage to Duško and Yuri, and to all other murdered colleagues, I wrote a text about journalism in autocratic societies and dictatorships. Its title was "Dancing with Death", and here is a key passage: *"That's what it's like when you live in a ravaged country and humiliated society. Instead of the courage needed for journalism, it is fear and trepidation that reign. And silence. Nothing that happens is unexpected, nothing that is said is shameful. However fabricated and false it may be. We live on a desert island where cowards rule, where the powerful and rich make the decisions, cursing through scandalous headlines – the worst of the worst. A few of us naïve souls won't give in, we do not want to see the desert around us or show the pain we feel from being crucified. Publicly we swagger, privately we weep. Because if we were to show fear, what would be left of those for whom we are their only hope. Those who cannot talk or write, but who have not stopped believing."*

However, my mother couldn't understand that. Now she was asking – why. Why does it have to be me howling at the moon and seeking justice? Why doesn't somebody else risk their neck? Why does it have to be up to me to change society, my mother asked, predictably concluding: You can't knock your head against a brick wall. Whenever she started on the subject, I would just turn around and go out, because I knew that any answer or explanation I might give would be futile, any word I said - pointless. Because her fear and trepidation were incurable. These feelings would not go away for as long as she was alive or until the dictator fell.

Words became especially pointless after I was ambushed. It was in the early morning hours of September 2, 2007, at the big, tenth anniversary party for our daily paper Vijesti. Around 3 a.m. I left the restaurant where we had been celebrating and walked towards my car. Just before I reached it, three men jumped me. The main guy was wearing a balaclava, the other two were holding baseball bats. At first, I thought it was simply a bad dream, that any minute I would wake up, sweating and terrified, but glad that it had all been a nightmare. When that didn't happen, I started defending myself, trying to wrest free from their grip. After five or six blows from the baseball bats--which left me, as later established by the doctor at the Clinical Centre, with a fractured cheekbone, contused meniscus and bruises on my body--I managed to break away and run back to the restaurant. Presumably deciding that I had gotten the beating I deserved and that they had been ordered to carry out, the thugs ran away.

I was never as curious as I was that night about – why? Even in those first few minutes after the assault. Why had somebody been so upset with me that they had to have me beaten up? Why was a different opinion and criticism so unwanted by anybody, even a dictator. Did he have children, I wondered that night, thinking about my mother and how she would live with this? Not to mention the children. And my wife. Why was the world so unjust that it gave the powerful the right to decide about other people's lives, violently if they felt like it?

In my mind I asked my mother why she had given birth to me and raised me to be so stubborn, so unwilling to pull back with my tail between my legs, even when my own life was at stake. In my mind, I asked my mother why they had beaten me with a wooden bat and not a metal rod; was that a sign that I wasn't that bad and that I deserved a milder punishment? I remembered Ali; had they beaten him like that or just tormented him to make him go to Vietnam? Or to agree to keep quiet?

Again I was curious and if I could have, I would have asked my mother all these things when she woke up the next morning and heard the news...But I couldn't, of course; there was no opportunity, because she just kept crying...And repeating through her tears that you can't knock your head against a brick wall and that this time I had survived but if I didn't keep quiet, the next time they would kill me. Like Duško, she kept saying, sobbing. In those moments, I thought about that evening on March 9, 1971, when she was rooting for Frazier and I was rooting for Ali, she for no freedom and I for freedom, already setting the stage for everything that was to happen.

I could have pressed the point and told my mother that all persecution, every act of injustice and every act of violence is, at heart, an attempt to deprive someone's right to free choice. I didn't do it, of course, because it would have been useless. In any event, my mother herself became sick of such a life sooner than the dictator did of his rule. And so she died before he fell from power. After that September evening in 2007, my mother spent the remainder of her life in fearful anticipation of receiving the worst possible news, probably wondering why her son was so selfish as to sacrifice the peace and tranquillity of those closest to him, his family, for his mission and profession. She died content - her dark fears had not come true and that worst of news had never arrived.

In his best-selling 1963 book *Man's Search for Meaning,* the renowned psychotherapist Viktor Frankl, who had survived the Auschwitz death camp, wrote: "*Don't aim at success. The more you aim at it and make it a target, the more you are going to miss it. For success, like happiness, cannot be pursued; it must ensue... I want you to listen to what your conscience commands you to do and go on to carry it out to the best of your knowledge. Then you will live to see that in the long-run—in the long-run, I say! —success will follow you precisely because you had forgotten to think about it.*"

Unfortunately, my mother didn't live to see the fall of the dictator and to get an answer that evening in Washington - again it was September, but this time 2022 - to the question she so often heard me ask and which she most often asked herself: Was there any point to it all? I stepped onto the stage of the National Press Club in Washington, from the 14th Street entrance, where I was to receive the Freedom of the Media award for my overall work in journalism, and in particular for the commentaries and opinion pieces I have been writing in Vijesti for years.

Here's some of what I said: *"I see this award as a small victory for trustworthy information over fake news; the award is also a victory for the rule of law over corruption and nepotism, it is a victory for the profession over organized crime, this award is the triumph of reporting in the public interest over trash and propaganda, and finally, this award is a victory for the moral over the immoral.*

"I hope that from the above you can see what I have devoted my life to, and what the most important topics our media group Vijesti has been focusing on every day for decades. Thank you to all journalists, editors and employees at Vijesti, thank you to fellow-fighters and partners. Without the sacrifice of all those mentioned, my own sacrifice wouldn't have any meaning or results. Last but not least, thank you to my wife and my children – only they know how much sweat, tears and yes, even blood was spilled for the result that has led to this moment."

But before I said these words, I mentioned my mother; I said that if she were with us that evening, even she would finally be pleased with me. Even she would have to admit that there was a point to it all. To Ali's curiosity, and to my own.

Mike Jempson

Mike Jempson began as a journalist in London's East End in the 1970s and was founder-editor of the *East End News* co-operative in 1981. A long-serving member of the Campaign for Press & Broadcasting Freedom, he organised Special Parliamentary Hearings into the Press in 1992, and from 1996 was director of the MediaWise Trust, the journalism ethics charity founded by victims of media abuse. A Visiting Professor in Journalism Ethics at Lincoln University, he taught journalism at the University of the West of England, and has trained journalists in 40 countries, with MDI, EU and UN agencies. A Life Member of the National Union of Journalists, he is editorial consultant to The Bristol Cable co-op. (www.mikejempson.eu)

DIVERSITY AND ME

Being brought up in a monoculture does wonders for your concept of diversity.

I was born in a rural English town about 25 kilometers southwest of London, into an Irish Catholic family. Our social circle was further limited because my dad was a policeman. In those days, the police and their families lived in social housing provided by the municipality. Few of our working-class neighbours wanted much to do with us. Besides that, we moved frequently. Before I left home I had lived in six different council houses in different parts of a very white, post-war suburban area.

These factors limited the building of friendships outside the home. However, with five sisters and two brothers, I used to say that we did not feel the need for friends. Within the family there were so many competing personalities and social groupings to contend with. I was part of the 'top two' with my elder sister. We felt hard done-by because we were given household chores long before the others, whose domestic servitude was diluted by the sheer weight of numbers.

My next sister down and I could resent our elder sister together and were thought of as 'terrible twins'. My next bond was with my first brother; we shared a bed. The eldest four were 'the Big Ones'; a three year gap separated us from the 'Little'uns' - three more girls and a boy. A gender divide was inevitable, and there were times when individuals or groups were in or out of favour with each other or with our strict parents.

I suppose a crude sense of social justice developed through the solidarity brought on whenever trouble threatened. I got my first taste of this when I was barely six years old at a Catholic primary school in what was then a military town. My older sister and I faced taunts and even stone-throwing from the non-Catholics at the state school. Once, after we'd had to take shelter behind a wall, my mother instructed me to always protect my sister.

When a fire broke out in the school, we were directed to a church hall for lunch. Teachers with croaky voices insisted that we eat in silence. My sister and I were caught whispering and were instructed to stand on our benches in different parts of the hall. When the meal was over, the teacher in charge administered a sharp smack across my sister's palm with a ruler.

He then strode around to me in the hushed hall and I got the same punishment. Fighting back tears I landed a punch in his face: "That's for hitting my sister!" I declared.

Surprised if not shocked, he lifted me up and carried me out through the fire exit to an alleyway where a wagon wheel was leaning up against the wall. Everyone else was back at school by the time he took me back. Rumour had spread that he had tied me to the wheel and whipped me. It was not true - but I had become a folk hero nonetheless. I remember being sat down on a window ledge in the playground and made a fuss over by the girls.

In the even tighter monoculture of a junior seminary I attended as a teenager, my sense of right and wrong was enhanced when we were suddenly banned from reading or even seeing newspapers. They were reporting in prurient detail a court case about a sex scandal involving the defence minister, who had apparently shared a lover with a Russian intelligence officer. Outraged at this censorship, I got the papers smuggled in through workmen before abandoning plans to become a priest.

In those days, compulsory testing at age 11 filtered children with more academic potential for free attendance at a grammar school until age 18. As one of only two local boys who passed the exam, our choice was limited to the nearest Catholic one. We found ourselves at the bottom of the pile, looked down upon by those whose parents paid fees, and especially by those who were boarding at the school. The discovery that you lived in a council house pushed you even further down the social scale.

Yet in our crowded home we provided support for those in need, and even took in Yoruba and Ibo exiles during the Biafra War in 1969. My father's links to police forces from Africa and Asia also helped open our eyes to the wider world. I volunteered with the St Vincent de Paul Society, which comforts those in need, and learned that even in respectable middle-class areas life could be tough if you were disabled, old and lonely, or suffered mental ill-health.

I progressed to a more egalitarian technical college before going on to university. These changes brought me into contact not only with girls who were not my sisters' friends from convent school or church, but even with people who did not share my Catholic faith. I discovered that, contrary to our bizarre notion that they were weird for going to church voluntarily, they could be fun to hang out with. (For Catholics, going to church was an obligation.)

I gradually emerged from my shell, without entirely discarding it, at Sussex University during the years of student revolt from 1966 to 1969, but I still had a sense of being an outsider in the big bad world. For the first time I met rich people and discovered that even the most upstanding and well-heeled English harboured deep-seated prejudices. The wealthy parents of my girlfriend disapproved as much of my Irish-Catholic heritage as my leftwing views.

My first job was teaching religious education and creative writing in a Buckinghamshire village secondary school. I experienced the hypocrisy of other respectable folk, from teachers to church-going country folk. They did not like my replacement of Bible studies with comparative religion, nor my efforts to explain to curious children the religious and political strife which had caused British troops to be sent into Northern Ireland. The out-of-school social justice activities I organised for the children also upset some in the village. Advertisements were placed in the local paper saying I was selling off items from the cottage I rented, drug detritus was planted in my kitchen, and a taxi was sent to take me to the airport at dawn. These were messages that I was no longer wanted in the village. Some people prefer their monoculture undisturbed.

It was much the same at my next job in respectable Tunbridge Wells in Kent, where the Catholic priests had upset the locals by allowing the basement of their presbytery to become a shelter for the homeless. The site had quickly descended into a drug den and I was invited in to sort things out. Initially, it was too dangerous to live there, so I earned a bed by working the night and early morning shifts at a nearby Cheshire Home, one of many set up by war hero Group Captain Leonard Cheshire to care for the disabled. I was immersed in the types of social conditions that society found difficult to cope with.

Gradually I won the confidence of the inhabitants of the basement and set it up as a Cyrenian project, named after Simon of Cyrene who helped carry Christ's cross; we called it The Well. I lived there with as many as 27 ex-servicemen, alcoholics, young offenders, drug addicts and rejects from psychiatric hospitals at any one time. They were vilified by many locals as the mad, the sad and the dangerous to know, and by identifying with them I branded myself as an outsider. With advice from two other outsiders, the secretary of the local Communist Party, who had only one arm and was married to a Vietnamese exile, and a gentle vegan anarchist who ran a cutlers shop, I learned how to engage with the media to challenge and change people's attitudes.

It was a skill I also applied in my next job as a youth and community worker in the East End of London, where whole communities were being abandoned as the river docks closed down and developers moved in. The racism that had once been directed against Gypsies, Huguenots, the Irish and the Jews was now being turned against Black people and the Muslim Bangladeshi community.

I tasted my own share of prejudice during my relationship with a Black single mother of three during the early 1970s. She was spat at by other young Black women for going with a White guy. Nor did our white neighbours approve and they reported me to my employers.

In 1974, when Irish republicans bombed taverns in Guildford and Birmingham, there was downright hostility to Irish communities - not least in East London, where many of the leading community and trades union activists were of Irish descent. As an act of solidarity I decided to assert my identity and take up Irish citizenship. I quickly discovered that just carrying a green passport qualified me to be stopped and questioned every time I left or re-entered the country. Yet I was the same person who had previously travelled on a British passport, which the authorities had required me to relinquish.

Ignorance was at the core of so many negative attitudes towards 'the other' - making people prey to those who would manipulate them for their own purposes. I also learned how easy it was for well-meaning liberals and leftists to respond with knee-jerk reactions to those who did not fit into their orthodoxies. Information and education would be essential to changing minds and attitudes and providing motivations for this change.

Having fed plenty of good stories to the local newspaper, I was eventually hired by them in 1977. I soon discovered that editors do not always uphold the ethical codes to which they pay lip service. As a reporter I saw how revolting and complex racism can be. When I asked my editor why, in one of London's most multicultural areas, we had no Black reporters, he replied "You don't know whose side they are on." And when my reports of racist attacks became too frequent he stopped running them on the front page, saying they were too depressing and upset the advertisers.

In the early 1980s, I helped set up and edit a rival local newspaper. At the *East End News* co-operative we championed as wide a range of talents as we could, launching the careers of numerous Black and Asian journalists and photographers who went on to do well in the mainstream media. To counteract their lack of representation in conventional local papers, we featured a weekly Black Voices page with contributions from local activists. It was to form the basis of Britain's most successful Black newspaper *The Voice,* launched by members of our co-operative.

Women members ran their own What's On column but also tried to ensure gender equality throughout the paper, especially in the sports section: We were the first local paper to have women covering football.

In the early 1990s, I was invited to contribute to media courses at a polytechnic in the West of England. I observed that many of the Black students felt marginalised. I organised a session in which all the White students were to sit silently on one side, and all the Black students on another, free to speak about their experiences of life, if they wished.

One Jewish student asked where he should sit. I told him that was a matter for him to decide. He chose to sit with the Whites. A Lebanese student asked where he should sit. "I look White," he said. "But when people hear my name they assume I am Black." Again I said it was his choice. He chose to sit with the Blacks.

There was an uncomfortable silence for a while, and then some of the Black students began to talk about their lives. One spoke very powerfully about her anxieties from the moment she got up and left the house. She described the looks and treatment she received in shops and on the buses.

Afterwards the Black students were positive about the session. I was struck by the fact that they spoke about feeling "grateful for being given permission to speak". Their language said it all. Meanwhile some White students, shocked by what they had heard, accused me of trying to break up friendships. I asked them why they did not know about the racism their friends had experienced.

All that had gone before helped to inform my later career as Director of the journalism ethics charity PressWise, now The MediaWise Trust. It was set up by people whose lives had been damaged by inaccurate or intrusive coverage by the mainstream media. Many of these victims of media abuse were women or the most vulnerable members of society. It put me in good stead to work with the Media Diversity Institute as a trainer, seeking to challenge, and to change, entrenched and often unconscious prejudice among media professionals.

We all like to think that we are well aware of the world and all its wiles, and secure from the weaknesses of our fellow citizens. In the mid 1990s, at a conference in Greece on The Media and the State, I recall remonstrating with a French member of the European Parliament who had blamed the media for the 1993 suicide of French Prime Minister Pierre Bérégovoy. To the amusement of the assembled journalists, I declared that "The only difference between politicians and journalists is that politicians think they know all the answers, and journalists know that they know all the answers."

People tend to have a certain intransigence in our view of ourselves. Maybe we need that level of confidence to cope with all the things that we see and hear, not least the bullshit of so many politicians, and the excuses of so many public figures and public servants when things go wrong.

Our industry is little better. Corporate media lawyers in the UK have warned us not to admit to errors for fear it may cost the company dearly. No wonder members of the public feel helpless and alone when we report about their lives and get things wrong, or rely upon easy stereotypes to get messages across, with little thought about how that might affect the lives of those involved. Our task should be to challenge and not simply amplify the intemperate or inaccurate language used by politicians to play on people's prejudices. We are supposed to offer verifiable information - not reinforce ignorance.

So how do you implant new ideas among colleagues who are reluctant to admit that they don't know things? It was a problem we had to face when introducing the idea that children's rights are a potential source of stories during trainings sponsored by UNICEF in the former Soviet Union.

We wanted participants to acknowledge their ignorance and to realise the importance of filling in the gaps in their knowledge. We also wanted them to appreciate that such knowledge could add depth to their stories and authority to questions they might ask of experts.

Since most journalists are both inquisitive and competitive, and enjoy a bit of fun, we adopted the format of the television game show as a learning method.

Participants were divided into teams. One by one, each person picked a number linked to questions devised from information needed to report authoritatively on a wide range of issues affecting children - the law as it related to adoption, for example, or the age of consent for sex, or aspects of the criminal justice system. They could choose to answer alone, or with help from their team mates for a reduced number of points. Other teams could win points with a challenge. Soon, in the battle to win a box of chocolates, they forgot they were displaying their ignorance. In the end, the full list of questions were shared and friendly rivalries resolved as they researched the correct answers.

We adopted a similar interactive-learning approach when introducing the concept of diversity. Using the 'pet hates' prevalent in the particular society, we would overload a 'life boat' - often a couple of tables pushed together that would barely hold all the participants - with a range of characters whose 'problematic' identities were leavened by a redeeming feature or skills. We'd have a gay doctor, for example, or a Roma carpenter. Cast adrift from a sinking liner, the boat would only be able to stay afloat and reach the safety of the nearest island if some of those on board were thrown into the shark infested waters.

Each person would plead for their lives before a vote was taken. Prejudices quickly came to the fore, whether or not participants remained in character. We added a fresh dimension to this scenario. All those thrown overboard were taken to another room - 'rescued' by another craft with a crew who knew where the nearest island was and had room for a limited number of extra passengers. Those once rejected now had to chance to vote for which of their persecutors could join them on the rescue craft. Now, prejudices aside, it was people's practical skills that mattered most.

This telling exercise generated much discussion, and some trauma. Seasoned journalists were surprised at how quickly their own prejudices had surfaced, and gave them all pause for thought. In Azerbaijan, constantly in conflict with neighbouring Armenia, participants expressed remorse about having instantly rejected a pregnant Armenian. They also realised that a doctor's sexuality should be less of an issue than their abilities.

In a booklet for Europe's SOS Racisme movement, "All The Voices/ Todas As Vozes", Portuguese journalist Ana Cristina Pereira and I shared our views on diversity and the media. In the opening paragraphs I attempted to illustrate what happens when people are denied a voice in the public sphere.

'You are sitting outside a cafe among a mixed social group discussing the latest big issue. Everyone has an opinion, and 'facts' to back up their convictions, but there are constant challenges from others who think their views and anecdotes offer a better analysis and solution. The topic may be gay marriage, economic downturn, unemployment, immigration, the latest war, global warming - something that affects us all. The debate is spirited; everyone seems to be enjoying the wrangle so much they do not notice their coffee has gone cold.

'And they do not seem to notice you.

'You have your own version of events, and an opinion to match. And this time it is based on personal experience rather than high theory. But no one wants to hear it. Every time you try to intervene, someone else butts in. This is worse than frustrating. The more you try to be heard the more annoying it becomes. It is as if you are invisible. It is as if they do not want to hear what you have to say.'

In circumstances like these frustration quickly turns to resentment, then anger. And when you are still ignored, violent retaliation is almost inevitable.

A female colleague and I tried to illustrate this with a version of my Black and White college experiment in some of our MDI trainings. Having carefully primed a couple of women participants, we would suddenly cancel a scheduled session on the grounds that some women had expressed some concerns about treatment they were receiving. The men were instructed to sit on their hands – literally - and not speak during the session. The women would be invited to come forward and speak freely about their treatment by men. And they did. Sometimes it was fun, sometimes painfully intimate. It always made the men extremely uncomfortable. Few could contain their frustration and would angrily demand the right to reply. At the end, we pointed out that the purpose of the exercise was to help them understand what it feels like to be forbidden a voice. The women needed no such lesson.

Promoting the message that everybody has a right to be heard is often an ongoing struggle. When people feel threatened there is a tendency to revert to an atavistic nationalism. As journalists we must strive to keep the door open to everyone, to confront ignorance and encourage understanding.

That is especially difficult to do when newsrooms themselves are a monoculture, rarely reflecting the audiences they serve. And it is especially difficult when powerful forces in society object to being held to account by the Fourth Estate. Our essential task is to provide citizens with the information they need to make well-informed decisions about their lives and the way they are governed. It gets tougher by the day when we are attacked for presenting unpalatable truths.

But these are not just professional matters. We need diversity in all our lives. It adds a richness and a sense of belonging to know that you are part of a human chain that stretches around the globe. There are vast gaps in the knowledge we were taught at school and our ignorance is a liability which diminishes respect for those who do not share the world view we inherited.

My children have godparents from Armenia, France, Germany, South Africa, Tanzania and Trinidad, as a constant reminder that they are part of a far wider network of cultures than those on their doorstep. And on my 70th birthday, my house and garden were filled with guests from at least 21 countries alongside family and friends closer to home - so very different from the monocultural world in which I was brought up.

In a poem I wrote in 2000, which seeks to honour diversity, I tried to sum up how journalists can cope with the realisation that their culturally specific view of the world is not all that there is.

THE OBJECTIVE 'I'?

(The eye of the journalist)

When we report the world
we describe a kaleidoscope.

The essential elements may always be the same
but each person has a different view.

Each time each person looks,
the pattern changes,
as do the circumstances of the viewing
and the language each chooses
to interpret what we see.

Only one thing is certain:
there is no one, simple,
accurate description.

The best we can offer is an honest account
of the impression we gained
from our tunnel vision,
and let others have their say.

Perspective comes
when we acknowledge
that those
without access to the kaleidoscope
have a different tale to tell.

Remzi Lani

Remzi Lani is the Executive Director of the Albanian Media Institute. Lani has a long career in journalism working for "Zeri i Rinise"-Tirana, El Mundo-Madrid, Zeri-Pristina, and the Alternative Information Network–AIM. He has also written articles on Balkan affairs for different local and foreign papers and magazines. Lani has been an expert for the International Commission on the Balkans (Amato Commission) and is a member of the European Council of Foreign Relations. Lani has vast experience working on media freedom in the Balkans, Caucasus, Middle East and Africa. In 1990, he was a founding member of the first human rights group in Albania, the Forum for Human Rights. The Albanian Media Institute was one of the first two MDI Balkan Reporting Diversity partners.

A BALKAN JOURNEY ON DIVERSITY

It was early June 1997, a month that Albanians won't easily forget, as a curfew was in effect following the civil turmoil that had kicked off in March earlier that year. All the while, 11 foreign armies patrolled the streets of Tirana at their pleasure, just like in an absurd theatre play in which no one understands who is fighting whom. Precisely during those days, after crossing the border between Albania and Montenegro with the help of local fishermen, Milica Pešić arrived in Tirana. Our joint efforts to secure her an entry visa to Albania had failed, partly due the fact that the Albanian state at that point had almost ceased to function altogether, and partly due to the fact that back then it was no mean feat for a Serbian to visit Albania. It required an incredible amount of paperwork, and many official signatures and seals. However, in an Albania drowning in anarchy, the idea that one must have a visa to enter the country did not make much sense.

Milica arrived in Tirana and we met at Fidel Cafe, a modest bar where journalists used to get together without even arranging it in advance; one would just show up and sit at the table they liked most, or at whichever table they had more friends sitting around. I had known Milica from a few years earlier when we both used to write for AIM (Alternativna Informativna Mreza-Alternative Information Network). This was a network of journalists from the Balkans, most of them from former Yugoslavia, who in the midst of bloody conflicts across the region refused to bow to the media controlled by nationalistic autocrats and tried to provide an independent and unofficial view of events.

A few months before her visit to Tirana, Milica, who at the time was based in London, had invited the newly established Albanian Media Institute, which I was managing, to take part in the Reporting Diversity project, along with the Center for Independent Journalism in Budapest, a Russian organization based in Saint Petersburg, and others. I gladly accepted the proposal. Unfortunately, due to the shutdown of the Tirana airport during the March turmoil, I could not participate at the first meeting of the full group, which had been held in Russia.

Now we were sitting at the Fidel Café and in no time the table was filled with journalists. They were polite and friendly to each other while sitting there, whether they fancied themselves as right-wing or left-wing, pro-government or against it. But come the evening hours when they would be writing their newspaper articles, they would revert to accusing each other of being servants of the regime or mercenary scribblers for the opposition, only to get together the next morning at the same table sipping coffee and striking up a conversation as though nothing untoward had happened.

Amidst all this, Milica was trying to explain to them what was meant by media diversity, hate speech, negative stereotypes, why it was important to achieve gender balance in the media, etc, etc, and would ask them questions about their jobs and their personal experiences in the newsroom. Truth be told, most of them were more intrigued by the fact that Milica was Serbian, an anti-Milosevic Serbian at that, rather than by what was saying. Some of them had never met a Serbian, let alone conversed with one in the center of Tirana.

Without digressing any further, I must point out that the first handbook on Reporting Diversity in Eastern Europe was produced thanks to this project, published first in Albanian, and later in Hungarian and Russian. In the archives of the Albanian Media Institute, we still have a copy of this handbook, which looks like a boring bundle of A4 paper sheets stapled together--not unlike the makeshift textbooks used by the Department of Philosophy of the University of Tirana when I was a student in the early 80s. Nevertheless, I was later told by Milica that this project was the starting point for the establishment of the Media Diversity Institute (MDI).

By the way, while Milica was meeting people at the Fidel Cafe, the foreign ministry called to say that they had approved her Albanian visa.

Almost simultaneously, ACCESS Sofia, a very active Bulgarian NGO, had initiated an interesting project named Balkan Neighbors. A group of experts from all the countries in the Balkans, from Albania to Greece, from Bulgaria to Turkey, including the countries that had come into being following the dissolution of what was still called Yugoslavia, would monitor the media in their respective countries to get acquainted with and analyze the portrayal of their adjacent and distant neighbors. Our Bulgarian colleague Roumen Yanovski, known for being scrupulous when it comes to his work, published a quarterly newsletter with the reports drafted by the experts of each country. The countries of the former Yugoslavia were still engulfed in conflicts and the media were dominated by negative stereotypes. Hate speech was almost the norm. L'enfer, c'est les autres. The "Others" were primarily the neighbors, with domestic ethnic minorities a close second.

In his 1995 report on the role of the media in the origins of the wars in the former Yugoslavia, UN emissary Tadeusz Mazowiecki came to the conclusion that the media were to blame for stirring up racist and ethnic hatred, thereby directly contributing to the outbreak of these wars[1]. It is no coincidence that in his 1999 book Forging War, the Balkan expert Mark Thomson paraphrased von Clausewitz's well-known expression

[1] Mazowiecki, T. (2005). Special Report on the Media in Former Yugoslavia.

as "War is the continuation of television news by other means."[2] The "campaigns" of the media were the forerunners of military campaigns; the mercenaries of the microphone and pen led to the mercenaries of the Kalashnikovs and landmines. The historian Timothy Garton Ash labeled the Milosevic regime a "TV dictatorship."[3] Now, more than two decades after the end of these bloody conflicts, we have achieved the necessary distance for a serious examination of the role played by the media. What is still needed is a deep analysis of the semantics of the wars: the establishment of nationalistic myths, the projection of the image of the Other, the use of hate speech and hate silence, and so forth.

The image of the next-door neighbor has continuously intrigued me, and that was the reason why I decided in 2015 to get back to this topic, some 15 years after the completion of the ACCESS project. At that point, with the wars having been left behind, the question became how the Balkan peoples view one another in times of peace. How do we report on our neighbors when the Balkan conflicts are a thing of the past and the countries of the region find themselves in the process of Euro-Atlantic integration? What is the image of the Other in the media of the region?

How are minorities in the country perceived? Are they a Trojan horse or a connecting bridge? What is the impact of the process of European integration on the way countries of the Western Balkans see each other? What is the role of new media and social media in creating perceptions of one another? These were some of the questions that needed answering when we started this new project in 2015. In summary, the answer was that despite the changes of the last decade, the way Balkan peoples view each other can hardly be called amicable. A number of negative stereotypes and prejudices vis-à-vis one another are still strong.

---

[2] Thompson, M. (1999). Forging War: The Media in Serbia, Croatia, Bosnia and. Herzegovina. *University of Luton Press.*

[3] Brunner, N. S., Gredelj, S., Hodžic, A. & Krištofic, B. eds. (2000). Media and war. *Centre for Transition and Civil Society Research, Belgrade.*

Compared to the first Balkan Neighbors project, Balkan Neighbors 2.0, as we called it, covered a smaller geographical area. Slovenia, Croatia, Bulgaria and Romania had joined the EU and escaped the Balkans. I remember that we had to postpone the publishing of the book for a few weeks to include an unexpected and interesting case study: the flying of a drone carrying a flag representing a map of Greater Albania over the Belgrade stadium by an Albanian youngster, an incident that was reported extensively by media outlets all over the region and instigated an 'internet war' between Albanians and Serbs[4]. Nationalistic propaganda mobilization in Belgrade, Tirana, Pristina, Banja Luka reached fever pitch. At the time, I wrote that the Balkan wars were over on the battlefields but were still raging on the internet. Cyber-nationalism had reached our shores.

The exit from communism was followed, among other things, by a departure from unanimity, uniformity, unity, homogeneity – very familiar terms to those who have lived under that system in Russia, Romania, Yugoslavia, or elsewhere. In the case of Albania, it was also an exit from totalitarianism, the most extreme form of communist control, a real-life application of George Orwell's Big Brother. Any step out of line--a colorful dress, a careless hairstyle, a pessimistic poem, an ambiguous comment--was just too dangerous. One for all, and all for one! Voter turnout in Albanian elections stood at 100 percent, while 99.99 percent of the voters cast their ballots for the uncontested candidates of the sole political party, which meant that officially, in many elections only a single vote was reported to have been made against the party's candidate.

Pluralism was a word that was nowhere to be seen in newspapers, nor heard on the radio. Diversity was a minefield. Whoever endeavored to walk that path risked a lot. Minorities constituted a threat to society, but that was carefully kept under wraps, and they were treated like a mere façade.

---

[4] Albanian Media Institute, Remzi Lani ed. (2015). Reporting Neighbors in Balkan Media. *Albanian Media Institute, Tirana.* https://www.institutemedia.org/reporting-neighbours-in-balkan-media/

The transition to a democratic society marked the end of the totalitarian regime and the first steps towards pluralism, or differently put the first steps towards diversity. In the meantime, a series of bloody conflicts in former Yugoslavia contrasted starkly with these developments. Minorities were no longer mere façades of socialist harmony, but rather Trojan Horses working for the enemy neighbors next door.

It was precisely in this context that, at the beginning of the 90s, training programs for journalists focused strongly on the topic of diversity, applying two main approaches. The first involved Reporting on Minorities–ethnic, cultural, linguistic, religious, etc. The second involved Reporting Diversity.

It is fair to ask: what is the difference between these two approaches? While Reporting on Minorities focused generally on one of the specific minorities, Reporting Diversity adopted a more comprehensive, holistic approach. While Reporting on Minorities had a protective approach in terms of promoting anti-discriminatory policies, Reporting Diversity adopted a more pro-active, more inclusive approach. We live in a reality of multi-color diversity, and in the final analysis the media is duty-bound to reflect this reality – this is in a nutshell the philosophy of Reporting Diversity. The Media Diversity Institute is a product of this philosophy and has done more than any other organization to promote diversity from the Balkans to the Middle East, from South East Asia to the Caucasus.

Old habits die hard. Young democracies have no doubt achieved a great deal over a relatively short period of time, but they have still continued to suffer from old ailments. Past traditions, habits and beliefs are still strong. One of these traditions is *majoritarianism.*

Dr. Stockman, in Ibsen's play *The Enemy of the People,* says: "The most dangerous enemies of truth and justice in our midst are the compact majorities, the damned compact majority."[5]

[5] Ibsen, Henrik. An Enemy of the people. Translated by R. Farquharson Sharp. https://www.gutenberg.org/files/2446/2446-h/2446-h.htm

A strong culture of majoritarianism is still dominant in the Balkans. Minority rights are proclaimed and promoted, but they often are seen as concessions, if not presents - gifts that the majority offers to the minority. If you are in Albania, you will hear politicians declaring that "we have granted full rights to the Greek minority". Question: who are the "we" who grants these rights? If you are in North Macedonia, you still encounter a strong feeling among the Macedonian majority that the Ohrid Agreement was imposed by Washington and Brussels. The rights of Albanians deriving from this agreement are seen as concessions that the majority was obliged to grant under pressure. Unfortunately, the media is one of the pillars of this culture of Balkan majoritarianism.

I like very much a famous quote from Sub-Commandante Marcos of Zapatistas: "Marcos is gay in San Francisco, black in South Africa, an Asian in Europe, a Chicano in San Ysidro, an anarchist in Spain, a Palestinian in Israel, a Mayan Indian in the streets of San Cristobal, a Jew in Germany, a Gypsy in Poland, a Mohawk in Quebec, a pacifist in Bosnia, a single woman on the Metro at 10 p.m., a peasant without land, a gang member in the slums, an unemployed worker, an unhappy student and, of course, a Zapatista in the mountains. Marcos is all the exploited, marginalized, oppressed minorities resisting and saying `Enough'. He is every minority who is now beginning to speak and every majority that must shut up and listen."[6]

If there ever were a topic that would stand out in the Balkans in terms of the number of papers and books published, conferences and workshops organized, it would definitely be *hate speech.* And for good reason. As Adam Michnik puts it, "The Balkan war first started in the newspapers, radio and television stations."[7] The term Media War was first coined in Bosnia; it was later used in Rwanda, and then unfortunately became an integral part of handbooks and manuals that analyze the role of media in conflicts.

[6] https://www.goodreads.com/quotes/259994-yes-marcos-is-gay-marcos-is-gay-in-san-francisco
[7] Michnik, A. (1995, Summer). Samizdat goes public. *Media Studies Journal*, New York. p. 74.

Sadly, historic knowledge and present experience provide rich material concerning the mechanisms of generating and amplifying hatred. Especially in the Balkans, but also elsewhere.

The first step is an exaggerated, artificial differentiation between the majority of the population and a minority group, the separation of *Us* and *Them*. This includes an over-emphasis on the features that distinguish or supposedly distinguish the minority groups from the majority. Instead of a source of richness, difference becomes a stigma and a stain.

The next step is separation of the two groups by cutting off the bridges between them. The Others, now seen as a distinct, homogenous group, become viewed as representing aggression, danger and crime; they are associated with poverty, sickness, weakness, laziness. Generalizations become routine; a crime committed by a member of the community becomes viewed as characteristic of the whole group. The process starts with prejudice and ends with radical rejection: the normality and humanity of the "Other" are gradually denied.

Simultaneous with the dehumanization process, the other side-"Us"-identifies itself only with the most positive features. Representatives of the dominant majority view themselves as champions of noble values that are threatened by the minority group. The "other" threatens, exploits and endangers "us"; the majority group becomes a "victim" that is obliged to defend itself. The victimization syndrome, which we have seen repeatedly during Balkan conflicts, is not a phenomenon of the past. It is still strong and present.

Albanesi antes portas, warned the Italian media 30 years ago while Albanians disembarked on Italian shores. *Invasion of Albanians*, warned the UK home secretary Suella Braverman 30 years later, in autumn 2022. The same technology, different times.

Also 30 years later, during the Covid 19 pandemic, the Albanian media raised the alarm about migrants at the gates: "...In Albania can enter "pigs and sows", illegal immigrants as well as Indian, Syrian, Afghani, Bangladeshi, Asian immigrants who are bringing with them the deadly virus," declared an article in a Tirana newspaper, as quoted by a report from the project Reporting Diversity 2.0, organized by MDI.[8] So is it really 2.0 or is it 1.0 all over again? This is the question.

Usually, when we talk about mechanisms of hate in the media we focus on "hate speech". I think it would also be interesting to analyze "hate silence". This, for example, is the treatment of the Roma, who simply do not exist in the Albanian media. Nobody talks about them. In this sense, hate speech is replaced by hate silence. The media influence their audiences not only through what they say, but, just as importantly, through what they don't say.

What we see today is the spread of unprecedented hate speech on the Internet. New media has offered an ideal platform for spreading hate speech because of its decentralised, anonymous and interactive structure. The image of the Greek as wily; of the Serb as an enemy; of the Roma as a thief; of the Vlach as a non-Albanian, and so on, is very present in the Albanian virtual sphere. Cyber-hate is the dark side of information technology. Cyber-hate knows no boundaries; its perpetrators are anonymous and fluid; its messages globally available.

It is 2021 and the Balkans, like the rest of the world, face the pandemic of COVID-19, practice vaccine diplomacy as much as they can, become part of the "vaccine war" against their will, and do not miss the opportunity to cultivate vaccine nationalism. And like all other countries, in fact more than others, the Balkans are infected by what is now widely regarded as an infodemia.

[8] Hysa, Dorentina. & Lani, Kristina. (2022). Monitoring report on Hate Speech in Albania. *Albanian Media Institute*. https://www.reportingdiversity.org/wp-content/uploads/2022/07/Monitoring-Report-on-Hate-Speech-in-Albania-12072022.pdf

Conspiracy theories and, along with them, misinformation have gone viral. (Ironically, the frequent use of the term "viral" itself means that we have actually been dealing with two viruses at the same time.) These tales begin with theories about the origin of the virus: according to some, the coronavirus came from a laboratory in Wuhan and was engineered by China; according to others, the coronavirus was created by the United States as a biological weapon; and according to still others, it was actually created by Big Pharma to make extraordinary profits from vaccines and medicines. Then, those promoting conspiracies and misinformation began linking 5G technology to the coronavirus and even accused Bill Gates of seeking to place microchips in human bodies through mass vaccination campaigns and thus establish total control over the human race.

And if the above theories are in fact global, and crashed on our shores as they swept across the world, local theories did not take long to follow, as is always the case. A so-called Albanian conspiracy theorist stated on TV that COVID-19 is a biological weapon spread by the "White Brotherhood" in a battle between the Illuminati and Donald Trump. A Montenegrin politician claimed that behind the coronavirus pandemic stands "a global Satanist pedophile deep state."

A survey from The Balkans in Europe Policy Advisory Group on the spread of coronavirus conspiracy theories in the Balkans, published in early 2021, reported that approximately 80% of the population believes in one or more of these fantasies and conspiracies. The report stated that the country in the region with the most supporters of conspiracy theories is Albania[9].

According to another survey, this one from the Institute for Development, Research and Alternatives in Tirana, "one third of the respondents believed that the 5G internet coverage network is one of the factors

[9] (2020). The Western Balkans in Times of the Global Pandemic. *Balkans in Europe Policy Advisory Group*. https://biepag.eu/publication/policy-brief-the-western-balkans-in-times-of-the-global-pandemic/

for the rapid spread of the virus, while 29% of the respondents believed that the vaccine would implant microchips in humans to track them."[10] Various data show that this is more or less the situation in other countries in the region.

How much does this situation have to do with what has long been said and written about the Balkans as the land of conspiracies? And what does it have to do with what the well-known political analyst Ivan Krastev calls "the rise of the paranoid citizen" nowadays[11], not only in the Balkans but worldwide? And, perhaps most importantly, what is the role of the new media and communications eco-system in the birth and spread of conspiracies and misinformation?

It was in a discussion session organized by MDI during the autumn 2021 Media Festival in Fazana, on the Croatian coast, in a room that was almost empty due to the pandemic, that I first used the phrase "*fake speech*". Of course this is a metaphoric term, and it is by no means an academic or professional construct. After hate speech arrived fake speech. More precisely, we now have fake speech alongside hate speech.

Fake speech, in my opinion, is a term denoting a dangerous cocktail of fake news, disinformation / misinformation / mal-information, and conspiracy theories. This booming avalanche is the core of what is widely regarded as the Information Disorder.

Eric Schmidt, former chairman of Alphabet, Google's parent company, is quoted as saying: "The internet is the first thing that humanity has built that humanity doesn't understand..."[12] The cyber-utopia we fantasized about at the beginning of the last decade, when we naively celebrated

[10] (2020, October 12). Majority of Albanians refuse a COVID-19 vaccine, says survey. *Euronews Albania*, https://euronews.al/en/majority-of-albanians-refuse-a-covid-19-vaccine-says-survey/

[11] Krastev, Ivan. (2017, March 16). The rise of the paranoid citizen. *New York Times*. https://www.nytimes.com/2017/03/16/opinion/the-rise-of-the-paranoid-citizen.html

[12] Oxford Reference. https://www.oxfordreference.com/display/10.1093/acref/9780191826719.001.0001/q-oro-ed4-00017947;jsessionid=F0BE826CAC151BD610CA0784063343BB

a wave of Facebook and Twitter Revolutions while China cynically perfected the Internet Dictatorship, seems to have been gradually replaced by cyber-realism. And it is indeed realistic to accept that the Internet is something we do not understand.

However, the 2.5 billion citizens of the Republic, or rather, the Kingdom of Facebook, have experienced on the one hand a strong dose of previously unknown freedom and, on the other hand, something of a casino-type addiction that paradoxically offers an illusion of freedom. The Balkan peoples are active citizens of this space, whether using real names or hiding in anonymity. (I have to disclose here that I am not a citizen of Mark Zuckerberg's virtual empire, but I spend quite a few hours online every day).

Mark Deuze, a well-known media studies academic, writes that "we do not live *with*, but *in* media."[13] Long gone are the times when we lived *with* media and in front of us stood a vertical media system whose operating keyword was *transmission*. Now, we live *in* media; in fact, we are part of a horizontal media system, the operating keyword being *share*. And perhaps what is most important here is not the lack of hierarchy, but actually the lack of rules. Paolo Mancini, the well-known media systems researcher, brilliantly defines the situation when he says that what we see today is the de-institutionalization of the media and communications system.

What interests me in this context is how conspiracies and misinformation spread massively on the web, and in the case of the Balkans, invaded it.

The term "fake news", which is actually misused by Donald Trump and others, metaphorically resembles a fast bike that transports, aside from short-term lies of the day that will be forgotten tomorrow, long-term conspiracies that thrive for a decade or longer. Labeling

[13] Deuze M. (2012). Media life. *Polity Press*, Cambridge.

something as fake news is an easy and convenient way to spread and amplify conspiracies. Especially in times of crisis. And especially in the Balkans.

This is to a large degree a symptom of a serious problem of the modern communications eco-system, which overwhelms individuals with excess information—known these days by the term "infobesity"—but finds them unprepared to navigate and orient themselves in this ocean of abundance. The latest Media Literacy Index[14] emphasizes once again that the citizens of the Balkans continue to be the most vulnerable in Europe to information manipulation, with these countries all ranking among the last ten on the continent.

Some specific issues make the situation in the Balkans particularly complex and problematic. It is not difficult to notice that our societies are firstly characterized by low trust, and secondly, are polarized to the extreme. Both of these factors create fertile ground for disinformation conspiracies of all kinds.

In our societies, which are marked by little trust in local institutions and leaders, individuals tend to seek out other authorities they believe they can rely on. In the vacuum created by distrust, questions raised are easily answered with simplified conspiratorial narratives.

The populist politicians who have invaded our political scenes present themselves as speaking on behalf of the people, on behalf of the whole people, even on behalf of the whole nation. In this context, those who are different, those who think differently, are viewed at best as sell-outs, or at worst as traitors. It is not difficult to notice that accusations of traitors and plotters "in our midst" have increased considerably in Balkan political discourse, from Albania to Serbia, from Bosnia to Kosovo.

[14] Lessenski, Marin. (2021). Media Literacy Index 2021: Double Trouble: Resilience to Fake News at the Time of Covid-19 Infodemic. *Open Society Institute – Sofia Foundation (OSI-Sofia).* https://osis.bg/?p=3750&lang=en

Mistrust and polarization fuel conspiracy theories, and conspiracy theories reinforce polarization and mistrust. When this happens, democracy erodes; diversity and pluralism are under threat. We witness this in the Balkans on a daily basis.

Seems that the Open Society is threatened by exactly what seemed like the Great Open. An aggressive and often blind threat. However, at least we have already realized that while for the pandemic virus there seems to be one or several vaccines, for the disinfodemic virus there can be none. We will have to look for immunity in developing critical thinking skills, building trust, promoting diversity and, above all, defending what John Stewart Mill calls "freedom of thought."

One of the most brilliant stories in Danilo Kis' *The Encyclopedia of the Dead* is undoubtedly *The Book of Kings and Fools*. The main character of this novel is not a human, but a book, entitled "The Conspiracy, or The Roots of the Disintegration of the European Society." Gracefully mixing fiction and nonfiction, the great Balkan writer has created an anti-story of *The Protocols of the Elders of Zion* and warns that the history of conspiracies and manipulations is not over. The title in particular sounds like a warning for today.

Rob Leavitt

Rob Leavitt is a Partner at Momentum ITSMA, an international business consultancy based in London, Boston, and Melbourne. He has worked for more than 20 years advising global technology and professional services firms on marketing and growth strategy. Previously, he worked with media, human rights groups, and Harvard and New York Universities to improve understanding of coverage of international and civil conflict, and support democracy, human rights, and global security. He lives in the Boston area, and has a Masters degree in Political Science from MIT and a Bachelor's degree in US History from the University of Pennsylvania.

BEFORE MDI... AND AFTER: AN ORIGIN STORY

I knew almost nothing about the Former Yugoslav Republic of Macedonia when I first flew to Skopje, the capital, in 1994. I flew in from Amsterdam on Palair Macedonian Airlines, on an ancient, Russian Tupolev Tu-154, hunched in the last row next to my friend Paul, a veteran metro reporter from the Providence Journal who jumped at the chance for what seemed initially like a great adventure. We did share a few morbid jokes on the flight in; the jet was painted bright red "so it would be easy to find when it went down in the mountains." A Palair flight had crashed the year before, killing most of the 97 people on board.

Our mission seemed noble, quixotic, and arrogant all at once. The ethnic cleansing of nearby Bosnia had continued for two years by then while the whole world watched. Sarajevo remained under deadly siege. Macedonia had avoided being dragged into the Yugoslav wars but tensions between the ethnic Macedonian majority and the Albanian minority were rising. United Nations, NATO, and nongovernmental conflict specialists were on high alert. UN peacekeepers, including 500 US soldiers, patrolled Macedonia's borders with Serbia and Albania.

Neighboring Greece was heightening the tension, too. The Greek government opposed the very existence of a state called Macedonia, hearkening back to ancient times and insisting that "Macedonia" was and is forever a part of Greece. In 1993, Greece launched a trade embargo, shutting off Macedonia's access to imports and exports. This exacerbated the already high unemployment, falling GNP, and growing social pressures that the Yugoslav wars had already generated.

Paul and I were on a scouting trip. The conflict resolution group Search for Common Ground had opened an office in Skopje led by a retired US diplomat. The organization knew local media played a huge role in fanning the flames of ethnic conflict in Bosnia, Serbia, and Croatia (among many other parts of the world). They wanted to identify opportunities to bring "media and diversity" ideas from the US that might help newly independent, post-Communist news organizations develop more inclusive approaches to local reporting.

Sure, give us a week, we'll figure it out!

My sensitivity to ethnic and social conflict emerged early. I grew up as a Jew in Worcester, Massachusetts in the US, an ethnically diverse and economically struggling industrial town. We were a small minority in town--about 5% of the population--but we had a tight community, pride in our achievements, and a strong ethic of social responsibility and "giving back."

I also grew up amid a quiet but lingering anti-Semitism: Periodic slurs, casual references to "the Jews killed Christ," pennies thrown at you as you walked the halls in middle school. It was nothing terrible but it was ever-present. Growing up in the long shadow of the Holocaust and seeing survivors in the synagogue meant you could never completely dismiss it either.

I was fortunate in having powerful female role models in those days of rising feminism. My mom was always active in the community and stood strong against the common sexist indignities of the times. Her mom, my nana, had lost her husband in her 30s and took over his struggling small business amid the Great Depression and made it work. She had lost a young son, too, but never let that slow her down.

My university education was another inspiration. I studied U.S. history amid the flowering of a new bottom-up approach to the discipline. History was about all the people, not just the white male politicians and generals and business leaders. There was a boom in women's history, history of the working class, new ways to consider the experiences of slavery, immigration, the devastation of Native Americans, and so much more.

I was fascinated by the first wave of Populism in the U.S. in the 1880s and 1890s. Here was a truly multi-cultural, multi-racial social movement demanding justice for farmers struggling against the railroad tycoons, miners and loggers working in brutal conditions, black sharecroppers being pushed back into slavery-like conditions, and women demanding a voice and a vote.

By the early 1900s, though, the movement had fizzled out after yet another great recession, political attacks, and the ultimate inability to overcome the deep fissures of racial and ethnic tension and hostility.

The fate of that original populist movement in the US foreshadowed the next 120 years of competing populisms of the left and the right.

Populism is always about "the people" vs. the elites running (and ruining) the country. Leftist versions typically crossed most other social boundaries, from the inclusive union and civil rights movements of the 20th century to the social and racial justice movements and the Bernie Sanders boomlet in the early 21st.

Right-wing versions have posited a more narrowly defined "real American" people under siege by devious elites (often with an anti-Semitic tone) in league with any number of other enemies undermining the country:

Immigrants, African-Americans, intellectuals, gays and lesbians, communists, and more. The rise of Trumpism and Make America Great Again is just the latest but probably the largest wave yet.

I met Randall Forsberg in 1983 and spent the rest of the 1980s following her unique lead. Randy seemed one of a kind; a powerhouse woman in the male-dominated field of military and nuclear weapons policy and strategy. She began as a secretary in a think tank, moved up to an analyst role, and then burst on the global political scene in 1982 with her brilliant and deceptively simple Nuclear Freeze proposal to halt the nuclear arms race in place.

Amid the nuclear nightmares of the Reagan age and the hyper-politicized debates between Disarmament Now and Peace through Strength, Randy was able to galvanize a broad coalition of activists, politicians, and millions of concerned citizens on all sides that played a central role in slowing the arms race and paving the way for Reagan and Gorbachev to step from the precipice.

Unlike many in the antinuclear left of the time, Randy was also a vocal proponent of human rights and security for all, not just for those opposed to "the American war machine." This meant opposing Soviet imperialism just as much as American imperialism – and standing up for the incredibly courageous dissidents and democrats in central and eastern Europe.

As the cracks in the iron curtain began to appear in the late 1980s, I leaped at the chance to sneak into Prague for a secret gathering of peace and human rights activists east and west. The goal was to show solidarity with Charter 77, the Czech dissident group led by Vaclav Havel and other prominent artists and intellectuals.

Not surprisingly, we were arrested and thrown out of the country. The secret police knew we were coming. They had arrested many of the

Czechs before we even arrived. They threatened us when we first tried to meet. And then they arrested the entire activist group at our second meeting attempt at Jiri Dienstbier's apartment. (Already in prison while we sat frantically drafting a statement of outrage in his living room, Dienstbier would soon become Foreign Minister in the first post-Communist government under Havel).

Along with the arrest, three moments stood out. First, amid the cat-and-mouse with the secret police following the initial threats ("you should not associate with these criminals"), our main thought was how to get in touch with *The New York Times*. Protests always look to the media. The local state-controlled media had already branded us anti-socialist agitators.

Second, a few hours into the interminable wait to be processed at the central police station, we began agitating to be fed. Our guards huddled for a few minutes, then one came back to announce: "If you provide the money, we can take two of the women prisoners to get food for the group." Barely missing a beat, the women in our group launched immediately into a feminist protest. "Why should it automatically be the women who get the food?"

Finally, after being released with *persona non grata* stamped on our passports and threats to leave the country by midnight or face the (undefined) consequences, a few of us were able to gather at a local café before boarding the train to Vienna. A confused representative from the US Embassy (low-level CIA?) showed up to question us and couldn't seem to grasp the idea that peace activists from the West would also support the local anti-communist dissidents.

Just a few months later, I faced a choice: Randy had wrangled an invitation to Moscow for a few of us to explore new arms control and confidence-building measures with the Soviet Union's top two international relations institutes. While the Czechs continued their crackdown,

Gorbachev was pushing *glasnost* and *perestroika* in Moscow – his opening to the West and attempt to liberalize at home without giving up entirely on the Soviet state.

Should I test my recently marked-up passport, which now indicated that I was an anti-socialist agitator? Ultimately, I decided not to risk missing the opportunity so I rushed to get a new, clean passport. And the trip proved a perfect bookend to my adventure in Prague: We received VIP treatment by day with Soviet officials as we toasted to peace and cooperation in smoke-filled rooms in the capital and then tested the local black market by night as our local minders barely pretended to care.

Fourteen months later the Berlin Wall fell, Havel became president and moved into the castle in Prague, and the cold war was over.

Working for Cultural Survival in the early 1990s, a small NGO focused on human rights and the environment, broadened my view considerably. Our mission revolved around the rights of indigenous peoples in the most marginalized societies around the world – native peoples in South American and South Pacific rainforests, African deserts, the Arctic north, and more. Founded by a prominent British anthropologist, David Maybury-Lewis, the group was led by another powerful woman, Pam Solo, a Quaker and veteran peace activist I had met during the nuclear freeze campaign.

Influencing the media was central to our work: How can we publicize the plight - and the essential dignity - of literally endangered peoples who, if acknowledged at all, appeared at best as exotic curiosities but more commonly as uncivilized savages? The growing awareness of the destruction of the world's rainforests provided a powerful hook for media attention and our work building sustainable Brazil nut-trading operations in the Amazon (we even created Rainforest Crunch candy) added to the allure. But the rights and dignity of the people we cared about too often fell to the end of the story.

I moved more fully into media education and advocacy in 1992 when I joined the Center for War, Peace, and the News Media at New York University. Founded by Rob Manoff in 1985, the Center initially focused on improving coverage of the US-Soviet arms race and arms control with a combination of media criticism and educational programs for mainstream reporters, editors, and producers.

With the collapse of the Soviet Union, nuclear weapons coverage remained on the agenda but we focused more on the fate of the former Soviet arsenal and proliferation risks in the Middle East and Asia. We looked as well toward reporting on the future of Europe, German reunification, regional conflict and security in Asia, and, ominously, the growing connection between ethnic conflict and media power, as evident in devastation in Bosnia and the genocide in Rwanda.

We also moved into Russia, opening a Russian-American Press and Information Center to promote informed and responsible journalism and help develop new media organizations as independent businesses. This meant working with Russian journalists as well as helping newly emerging women's, human rights, and ethnic minority groups voice their concerns and tell their stories in the new media environment.

We added another international dimension, too: Bringing together US and Asian journalists to explore regional security issues and challenges from cross-regional perspectives. I led study tours for international media groups to Washington, Honolulu, and Seoul to meet with academic experts, government officials, military leaders, and NGOs. We pondered the Vietnam memorial, Pearl Harbor, and the heavily armed "demilitarized zone" between North and South Korea. And we built connections and respect with top journalists from China, Hong Kong, Japan, India, South Korea, Indonesia, the United States, and others.

By the time I flew into Skopje, my personal and professional experience gave me confidence that I could help but the challenge certainly seemed formidable.

With support from Search for Common Ground and several charitable foundations, we put together a series of training and reporting projects focused on supporting more cross-ethnic, inclusive, and confidence-building journalism.

It was challenging but gratifying work. We brought in American journalists with deep experience covering diverse communities across the US as well as conflict zones around the world. We respected the difficulties of building new profitable media businesses but still called out examples of playing to local prejudices and going overboard with nationalist themes and symbols.

Adapting a powerful approach developed by the Maynard Institute in the US, we organized a month-long, cross-ethnic reporting project with young ethnic Macedonian, Albanian, and Turkish journalists on the impact of the economy on "ordinary people." As we had seen in Russia and other newly post-Communist countries, journalists were used to talking mainly to government officials, not everyday members of the community.

We arranged for their work to be published jointly across newspapers serving each of their different communities. We continued with additional projects exploring common concerns on health care, the environment, and the role of women in the local society. We built trust and confidence in good, fair journalism and created new opportunities for Macedonians from diverse groups to understand a bit more about their fellow citizens without prejudice, stereotyping, or a sense of inevitable conflict.

"In my entire career I've booked four trips to Macedonia," my travel agent mentioned as I booked yet another mission to Skopje. "All for you." My friends at home had little sense of what I was up to. One regularly mentioned, I think jokingly, that I must be in the CIA.

I have no doubt that local leaders and the broader international community deserve all the credit for keeping Macedonia from falling into the ethnic conflict abyss in the late 1990s. But I like to think we made a small contribution, too.

When I met Milica a few years later at a journalism conference in Moscow, the stars seemed to align for a more ambitious new initiative. Building on our Russian and Macedonian experiences, we had already launched a broader "Media and Conflict" program to address the destructive uses of media that were spreading across the post-Cold War world in the 1990s.

From my NYU perspective, Milica brought hard-earned experience from ground zero in Belgrade in the 1990s. She began her journalism career as a presenter on state-run Serbian TV, was fired for protesting from the inside against its cheerleading for ethnic conflict and war in the former Yugoslavia and helped set up an alternative media network to counter the devastating role of Milosevic-run media. Milica had moved to London, earned an MA in International Journalism, and was working with the International Federation of Journalists.

For Milica, journalism in the US, for all its faults, included a wealth of ideas, examples, and expertise that could help inspire a more inclusive approach to reporting. Bringing these approaches to media in other regions, she believed, could help lessen ethnic and other types of social conflict rather than egging them on.

I leaped at the chance for the Center to hire Milica. Within just a few months, leaning heavily on her contacts across Central and Eastern Europe, we launched a new Reporting Diversity Network to bring together independent journalists across the region to share experiences, develop new standards, and support hands-on reporting projects to put theory into practice.

The Reporting Diversity Network served as the launch pad for the Media Diversity Institute, and 25 years later I could not be prouder of the fantastic work that Milica and MDI have done. From the small seeds we planted in the 1990s, MDI has grown to play a powerful global role in developing and demonstrating the best kinds of inclusive journalism, exposing the worst, and helping marginalized groups and communities share their stories with the world.

The challenges, to be sure, remain daunting. The collapse of so many independent news organizations has created vast "news deserts" populated largely by (often right-wing) infotainment. The growth of Fox News and similar organizations in the US and elsewhere has demonstrated that divisive, resentment-based media can be highly profitable. The rise of social media has created a massive new platform for spreading hatred, harassment, and misinformation. The rapid spread of simple tools to use artificial intelligence such as Chat GPT and DALL-E promise new waves of deep fake disinformation.

Most ominous, the rising tide of authoritarianism has both relied upon and reinforced social division and "othering" while strengthening destructive media and legitimizing the "enemy of the people" narrative that undermines good journalism and threatens a growing number of journalists.

Indeed, just as our small NYU Center was trying to bring the best of US journalism to areas of social and ethnic conflict in the mid-1990s, the seeds of today's right wing, media-driven MAGA movement were beginning to sprout.

Rush Limbaugh, whose radio show had built a massive national audience by attacking and ridiculing "feminazis," "militant homosexuals," and black civil rights leaders (among other regular targets), burst on the political scene as a major force in the 1992 presidential election.

Right-wing populists led by Congressman Newt Gingrich used media savvy and attacks on "liberal media" to take power in the Republican Party in 1994.

Fox News launched in 1996 and within a few years became the central platform for conservative politicians to hone their message and build national support. By the time Barack Obama made history as America's first black president, Fox had become the de facto hub of the conservative movement, and, not incidentally, a megaphone for the increasingly overt racism that characterized the right-wing reaction to Obama's candidacy and election. Donald Trump laid the groundwork for his 2016 campaign on Fox News with regular appearances attacking Obama's legitimacy to even run for office.

The polarization was certainly not all one-sided. Extremist voices on the left joined the fray, especially on social media (although right wing TV and social media outlets continuously drew much larger audiences). And mainstream media leaders appreciated the ratings that the politics of anger could generate. As Leslie Moonves, chairman and CEO of the national TV network CBS famously said in 2016, "It may not be good for America, but it's damn good for CBS… The money's rolling in and this is fun… It's a terrible thing to say. But bring it on, Donald. Keep going." (Moonves was later ousted for sexual harassment during the #MeToo movement.)

By the time Trump and his allies tried to overturn his defeat in the 2020 presidential election, the convergence of extremist right-wing media and conservative politics seemed complete. For millions of Americans, the news of the day was dominated by an angry rhetoric of attack and betrayal, unfounded conspiracy theories, and outright lies: "Antifa activists" staged the attack on the White House, Black Lives Matter activists were burning down cities, immigrant hordes were overrunning the country, "real Americans" were under siege, and Trump really won the election.

Today, the fears we had about Macedonia in 1994 have come to life in America on a vast scale. "Culture wars" dominate local and national politics. Substantial segments of the public have lost trust in core institutions. Large numbers of both liberals and conservatives see their political opponents as threats to the country and accept that violence could be justified to achieve their social objectives.

Fanning the flames of civil conflict, right-wing media harp endlessly about liberal/radical/deep state/socialist/communist activists destroying our country with "open borders," "critical race theory," pedophilia, and trans-gender rights. Racist, anti-Semitic, and homophobic tropes appear with depressing regularity.

In contrast, mainstream and liberal media often fall into a pseudo-objective both-sides-ism that provides equal attention to opposing arguments – often highlighting the most extreme voices on each side. Or they focus on the "politics" of the debate, looking for the potential impact on upcoming elections rather than the actual impacts on the people most affected.

But we've seen important progress since the 1990s, too. The digital transformation of media has enabled a flowering of new voices and perspectives even as hundreds of traditional media outlets have gone out of business. Innovative approaches to civic journalism, non-profit newsrooms, and cross-organizational collaboration have worked to fill the void left by newspaper decline.

The best newsrooms have become much more diverse and inclusive; thoughtful and sensitive coverage of formerly marginalized communities has grown accordingly. Investigative reporting continues to expose abuses of power and hold the guilty to account. Journalists are taking full advantage of the vast array of new digital tools, approaches, and formats to produce powerful and compelling reporting on the most challenging and complex topics. New and urgent discussions about countering misinformation and bolstering democracy have risen to the top of at least some media business agendas.

For MDI, the work must continue – building on past success and demonstrating the way forward. Continuing to shine a light on the media manipulation that turns difference into division. Continuing to demonstrate the positive example of inclusive reporting. And continuing to nurture the next generations of students and reporters that we so need to pick up the torch.

Jean-Paul Marthoz

Jean-Paul Marthoz is a columnist at the Brussels daily Le Soir. He is the author, or coauthor of some 20 books, in particular The Media and Terrorism (UNESCO, 2017) and Fragile Progress (on the EU and Press Freedom, 2023). He has been Human Rights Watch's European Press Director and EU correspondent of the Committee to Protect Journalists. Between 2002-2022 he taught international journalism at the UCLouvain, Belgium. He sits on the Editorial Board of Index on Censorship magazine, the Ethical Journalism Network, the Bastogne War Museum and Belgium's public broadcaster's (RTBF) ethics committee.

MY STORY, MY WAY

Diversity? The term had a weird meaning for me when I was a kid. In fact, it was never mentioned in my little world, which was made up of a close-knit family that numerically dominated an isolated village in the Belgian Ardennes, which was itself dominated by the steeple of the Catholic church.

The media habits of my parents were not diverse at all, nor even ecumenical, but staunchly and unequivocally Catholic. My father faithfully read the conservative Catholic daily *La Libre Belgique*, my mother was an avid reader of a regional paper partly owned by the Bishopric. Both pored over religious news in the official church weekly, which printed the sermons, the Mass timetables and the imprimatur - that is, the list of books, newspapers and movies that a good Christian should favour or avoid.

Diversity? No, unity. Around the Church, the Monarchy and the ruling Christian Social Party.

My destiny was just like that of everyone else in the village. My cousins, my neighbors. Like me, they were born in a Catholic maternity ward, were protected by the Christian health mutuality, and if they were bright, they were sent to study at one of the severe Catholic secondary schools in the area. Mine was even a Little Seminary ensconced in an 11th century grey-stoned abbey planted in the middle of dark forests. The contents of my courses, the lists of my readings, were determined by the Catholic hierarchy. Diversity? No, uniformity. Around Catholic writers from Paul Claudel and Gilbert Cesbron to Graham Greene.

Thinking about those years now, I realize that I was perhaps the least destined to find myself, decades later, immersed in a world of political, ethnic, cultural, religious, and philosophical diversity. And enjoying it so much. How did this happen? What did it mean?

Belgium is a particular case. In fact, in the last 70 years the country has simultaneously experienced a process of inclusion and exclusion, of uniformization and separation. Since the end of the 19th century the political and philosophical institutions, the "pillars", as they were called, had organized and segmented politics, education and social life around Christian, socialist or liberal ideas. There were few cross-overs and mavericks were looked upon with scorn or mistrust. However, in the wake of the 1960s cultural and social upheavals, these lines began to blur. Journalists could start their career in the small-circulation *La Cité*, the organ of the Christian trade union, and then move to *Le Soir*, a large-circulation newspaper anchored in the liberal and secularist tradition. Over the years the country grew more diverse as it "welcomed" a growing number of foreigners - political refugees from dictatorial regimes like Spain and Portugal, but also, and more significantly, economic migrants, especially from Italy, Morocco and Turkey.

At the same time, the Flemish and Francophone communities that constituted Belgium and were supposed to relish the national motto "Unity makes strength" started a process of separation from each other, the result of pent-up grievances over the dominant use of the French language by the ruling classes in a linguistically diverse country. Normally as an alumnus of a Catholic secondary school I was pre-programmed to study in the beautiful historical city of Leuven in Flanders, where the prestigious Université catholique de Louvain was founded in 1425. But I could not. The year I left my "collège" in 1968, nationalist politicians and Catholic bishops decided to cut it into two separate institutions. French-speaking students were compelled to move to a new location some 20 miles away, on pastures situated in French-speaking territory, on the other side of the newly established "linguistic border". Diversity? Segregation. At the same time political parties and a number of civic associations split up along linguistic lines, as if language trumped ideologies-socialist, Christian democrat, liberal - that were supposed to be inspired by universalist values.

Years later, in November 1998, when I attended my first event organized by the Media Diversity Institute, at the Freedom Forum in London, all these memories were floating in my head as I was listening to Michael Ignatieff's reflections on the "narcissism of small differences". At this London conference centered on discussions about communal conflicts, I knew that the end of the sixties had been my "aha moment". Even though Belgium's linguistic battles had not turned violent, they had shaped my world views forever. I had become a universalist, whatever that meant. I was for the free expression of cultural differences and for equality for all linguistic groups. And therefore, during the Franco dictatorship in Spain, I supported the Catalan and Basque demands that people be able to speak their own languages. But I was suspicious of - and hostile to - the idea of identities and communities based on - or leading to - diffidence and exclusion.

Even before that London conference, I had had intense discussions with MDI's founder, Milica Pešić, who had been working with New York University's Center for War, Peace, and the News Media. As a journalist, I was appalled at the role that "hate media" had played in the former Yugoslavia in exacerbating what my former colleague in

Paris (and future member of the French Academy), Amin Maalouf, a Melkite Christian from Lebanon, had called “murderous identities”. The Srebrenica massacre and the genocide against the Tutsi in Rwanda shocked me profoundly as they upended the “never again” mantra that the international community had solemnly promised to uphold after the Second World War.

For my family, which had been active in the anti-Nazi resistance, the Holocaust constituted the most extreme example of identity politics. Thanks to their warnings, very early in my life, the risk of genocide, of “eliminationism” as historian Daniel Jonah Goldhagen would call it in his 2009 essay *Worse than War*, the claims for population homogenization with its consequent exclusion of minorities, became the central reference in my definition of identity and of diversity.

The fear that identity claims can lead to civil strife or - even worse – to ethnic cleansing and genocide conditioned my analysis of many communal conflicts. As a journalist I was particularly concerned by the general failing of the press when confronted with evident signs of radicalization, hatred and atrocities. *Why didn't The Press Shout?* This question, the title of a book on American and international journalism during the Holocaust, haunted me. “Policymakers, journalists, and citizens are extremely slow to muster the imagination needed to reckon with evil”, Samantha Power wrote in her groundbreaking book, “A Problem from Hell”. These reflections would lead me to advocate for a form of journalism of anticipation and alert, for the “responsibility to report”, as Carleton University professor and ex-reporter Allan Thompson calls it, on the risks of genocide, in line with what the UN General Assembly would call in 2005 the “responsibility to protect” populations in danger.

FUSION

For me, diversity meant exchanges, encounters, fusion. The first foreign country that I visited was Mexico in 1971, and I was thrilled by its celebration of mestizaje, the miscegenation of "races" and cultures. This hybridization expressed itself in the Place of the Three Cultures, called Tlatelolco in Nahuatl. In the middle of the site stood an Aztec pyramid and a Catholic Church, surrounded by modernist high-rises that were supposed to represent the unique diversity of Mexico.

Even as I was aware that this mestizaje had mostly been the result of the violence of colonization, I concluded that it was an invitation to share and mix and enrich lives. This mestizaje was also present in Mexican cuisine, which blends ingredients and recipes drawn from pre-Columbian times, the Spanish colonization and the French influence into divinely delicious and complex dishes. It enriched the country's arts and literature, from Frida Kahlo's paintings to Carlos Fuentes' novels. It did not mean fusion or homogenization, but in Carlos Fuentes' words, "the duty to invent a great innovative synthesis of the times which had marked us", by respecting in particular the contributions of Mexico's Indigenous cultures.

I experienced the same process intellectually. I came from a practising but very open-minded Catholic family. My mother viewed her faith, to some extent, as an accident of birth. "I am a Catholic, perhaps because in Belgium most people are. If I had been born in Morocco, I would have been a Muslim, I suppose". The dogmatic teachings of the Church were softened by contact with the works of enlightened philosophers, novelists and journalists as well as progressive and socially conscious activists in the Christian workers' movement. *Esprit*, a leading intellectual review founded in the 1930s, became my inspiration. Its founder, Catholic philosopher Emmanuel Mounier, opened its pages to non-Christian authors who shared his aspirations and hopes for justice and freedom.

I was seduced by the idea – drawn from my own experience but also from my readings of Bertrand Russell or Albert Camus – that every person could grow and break free from the shackles of their own community, social class or religion. Diversity went hand in hand with freedom of conscience, the right to choose your own beliefs.

My best intellectual companions in these university years were mostly liberal Jewish thinkers. They were sometimes dissidents or contrarians in their own communities, from Baruch Spinoza to Hannah Arendt. They dared to confront the dogmas of their tribe and by doing so they created brilliant, humanistic reflections on our societies and our fate. Dissent was part of diversity.

CLOSED IDENTITIES

On my return from my Mexico study trip in 1971, I was struck even more by what I saw as the mediocre arrangements carving up my country along linguistic lines. The media reflected this growing separation. On the two sides of the language border, coverage of the country became compartmentalized, while the real world, in both communities, was growing increasingly diverse. New migrants were coming in and were expected to blend into one of the two communities, to become French-speaking or Dutch-speaking Belgian residents or citizens.

I hated this separation. I saw it as an attack on the values in which I had been educated. It denied the past that I had been taught to respect and honour. During the Second World War, my father and my mother had been part of the Resistance. It was the moment in their lives that transcended everything else and in fact reflected their understanding of "unity in diversity". "I will always prefer a Flemish anti-Nazi resister to a Walloon or Francophone pro-Nazi collaborator", my father would say when questioned about his loyalty to the Francophone cause.

Linguistic diversity, yes, but first and foremost unity in sharing the values of freedom and humanity. In the mid 1990s, at a seminar in Ohrid, Northern Macedonia, sponsored by New York University Center for War, Peace and the News Media, I repeated my father's quote, to great effect, when confronted with a local journalist for whom ethnic nationalism trumped humanism and ethical journalism.

LE GRAND LARGE

In the early 1970s, I booked a flight to, of course, Mexico. But as I could not get a residence permit there, I tried my chances further south, in Costa Rica, which welcomed me with open arms. While teaching French at the state university, I started my journalistic journey at a new leftwing political weekly, *Pueblo*. Run by a former Catholic priest, it was staffed with political exiles from Central America and Chile. I also freelanced for the expatriates' weekly, *The Tico Times*. My editor-in-chief was a woman, an exception in the world of journalism at the time. Derry Dyer was brilliant and congenial and she started a pattern in my career in which, for half of my working life, I was supervised by women.

The Tico Times was a liberal paper dedicated to civil rights and equality. Despite its reputation as the Switzerland of Central America, the only democratic country in the region, Costa Rica was still struggling to include its Black citizens, heirs of marooned slaves who had escaped from sugar plantations in the Caribbean. *The Tico Times* opened its columns to intellectuals from the community of African descent. In fact, this gringo newspaper was one of the few media venues in town where Blacks had a voice.

It was a political and ethical choice. But it also reflected a philosophy of public interest journalism, the way the Commission on Freedom of the Press, chaired by University of Chicago president Robert Hutchins, had defined it in its 1947 seminal report *A Free and Responsible Press*. Among its recommendations, the report called upon journalists to "project a representative picture of the constituent groups in the society". Diversity was a matter of justice, but it was also an intrinsic corollary of the first commandment of public interest journalism: to provide, in the Commission's words, "a truthful, comprehensive, and intelligent account of the day's events in a context which gives them meaning".

As a journalist, I saw diversity as a necessary ingredient of any story aspiring "to provide the best obtainable version of the truth", to quote Carl Bernstein of Watergate fame. Could the press do that without being itself a reflection of the diversity of the societies on which it was reporting?

When I was hired by *Le Soir* in 1980, I entered a newsroom that was politically and philosophically diverse but less so in other ways. The effort to increase gender diversity was in its infancy but was gaining strength. If there were still only a few women on the staff, they held very visible positions: among them were a daring war reporter, the editor of the sprawling economics department, and a talented political editor. However, most of the journalists were still white, middle-class, secular. The paper was liberal and vocally anti-racist but, with the exception of two Lebanese journalists on the foreign desk, the staff did not include anyone from the migrant communities, even though these already represented a significant part of the increasingly cosmopolitan city of Brussels.

COMMUNITY JOURNALISM

How could we accomplish our essential mission and pretend to "tell the truth" if we did not have journalists "issus de la diversité", who would help us understand what was happening in all the communities that made up our society? Since my early days in journalism, I had been fascinated by the US press. And I closely followed the journalistic experiments on the other side of the Big Pond, from the Pentagon Papers to the Watergate saga, in particular, when *The New York Times* and *The Washington Post* dared to stand up to the Nixon administration, which governed from 1969 until 1974. But I was also attracted to reporting initiatives that journalistic scholars at the time called "community journalism".

The US is a country of immigrants. Decades before their Belgian or French colleagues, US journalists had been confronted with the challenges of reporting on a very diverse society. On its Black community of course, but also on a country made up of hyphenated Americans; Jewish-Americans, Irish-Americans, Mexican-Americans. How did US journalists address these stories? I had read with awe and admiration *Black Like Me*, a non-fiction book by John Howard Griffin, a Texan journalist who in the 1950s had darkened his skin to roam the Deep South and tell the story from the perspective of a Black subjected to segregation and the "hate stare" of white racists. His project demonstrated that undercover journalism could be crucial to diversity reporting.

Others immersed themselves not among the victims of discrimination but among the victimizers, by infiltrating the Ku Klux Klan and other extremist groups. These were dangerous but important investigations. In these tumultuous years, reporters from *The New York Times* or from the very few liberal Southern newspapers were considered by segregationists to be "enemies of the people", part of the elite "lying press" that deserved to be mobbed and punched.

The will to "project a representative picture of the constituent groups in the society", as the Hutchins Commission recommended, did not necessarily require such daring methods. In most cases, it simply meant to get out of the newsroom, meet and mingle. "Roll down your window", advised Puerto-Rican journalist and *New York Daily News* columnist Juan Gonzalez in a book that described the way he covered Latinos in the US. His beat was community journalism at its best, immersing himself in the ordinary, day-to-day life of a community, chit-chatting with regular people, walking leisurely around neighborhoods, observing the small signs of change that reveal trends and developments: the replacement of a Latino shop by a Korean restaurant, the Babel-like diversity of languages among parents waiting for their kids at the local schools.

As Gonzalez elegantly wrote: "The outsider who wanders into one of these outcast neighborhoods by accident only registers garbage and loud music. And with a roar of his engine, the stranger is gone. But if he had rolled down his window and listened for a moment to the melancholy lyrics of the music, or stepped out and bought a coffee, he might have learnt something about his own humanity."

Unfortunately, in Belgium very few of the journalists assigned to cover a specific community practiced this form of "slow journalism" and grassroots reporting - at least in the media where I worked. Journalists who were supposed to cover the Muslim communities mostly visited "les quartiers" when there was an "incident". Or at the beginning and end of Ramadan. Their main contacts were the community's established leaders who at times were ignorant of - or disconnected from - the reality on the ground.

THE INVISIBLES AND "DEPLORABLES"

The pattern even applied to a form of diversity that is rarely mentioned in our neoliberal times: social class. Most media in Europe missed the story of rising rancour and a sense of disenfranchisement among lower-income whites. The "deplorables", as Hillary Clinton infamously called them in 2008, the pro-Brexit "chavs" in the UK, or the Yellow Vests that rocked the initial days of President Macron's presidency, were mostly absent from the mainstream media.

There had been warnings. In France, the eminent social scientist Pierre Rosanvallon had written about these people that he called the "invisibles". They were mostly white people, blue-collar, often veterans of a downsized manufacturing sector, who felt left behind by globalization, migration, culture wars and technological disruptions. Who had taken the time to talk to them? Studs Terkel, the legendary author and radio host in Chicago, had done so in his iconic books *The Great Divide* and *Working*, interviewing with a sympathetic ear a chorus of people usually forgotten and sidelined by the media. But he was a lonely figure in the world of mainstream media.

All these issues popped up in 2018 during an event convened by MDI at the Perugia International Journalism Festival to discuss the rise of the far right and the press coverage of populism. Was the press part of the problem by being too close to the liberal global world and too oblivious of - or even too dismissive of - the "white tribe"? The press, or at least a significant part of it, was taken off-guard and was definitely at fault: not only did it largely miss the "invisibles" and the emergence of populism, but it also took time to report properly on the most violent groups. "The coverage of the far right is not really a cause for cheers in the mainstream media", I said at the gathering. "In many countries violence from far-right groups has been underreported, compared to the coverage of Islamist terrorism, and often framed in a way that tends to misrepresent their danger to democracy." I mentioned in particular the coverage of the October 2015 attack against the Christian Democratic candidate for the Cologne municipality by a far-right thug. It was so underreported that I headlined my column in *Le Soir:* "Don't worry he is just a neo-Nazi". Imagine the media frenzy if he would have been a Muslim! Diversity reporting implied consistency and excluded double standards, said the speakers at the event. I could not agree more.

QUOTAS AND THE TRUTH

Starting in the 1980s, the press tested other ways to tackle diversity. How about hiring a number of reporters and editors from the "other" communities, up to a percentage of the newsroom, so that the staff would more or less closely reflect the demography of a rapidly diversifying nation? In 1980, I had been to the US on a Fulbright Scholarship to study the press. And I had met a couple of African-American journalists and members of Congress who expected a lot from newsroom diversity. Some were speaking of the need for quotas of "ethnic journalists" in newsrooms. Many were insisting on the need to give more visibility to non-Caucasian anchors on TV.

These suggestions were well-meaning and in fact rather obvious. But I was concerned by the risk of assigning journalists to specific beats not based on their skills or desires but on their ethnic or religious origin. Ethnic-minority journalists assigned to cover their communities faced a difficult task. If they reported any inconvenient truths, they and their families took the risk of being more or less excluded from their community. Over the years, however, diversity was adopted as a mantra in many media circles. It became a central tenet of journalists' unions and an organizing principle in public broadcasting. It led to hiring rules and editorial guidelines.

These efforts achieved some success. In Francophone Belgium, in the first decade of the third millennium, two women from the Maghreb anchored the most popular evening news programmes on both the private and public TV channels. One of them, Hadja Lahbib, is now Belgium's foreign minister.

Rising visibility, however, did not mean that newsrooms were numerically more diverse. If the proportion of women kept rising, other indicators of diversity were lagging. While the population of residents of African and Arab origins was growing, the numbers of journalists from these communities remained disproportionately low, in part because few people from these groups considered journalism a promising career. Many more preferred to join political parties or chose more prestigious professions, like medicine, business and the law.

CULTURE WARS

In fact, although a majority of migrants had found their bearings, identity had become a hot-button issue. The growth of Islamist movements on one side coincided with the rise of nativism on the other side to give an ominous meaning to diversity. For these identity-driven groups diversity was no longer seen as a promise of equality and respect for the common good. The former confused it with assimilation and therefore as the denial of their most essential norms, beliefs and values while the latter perceived it as a threat to their once-dominant national culture.

Newsrooms became battlegrounds. Some tabloids and talk shows fed intolerance and bigotry, seemingly ignorant of the International Federation of Journalists' Global Charter of Ethics: "Journalists shall ensure that the dissemination of information or opinion does not contribute to hatred or prejudice and shall do their utmost to avoid facilitating the spread of discrimination on grounds such as geographical, social or ethnic origin, race, gender, sexual orientation, language, religion, disability, political and other opinions". The more respectable media were accused by one side of being racists and by the other side of being "politically correct wokists". In Belgium's Francophone part, which is highly influenced by France's controversies, journalists felt obligated to define themselves as pro- or anti-headscarf, pro- or anti-Islam. The publication of the Charlie Hebdo cartoons and the subsequent terrorist attack against the satirical weekly on January 7, 2015, framed the controversies and froze attitudes in increasingly polarized camps. Social media harassment fanned these battles, leading some journalists to avoid the touchy subjects of migration or religion altogether. In contrast, others took sides and often crossed red lines by jettisoning the journalistic principles of independence and impartiality.

There was no way out of these battles without reaffirming core principles. This is the message that was conveyed at one of the most interesting MDI events I attended. In January 2019, at the Brussels International Press Centre, I moderated a distinguished panel of journalists, lawyers and scholars who addressed the issue of "reporting religion in the populist era". Auckland University of Technology's Verica Rupar, Human Rights League Director Pierre-Arnaud Perrouty, Reporters Sans Frontieres President Pierre Haski, US-based religion expert Kimberly Winston and the European Commission's David Friggieri candidly analysed the frames, routines and assumptions of religion reporting. And they confronted the challenges and dilemmas of free speech and responsible reporting. These exchanges highlighted the need for all of us to constantly reflect on our biases, to discuss them openly, to think from the standpoint of someone else, and to embrace complexity where too often Manichean or binary positions prevail.

I still see that event as emblematic of my own reflections on diversity. It stressed the potential of finding the common ground underlying our differences and of turning these differences into an asset and a lever of journalism. This is what my newspaper, *Le Soir*, had been doing in recent years when it was collaborating with Flemish media *Knack* or *De Tijd* to investigate public interest stories, from the Panama Papers to corruption at the European Parliament. Their combined strength anchored in diverse networks of sources and cultural references produced outstanding journalism. Diversity and unity, freely crossing its linguistic border to work together, was possible in my own country. It reminded me of the discussions I had held with Milica Pešić on "multi-ethnic reporting", assigning journalists from different communities to work together on issues of common interest, like the environment or social issues. My journey on the road of inclusive journalism had come full circle.

That night, at the prestigious Residence Palace in the heart of Brussels' EU neighborhood, "sharing" was the key word and the roadmap for a journalism of diversity: sharing the best of our own idiosyncrasies, but also our doubts and our fears. Sharing above all those common values that we think are universal and without which we could not imagine a common humanity and a common destiny.

Dr Jovanka Matić

Dr Jovanka Matić was a journalist before moving into the academic field of media and journalism, working at the Yugoslav Institute of Journalism and the Institute of Social Sciences in Belgrade. Matić is the author of three books and about 100 articles dealing with the role of media in transition processes and conflicts, the media system of Serbia, media policy, media coverage of political issues, audience studies and journalism culture. Matić holds a PhD degree from the University of Belgrade, a MA in communications from Simon Fraser University, Canada, and a BA degree in journalism from the University of Belgrade.

POLITICAL DIVERSITY IN THE MEDIA AS AN ISSUE IN THE PROFESSIONAL LIFE OF A MEDIA RESEARCHER

The year is 1982. I am in Canada. I came from Belgrade, the capital of Yugoslavia, to study for a master's in communications. A $500 scholarship affords me little. I live in a shared basement, do not dare going to a dentist, never use a taxi, and wear only clothes that I brought from home. In the four previous years, I worked as a journalist at a national weekly paper, used to fly to different parts of the country at least once a month, spent a four-week vacation in Paris, and smoked the most expensive cigarettes. But I do not mind. Everything is new and exciting. I am 28. This is the best year of my life so far.

My main academic interest is in the news: what is the relationship between news and social change? I know well the limitations of journalism in Yugoslavia. It is a communist country, but different from others in Eastern Europe. Based on collective or what was officially called "social" ownership rather than state ownership, on participation of all employees in business decision-making, on a guiding instead of a direct governing role for the Communist Party, Yugoslavia was an alternative to a Soviet-type system. Orwell's "1984" was widely read among my colleagues, but we all thought that it did not concern us. Yugoslav media are "something in between" the East and West. They are public enterprises, active in the market and free in hiring their staff. Most respected journalists are well-educated and liberally oriented.

Yet, the official ideology lays down clear lines of acceptable discourse in the public sphere. The ideas of socialism, workers' self-management, "brotherhood and unity" as the dominant relationship between numerous ethnic groups, non-alignment as the foreign policy strategy and the role of Tito, who is simultaneously the country's president, the Party's leader and the supreme military commander, are all beyond criticism. Discussion of the way these ideas work in practice is allowed but only if it is initiated by official organizations, all under the eye of the Party, careful to prevent ideological deviances.

The circumscribed autonomy of media served the population well as long as the country was progressing economically, which it was in the 1960s and 1970s, owing to Western financial aid. The first serious cracks in the system started appearing after Tito's death in 1980.

In Canada, I comprehend the complexity of the social roles of media and view journalistic practices from new perspectives. I gain new knowledge about the importance of media pluralism and content diversity for social development, but also about concerns over the belief that the free market by itself can bring freedom of expression and fully meet consumer needs.

I learn that the concept of the "objectivity" of news was born as journalistic credo at the beginning of the 20th century, after a long period of political partisanship, and as a means of bolstering the commercial interests of owners of mass-market daily press outlets: they could reach a wider audience with neutral and diverse news than with one-sided political content. Decades later, the main business of media in established liberal societies is selling the audiences to advertisers. This business model gives the media independence from the political powers-that-be, but makes them dependent on the economic logic of capital, mass production, mass consumption and the commodification of every human need and product. In these societies, the news can be objective and still serve as an ideological institution.

I learn that the process of representing the reality in the media, inevitably selective, consists of choosing from among the available facts and organizing them to create meaning. The result is the promotion of a certain way of interpreting reality - one of many possible ones. These routine journalistic practices are deeply embedded in dominant social values and cultural assumptions on how the world functions and how society should be organized and governed. The media do not simply reflect the consensus on fundamental issues but produce it on a daily basis and thereby reproduce the existing social structures and relationships. They accept the given institutional arrangements - such as dramatic differences in wealth distribution - as natural, neutral, commonsensical and universal when in fact they favour the interests of the most powerful social groups. This attitude is generally adopted even by those who benefit least from these arrangements. Thus, the news media act as the agents of the status quo and as key actors in the process of social control.

I also learn about different strategies designed to oppose the ways in which media can obstruct social change. These strategies include diversification of ownership structures, allowing for various forms of public and community media to thrive; limitations on the concentration of media ownership to prevent monopolies; protections for independent media that give voice to minorities; proactive encouragement of a diversity of media content; and broadening sources of media financing beyond advertising.

NATIONALISTIC NIGHTMARE

The year is 1993. I am in Belgrade and work as a media researcher at the dying Yugoslav Institute of Journalism, planning to get a new job at Serbia's Institute of Social Sciences. Yugoslavia does not exist anymore. Everything it stood for has turned to ashes, literally. Slovenia departed after a short war. Now the fight rages in two other former Yugoslav republics, Croatia and Bosnia-Herzegovina. Yesterday's united "working people", the fundament of the Yugoslavia I was born in, over years transformed themselves into antagonistic Serbs, Croats, Slovenes, Bosnians, Macedonians, Montenegrins and Albanians.

Now, my country is Serbia - one of the rare parts of Eastern Europe in which the former Communist Party, reformed to become the Socialist Party in order to match the proclaimed new order of political pluralism, won the first multiparty elections in 1990. Eastern Europe overall is consumed with the transition towards a market economy and pluralistic parliamentary democracy. Serbia is on a different path. It is engaged in the process of building a nation-state, based on the *etatization* of the economy and the autocratic rule of a nationalistic and war-oriented Socialist Party and its leader, Slobodan Milosevic. With the country isolated because of UN sanctions, crime and corruption are flourishing.

Inflation reaches a history-record peak. My salary is now in the millions of dinars. Actually, it is worth about ten German marks. For these millions I can buy less in the afternoon than in the morning, if there is anything at all left to buy in regular shops. People live by spending their savings, doing additional jobs, buying on the black market, or receiving goods through charity. Petrol is sold in plastic bottles at street corners. I smoke the cheapest cigarettes, smuggled from who knows where. This is the worst year of my life so far. (The 1999 NATO bombing is still years in the future.)

The media are among the strategic pillars of the regime. The largest and most popular outlets have been transformed from their previous status. They are state-owned, state-financed and state-controlled, and they function as a classic propaganda apparatus, now in the service of the ruling party instead of the working class. Their crucial aim is to foster ethnic and political homogeneity in order to help achieve the regime's ideal of "all Serbs in a single state". They use intolerant and militant rhetoric. Every day I wonder anew how people I previously knew as clever, educated and generous have become part of this horrible world of journalistic dishonesty.

Yet, some journalists refuse to take part in such "patriotic journalism". They were either fired or left the state media, and some of them established independent media organizations. These outlets are small, poor, badly equipped, and boycotted by advertisers, and they survive largely because of international donors. Still, they nurture high professional standards and cover topics that the state media barely mention or hide altogether.

With a co-author, I wrote my first book - an analysis of TV coverage of the 1992 national elections. It compared the news shown by the state's national television network and an independent Belgrade-based television station. These two news organizations offered completely opposing pictures of the election process, the crucial issues confronting voters, the candidates' political platforms and promises, and the images of the leading political personalities.

The national state television was openly and sharply skewed towards the ruling Socialist Party and its allies, especially the extremely nationalistic Radical Party. It gave the ruling party twice as much airtime when reporting on the elections than the main opposition. The ruling party was presented overwhelmingly in positive terms, while the strongest opposition party was portrayed exclusively negatively.

For the ruling party, the main electoral issue was the need to defend what it viewed as Serbian national interests from ethnic enemies in Croatia (i.e. Croats) and in Bosnia-Herzegovina (i.e. Muslims) and from the anti-Serb-oriented international community (i.e. the West), which did not want a strong and independent Serbia in the Balkans. It promoted itself as the only guardian of these interests, the best established, most popular and only political actor that could govern effectively. It labeled the opposition as traitorous, ready to sell out the national interest to foreign powers, and described it as incapable, unpopular, disorganized, immoral and dangerous. The entire news programming on state television – the choice of domestic or foreign news topics unrelated to the elections, the visuals of political rallies, the selection of politicians' sound bites – all supported the ruling party's positions.

Independent television gave more time and positive publicity to the opposition, although it ignored the Radical Party altogether because of its extreme nationalistic positions. For the main opposition party, the key election issue was a need for a democratic regime instead of the slightly reformed communist one. It promoted an end to the wars, the introduction of a market economy and a functional multi-party parliament – which would save Serbia. Independent television reports focused on the harsh consequences of the government's policies on the everyday lives of citizens rather than on ethnic issues. Its entire slate of programming gave more sense to the opposition platforms than that of the ruling party.

The majority of voters across Serbia had access to only one version of the election coverage – that of the state-controlled national television. The independent television programming was seen only in Belgrade and its surroundings.

The lack of media pluralism and the absence of representation of diverse opinions, ideas and interests of various political actors were great assets to Milosevic's ruling party. They contributed enormously to its electoral victories not only in 1990 and 1992, but also in subsequent national elections in 1993 and 1997.

Along with other media experts, I had to fight for a simple idea: favoring and idolizing one political force and discriminating against and demonizing another was not journalism. It was political propaganda. It prevented voters from being able to make informed choices. It made multiparty-elections meaningless.

MEDIA TRANSITION TURMOIL

The year is 2000. The day is October 5. I witnessed the most important political event in my life - the collapse of the nationalistic Serbian regime. A massive political rally in front of the Parliament demonstrated the popular rage against the Serbian ruling party and its president Milosevic, who tried to fake the results of the presidential election. I was hit with a lot of tear gas, from which I could not see clearly for hours, but that was an irrelevant and miniscule price paid by thousands of citizens in exchange for such a great gain. Serbia soon got a democracy-oriented government and started down the road of post-communist transition. There was great hope that the country had irrevocably left behind the authoritarian, war-oriented, nationalist dead-end in which it had found itself and was on the path to a democratic, well-organized and prosperous society.

The regime-controlled media changed editorial policy overnight. Starting on October 6, they all - with one exception - began criticizing yesterday's ruling party and its policies, promoting the new ruling elite as the long-awaited saviour heralding a bright future. However, the painstaking work of systemic media change had yet to start.

I was an active part of the media community arguing for a thorough reconstruction of the media system. Media reform, media pluralism, public broadcasting, independent regulator – these were the buzz-words of the decade in all professional conversations on the media. Still, there was no agreement on the optimal direction for the media transformation - neither in the media community nor among the new political rulers. Short ("The media are free") or very detailed media law? Exclusively private media or some public media? Lustration of former war propagandists or not?

Ten years earlier, after the fall of the Berlin Wall, when countries in Eastern Europe launched their media reforms, Western scholars of critical communications argued that the development of private comm-ercial media was not by itself a sufficient guarantee of free and diverse media. They hoped that the East would not allow market-oriented media to be a dominant element of the post-communist media scene. Most radical scholars expected that the social circumstances in new democracies would allow for the development of different kinds of communication institutions and media infrastructures than in Western societies.

These expectations failed. The experience of media reforms in post-communist societies showed that there was no shortcut to a free, autonomous and democratic media system. All of them finally accepted a model of media transformation that was to make them similar to the media in Western Europe. This approach rested mostly on the liberal idea that market competition among multiple media voices inevitably leads to content diversity. Yet, it included limits on media ownership to avoid monopolies and insisted on the creation of public service broadcasting.

However, the idea that the post-communist media would play the leading role in the democratization of the whole society, which had been taken for granted, did not turn out to be the case. Instead, the country's new political elite held the greatest influence over the process of becoming a democracy. It used this power to limit the development of democratic structures within the media system.

Along with other post-Yugoslavia countries, Serbia accepted the model of Western Europe as an example to follow. I found myself in a peculiar position. In my work, I advocated for the need to develop the dominant market-based media system, whose shortcomings I had analyzed in my master's thesis 20 years before. However, the repression of critical thinking and promotion of controlled patriotic journalism, as leftovers from both the communist and nationalistic perceptions of the role of the media, were so strong that the development of the media system based on private commercial media and the abolition of the state control, seemed a great achievement. In addition, the model I promoted also included restrictions on the concentration of media ownership, incentives for both structural and content diversity and, especially, the establishment of public service broadcasting as a new media institution very much different from state-run radio and television.

In this period, I also supported, advised or participated in many kinds of training of journalists aimed at sensitizing them to the need for including ethnic and political diversity in their stories. This training was organized by domestic NGOs and professional associations as well as international ones, including the Media Diversity Institute.

During the first decade of these reforms, the media transition went poorly. Serbia continued to lack the crucial conditions for positive changes: a stable economy allowing for a developed media market, a consolidated democracy based on a broad social consensus, adequate legal and institutional frameworks, and a professional workforce bound in solidarity to the goal of defending journalists' rights.

Numerous democratic governments never made media reforms a priority. They never developed a coherent media policy oriented toward dismantling the financial dependence of the media on the state and towards disabling political influences on media representation of the social spectrum of opinions. They all preferred to use the major media as a resource in mobilizing political support, justifying this behaviour by citing a matter of the utmost public interest – the consolidation of democracy.

It took a lot of psychological strength for me to continue fighting for media reforms, now hindered by democracy-oriented politicians, yesterday's opposition figures, whom I had supported all along in elections and trusted when they professed sympathy for free media and political diversity. I worked day and night, analyzing the reporting of major media and demonstrating how they fail in their main roles: providing a credible and balanced picture of events and issues, serving as a watchdog on the authorities, and acting as a forum for public debate. None of my research results provoked a serious debate on media policy, even when they gained considerable publicity. Once, when I concluded that the news program of the public television network discriminated against women because they very rarely appeared in news stories, its editor-in-chief countered my conclusion with the irrelevant claim that there were more females than males among the public television journalists.

The dismissal by the political and media elites of criticism of their work coming from various sides had more serious consequences than my personal frustration. A feeling of disillusionment with all political parties was spreading among citizens, combined with a downward trend in appreciating the benefits of democracy. Among journalists there was a growing doubt that Serbia was even capable of having autonomous, professional and multi-perspective media organizations.

NEO-AUTHORITARIAN DOWNWARD SPIRAL

The year is 2012. The neoliberal policies of the democratic governments in the previous decade, and the politicians who championed them, are rejected by voters. The authorities did not keep their promise that Serbia would become a normal country – a boring one, without negative news for the front pages of the international press. In addition, Serbia is one of the poorest European countries, although it is a prospective EU member.

Serbian voters returned to their traditions this time and expressed a preference for a strong nation-state that would guarantee economic security. A former high official of the Radical Party, Aleksandar Vucic, soon becomes the leading figure among the new group of authorities. He previously served as the Minister of Information in the Milosevic government and personally conducted censorship of the media during the NATO bombing. In the meantime, he established a new Progressive Party, abandoned his former chauvinist stances and put a pro-European hat on his head.

From 2012 onward, the government is formed by the parties that ruled during the nineties, the part of the former Radical Party reformed into the Progressive Party, with the Socialist Party as its ally. Given a new chance to govern, they use it to bring back many values, policies and institutional characteristics of the authoritarian regime. They define October 5 as a negative turn in Serbian history and blame all the country's problems on the treacherous and greedy governments established after the year 2000. They never speak about their roles in the period before 2000.

The important difference between Milosevic's and Vucic's Serbia is that the latter gets wide support from the European Union, both economically and politically, resulting in some economic stabilization of the country.

The EU nourishes a typical stabilitocracy regime in Serbia whose only task is to preserve peace in the Balkans, even at a high cost for Serbian citizens – the killing of democracy.

The Progressive Party rules through state-capture and media-capture. The state is extremely centralized and all important decisions are made in one place, disregarding the divisions of power designated in the Constitution. All state institutions are colonized by people loyal to the party. Vucic has personal control over the key levers of power. He has exerted his influence far beyond his constitutional responsibilities, first as Prime Minister, and from 2017 as President of Serbia.

Vucic personally holds a monopoly on public discourse. He defines the official stance on all important social issues, which he disseminates to the public himself in very frequent public appearances. The mainstream media and a massive army of party trolls, active on social networks, spread his messages.

The news media are again divided into two camps. The first includes the most popular media – all five national television networks, along with the public service broadcaster, and seven out of nine national daily papers, with strong online news portals. The latter camp consists of two cable TV channels, two dailies and several weekly news magazines.

The first camp acts as a typical propaganda tool of the regime and is privileged in many ways, especially in terms of finances and access to information. It brutally promotes the ruling party, all of its policies, and President Vucic in particular. It either ignores all negative outcomes attributable to the government or ascribes them to the wrongdoings of enemies of Serbia and the Serbian people, enemies of the Progressive Party, and enemies of Vucic and his family. The enemies include the 2000-2012 democratic governments and all critics of the ruling party, ranging from international actors and neighbouring countries to domestic opposition parties, civil society organisations and activists, and independent media owners and journalists. The leader in demonizing critical voices is the tabloid press, which is openly anti-Western and strongly pro-Russia oriented. On the day of the outbreak of the war in Ukraine, the most influential tabloid ran the title "Ukraine attacked Russia" on its front page.

The other camp follows the tradition of independent media from the 1990s, promotes itself as a guardian of the public interest and nurtures a critical attitude toward the government. The ruling party boycotts the independent media. Its representatives steadfastly refuse to give statements and interviews to these organizations and never accept invitations for live studio appearances. These media are economically distressed and under constant pressure from the government and party representatives, as well as from the regime-controlled media. They are regularly labelled as traitors and servants of foreign powers.

During the development of the Serbian hybrid regime, I was involved in many public events aimed at informing both the domestic and international audience about the process of media-capture. Together with other colleagues from the Balkans, in 2014 I spoke at the conference in the EU Parliament, but only a few MPs were interested in the problems of the media in our region. In 2018, I participated in the Perugia Journalism Festival's panel "Fascism is back. Is journalism part of the problem or of a solution?", organized by the Media Diversity Institute, criticizing the EU's "stabilitocracy approach" to Serbia. It raised concerns among international journalists.

My greatest effort in opposing manipulative functioning of the Serbian media was participation in an expert group that proposed a set of reform measures in advance of the 2020 national elections, which the opposition parties threatened to boycott. A group of representatives from the EU Parliament organized a series of consultations between the relevant political actors in order to reach an agreement.

In my opinion, this was Serbia's last chance under this regime to introduce some normality into its political life and the everyday functioning of the media. The hope of our expert group was that the pressure from the EU could stimulate the Progressive Party to make some concessions and that the election results would normalize the work of the national Parliament, which in turn would halt the downward autocratic spiral.

None of our proposals were accepted. Most of the opposition parties boycotted the elections. For the first time in 30 years of multi-party political life, the new Parliament did not include any opposition parties.

The ruling party again rendered the elections meaningless. Without fair media reporting on relevant events and without representation of diverse political opinions, the elections simply affirmed the party's hegemonic position.

NO PASARAN

The year is 2022. I officially retired three years ago, due to a compulsory age-retirement for employees in public institutions. My pension is half of my last salary, which was about 1000 US dollars a month. But I do not mind. Many things are new and exciting. Within the year, I travelled to Italy, to Spain, to Croatia and for the first time to Britain and to Vietnam. I still work, participating in various projects. But I no longer have to follow the regime-controlled media for research purposes. My reservoirs for awful journalistic products are already filled up - no place left for new ones.

I gave myself a treat by ignoring the media reporting of the 2022 snap elections. Due to EU pressure, the government made some changes in the electoral process and conditions, but none of them address the ruling party's enormous advantages. Despite the odds being against them, the opposition parties were still able to win some seats. But they are in the minority, so their presence does not bear any influence on the way the Parliament makes decisions or on how the country is run.

I have new research interests. I am strongly convinced that the Serbian media system needs another radical reconstruction. There is also a need for the re-education of politicians, journalists and news audiences of both traditional and digital media about the necessity of *active and passive access* to media by local communities, a variety of cultural and social groups, and above all, of political actors with diverse interests, opinions and values. I want to be part of that process, which should be grounded in the new relationship between the media and audiences. I am not alone. Many others are willing to contribute.

I still believe that Serbia could give birth to some new communication structures that would stimulate and allow the news media to be the force of progressive social change.

Dr Snježana Milivojević

Dr Snježana Milivojević (PhD Sociology/Communication) is Professor of public opinion and media studies. She served as dean of Bayan College, Purdue University Northwest USA affiliate in Muscat, Sultanate of Oman, during the 2022-2023 academic year. Prior to that, Milivojević was a professor at the University of Belgrade - Faculty of Political Sciences where she chaired the Doctoral program in Culture and Media, MA program in Communication and was the founding chair of the Center for Media Research. She was international guarantor and visiting professor at the University of New York in Prague (2014-2018), co-director of the international post-graduate course Comparative Media Systems at the Inter University Centre in Dubrovnik (2011-2022), Fulbright visiting scholar at Columbia University (2012-2013), Chevening scholar at St. Antony's College Oxford University (2000-2001), and visiting lecturer at several European and American universities. Milivojević has participated in many international research projects and has published extensively in the fields of communication theory, political communication, cultural and gender studies, and media and public memory.

DIVERSITY POSTCARD

When I accepted a position I was unexpectedly offered from Bayan College in Muscat, the capital of Oman, I knew little more about the country than where it was on the map. Oman is a Sultanate, an absolute monarchy with very limited political representation. It is also a fast-developing high-income country. Both the academic and media cultures there were equally unknown to me. Comparative indexes of media freedom rated it very low, in line with the country's record on political and civil liberties. But the college is affiliated with the US Purdue University Northwest, and it offers the country's only BA and MA communication programs in English. I was assured that my international experience was welcome. Nonetheless, I suspected I was in for an epistemological challenge.

A few months after my arrival, some Omani colleagues asked me to briefly describe the country. Off the top of my head, I answered that it was "hot, friendly and slow". When asked to elaborate, I added a bit more to the picture.

Here, "hot" means more than the climate. The bright, sun-baked environment combines three large ecosystems: the desert, the mountain range and the ocean. The powerful meeting point of the three forms the background of the country's geography, history and identity. The heat dictates that many people must live in an air-conditioned world most of the year. Villages are pleasant if hidden in the mountains, but cities are hot and mostly oriented to life indoors. Even along the beautiful coastal areas, beaches are less widely used for swimming and more often for family outings in the evening under the stars. The country is in the northern hemisphere but due to the proximity of the equator winter is heavenly and summer is the ‘bad season’.

“Friendly” refers to the people, who are welcoming, open and proud of their heritage. The majority of the population is young, with 44% 17 years or younger, and less than 4% 65 and older. Older people really seem to be a rare species. Students are very respectful of authority, rarely critical and often quite naïve. Women have only had the right to vote and participate in political life since 1994. Yet women make up 50% of all students, around 17% of the workforce, the ministers for both education and higher education are women. A policy of universal education was introduced in the 1970s, but men and women are still schooled separately. Only at university do young people attend mixed classrooms and learn in inclusive teaching environments. Almost half of the population are non-citizens, expatriates from around the world. A constant visual, cultural and linguistic blend is the standard here. So, “friendly” also means tolerance and accepting of differences.

And “slow”. Everything always takes more time and does not move in a linear fashion. There are twists and turns and setbacks that proceed in a slow and circular manner. After my repeated efforts to have something done, the HR officer told me: “You want everything fast, doctor. Here is slow”. This slow pace helps changes seem natural and renders them more easily acceptable. But sometimes abrupt events intersect with those long, slow cycles, producing unexpected cultural outcomes.

Last December, long-overdue municipal elections, which were postponed during the Covid pandemic, took place across the country. These were only the third municipal elections in the country’s history—the first such voting took place in 2012--but the entire population now had access to e-voting. Unlike in many other areas of the world, the development of some social or political skills connected with lately introduced processes is now happening almost simultaneously with the learning of digital skills. Due to a very rapid digital transformation, the very young population is mostly unaware of the time gap between the centuries of election history worldwide and the newness of the digital. Quite often this mismatch resembles what Manuel Castells, a famous sociologist and interpreter of the Information Age, called the timeless time - time without socially meaningful ordered sequencing. Mixing different temporalities feels like living where the Middle Ages meets the cyber-future.

This fractured postcard corresponds to my fragmented experience of the country. It also reflects what differs from my usual environment and reveals how I discovered new dimensions of diversity. Soon after my arrival, I realized that I was not facing only particular new differences but a whole new environment of diversity. Environments are not passive wrappings. They are natural worlds which shape our perceptions, experiences and behaviors. But the environment, even when it refers to nature, is always socially constructed and is never just a background against which cultures develop. And it is from understanding the Omani environment that I slowly began understanding how it relates to diversity.

As one of the major crossroads of the world, this whole region has had a long experience with diverse cultural, ethnic, and religious traditions. Networks of maritime and continental routes that connected the Mediterranean region with the Middle East, Arabia, Far East and China originated around the overlapping of the Silk Road with routes for trading spices and incense. For centuries, these areas were also venues of intensive knowledge development and cultural exchange. But the present-day diversity results from migratory waves connected to the development of the Arab states of the Persian Gulf and the modern world's dependence on oil and natural gas from the region. The influx of experts and workers from both East and West over the past 30 to 40 years has entirely transformed society.

These migratory trajectories also shaped the social response to diversity, in effect producing multi-culturalism of a specific kind, where many cultures coexist around a politically and culturally privileged local culture. All societies are diverse. What distinguishes them is how these differences are treated and managed. An acknowledgment of the fundamental right to be different and to maintain individual and cultural identities is a recent development in pluralistic societies. It has transformed social acceptance into a political philosophy and a corresponding politics of difference in contemporary western democracies. Respect for differences means that recognition, inclusion and acceptance do not depend on the benevolence of individuals but are now social norms that serve as a cornerstone of late 20th century liberal multiculturalism.

The cultural landscape within which differences do not merge into a multicultural western liberal, secular core but into a religious, Arabic, fast-developing yet conservative and patriarchal culture presents another context for social diversity. This landscape impacts both the sense of what it means to be different and how these differences are treated.

LANGUAGE AND THE MEDIA

In her innovative work, American political scientist and feminist scholar Iris Marion Young connected social justice with the politics of difference. She argued that the liberal concept of human rights based upon the notion of a 'universal person' neglects differences among social groups and is in effect blind to gender, ethnic, national or other differences between them. Claiming that diversity is a resource, she argued for the equality of culturally and politically distinctive group experiences. Around that time, the media picked up the meme of 'diversity' and began explaining how the representation of race, ethnicity, gender, and identity in general relates to structural inequalities and not only to personal differences. The awareness that the visibility of diverse voices depends on the media positioned the media as one of the major battlegrounds of identity formation as well as part of the quest for more socially just societies.

This global momentum reached me during the wars in Yugoslavia, where diversity was weaponized in the propaganda of war. Throughout the Balkans, ethnic identity became a key identifier of social fragmentation and a source of conflict. In the midst of it all, the Media Diversity Institute initiated journalistic and civic educational initiatives paving the way for a more sensitive understanding of diversity. Later, in the spirit of post-conflict reconciliation, MDI started a media monitoring project focusing on the representation of ethnic minorities in major media across countries emerging from bloody wars and in some countries in their neighborhood. My motivation for becoming involved with the project was to help develop a methodology and a set of analytical skills that could be used outside academia by various professionals and activists.

I found that comparative research was the best strategy for documenting how ethnic differences became stereotypes and for explaining how they were politicized and misused to label some actors as social outcasts, some as political enemies and some as respected 'others', across communities. Therefore, the main purpose of the research was not to identify particular differences and how adequately or not they were presented in public life but to critically read media representations, hoping to raise public consciousness and promote tolerance throughout the war-scarred region. In a broader sense, the monitoring also aimed to document how media get instrumentalized and what they do and do not do to construct the social and political context in which identity and diversity gain meaning.

Critical reading of the media and their portrayal of differences was particularly important in a region where media images often essentialize identity. These images suggest that identity is characterized by some fixed, coherent, essential core; they ignore the fact that there are fractured, hybrid, mixed and even more complex forms of identities, and that nobody comes in one piece. Those various fragments are transformed into meaningful wholes labeled 'identity' only though the persistent work of representation. The message that identities, both personal and collective, need to be formed, constructed, negotiated and acquired discursively was and is crucial for a region in which wars were fought in the name of ethnic purity. Arguing that identities are human constructs does not mean that they are artificial or not real but underlines the importance of the sense-making practices through the use of media and language.

Living in different language communities offers the most obvious encounters with differences. I still remember my graduate studies in the Netherlands during the late 1980s, when I was studying in English and thinking in Serbian while being surrounded by Dutch and other languages at our international school. For all of us, English, the language of instruction and our lingua franca, was never just a medium of learning and communication. It was a conceptual tool and a major instrument for translating experiences across cultural contexts. A world that converged around language while diverging in many things was a reminder that discursive resources to comprehend and represent reality are the same as those used in constructing it. In the much simpler media landscape of the time, my daily media diet of reading The Guardian and watching the BBC grounded that frame of reference for understanding the world out there deeply within 'western culture'. Fluency in English was actually instrumental in domesticating cultural differences within the common linguistic space.

Now, almost 40 years later, technology has completely altered the linguistic experience. I am again living surrounded by different languages, in an Arabic-speaking country. This time the majority language is so remote from my Slavonic-originating Serbian that I cannot guess what anything means from listening to other people's conversations. But unlike before, it is much easier for me to navigate this linguistic environment. I have several translating apps on my phone to instantly scan and display the text or vocally translate messages into any language. Leaving aside the quality of the translation, which is always a major challenge, the sheer possibility of communicating through a local language without being able to speak it is a major novelty. In fact, the ability to communicate among people who find each other's languages equally distant, while they listen or read translations of messages on their phones as they receive them, redefines the meaning of the phrase 'language community'.

For me the benefits of this possibility went beyond causal everyday encounters. As dean of the college, I had to officially communicate in Arabic with the Ministry of Higher Education and had to rely on translating apps even when the discussion involved very sensitive issues. Of course, in addition to basic reading and writing, these communications required specific forms guided by cultural semantics, a fact I was not unaware of as non-speaker of Arabic. The official correspondence would always feature paragraphs of standardized greetings adhering to a formal etiquette not easily translatable into other languages. The same phrases had to be added to my English sentences when they were adopted for institutional correspondence. And this whole app supported communication worked smoothly.

I was born in Bosnia, the most ethnically mixed part of Yugoslavia, to parents who were from different parts of the country but spoke the same language. We then lived in Macedonia, where I was exposed to linguistic variety. I attended a 'Serbian school' in which we were taught in what was a minority language in Macedonia but also the majority language throughout the country of Yugoslavia. I have moved many times since then and have lived in countries where my name was difficult to pronounce. But the languages I encountered in that period were always sorted into families, with similarities among them even when they differed. Living in the Arabic-speaking world, a common linguistic territory of more than 400 million people spread across continents, I experienced a very distinct sense of being surrounded by difference. In addition to Arabic, common foreign languages there were Malayalam, Hindi, Tamil, Bengali, Urdu, Malay, Thai and many more with alphabets far more complicated and difficult to learn than the Cyrillic and Roman letters which I was used to. Without speaking any of the languages, I was daily reminded how these other tongues conceptualized the world differently and helped those speaking them to experience and represent it in diverse ways.

Since the emergence of newspapers, the major challenge for the media has been to represent complex reality and different points of view as a meaningful whole. From 1605, the year which marks the birth of newspapers, when publisher Johann Carolus started publishing regular news bulletins in the city of Strasburg, news media and journalism were giving voice and visibility to social plurality while acting on behalf of the public. Objectivity, fairness and impartiality developed over centuries as rules for professionalism, and institutional arrangements evolved to foster those ends. But only during the last decades of the 20th century has media professionalism extended to constructing rules of representation that ensure a fairer and more just portrayal of various social actors. How media represent reality and everybody in it affects identities and subjectivities because the work of representation disturbs relations of power in society.

The first newspapers in Oman were published in the 1970s, although beginnings of Omani journalism date back to the early 20th century when several papers were initiated outside the country at the island of Zanzibar. With such a short history, media quickly jumped into the digital transformation. When social media shook the media world, the general population did not have a long-established pattern of media consumption. In the current global media landscape, the digital revolution is carried out by new generations of media users who are digital-native, digital-literate and almost disconnected from legacy media use. Younger media users hardly remember the old media anywhere, but here there is no rich collective memory to rely on either. Almost everybody starts using new media as an absolute beginner.

Now social media are almost universally accessible and are used by everybody all the time. Restaurants operate only with QR codes; when you ask for a paper menu, the most you can expect is that waiters will bring you a tablet. In the fast-growing cities, nobody knows street names or addresses, and everybody moves around with the help of navigation apps and according to online geo-location. Many products, even traditional crafts, can only be bought through Instagram. State institutions and services used widely by everyone include everything from e-banking to applications for the Hajj to Mecca, with some of the pilgrims even being selected by digital lottery. WhatsApp is the preferred channel of communication for every purpose and among all age groups.

Media not involving journalism are also major sources of information and most people receive 'news' through friends, PR agencies or directly involved actors. New media habits and practices are being developed by generations of young people who are watching Netflix and don't even know that movies were once made for theaters. They are unfamiliar with the global history of film or popular culture and enjoy cultural geography organized around centers like Korean pop, Bollywood film or Dubai digital culture. All around the Gulf countries, the future is turning the region into a digital creativity hub as the oil economy loses importance and an immersive digital and virtual art scene is blossoming.

Concepts of media literacy and media competencies are being thoroughly reorganized. Generations of digital natives create new habits that represent a break from traditional cultural patterns. In some respects digital networks resemble traditional family or tribal ties, but are also establishing new patterns of communication. So young women and men who did not go to mixed schools are hesitant when they meet in person, but socialize easily on Instagram and WhatsApp. This digital transformation has rearranged social relations, and society is discovering its internal differences as much as what makes it distinct from others as a whole.

As Marshall McLuhan, the Canadian media theorist who was among the first to recognize the importance of media as technology, once famously said, the effect of each new medium is not in what it says but how it reshapes our symbolic environment and our entire social life.

THE CITY, PUBLIC AND PRIVATE SPACES

I love the city. According to Richard Sennett, an American academic who studied various aspects of urban life, the city is an urban settlement in which strangers are likely to meet and therefore a place where we tolerate those who are different. The city is a necessary environment for diversity, a stage to present and represent differences, to interact with others without fear of confrontation. It is the foundation of democratic life, the place where citizens learn to see and accept others regardless of their looks or behavior. Its streets, coffee shops, parks, squares and piazzas are open to all for spontaneous and non-hierarchical public communication. As public spaces, they are by definition inclusive and allow for equality of movement and the right to gather. It is where citizens are exposed to a variety of views and attitudes different from their own, where they learn that these differences are not threatening and therefore should be approached in a co-operative and non-combative manner.

The ability to negotiate differences without violence is one of the most important achievements of democracy, ensuring that when strangers or dissimilar people meet they do not fight over scarce resources or divergent opinions but interact with acceptance and respect. Tolerance is possible only when meeting strangers, passersby, accidental visitors, fellow citizens, neighbors, opponents and foes are all regular and ordinary experiences. This micropolitics of everyday life is partly based on indifference and partly on acceptance. The essence of it has not changed much from the ancient city of Athens to the metropolis in contemporary democracies.

Outside the cultural and political West, visibility and voice are differently entangled with publicness. Modern Muscat is a city developed mostly along large roads parallel to the coastline. The city is not structured around public squares or places for easy, everyday encounters, and its large distances limit the possibility of walking. The climate also dictates that activities mostly take place indoors, and spontaneous encounters occur mainly in big shopping malls. And traditional Muslim culture defines what is private and what is acceptable in public. I have often seen in the Gulf Arab countries how easily secrecy is mistakenly defended as privacy. This conception of privacy hampers public insight into gender relations and domestic practices and habits, which change more slowly than public mores, and stay under the discretion of the household or the traditions governing family relationships.

But things happen differently in the digital environment. Online content is externally monitored and the concept of privacy does not protect online data and behavior. Even shops and restaurants expect everybody to voluntarily reveal private data—such as a phone number, email or other contact details--after each purchase. I was surprised when I was asked to leave my phone number during my first time shopping in one of the Muscat malls. I even asked to see the manager to discuss it. The cashier was surprised that I made an issue over it and tried to explain that this was a standard practice. This discussion continued until the line behind me became quite long and I realized that everybody there was puzzled by my concerns and was looking at me.

This was one of my first "things-are-different-here" experiences. There were many more examples of striking differences in the treatment of virtual and actual privacy. While physical protection from actual visibility persists, online behavior is much more open. For instance, it is illegal to feature even an accidentally taken photograph of a women in the street without her explicit consent, many private villas still have high wall, and both white male dishdasha and black female abaya are forms of dressing that shield people from the gaze of others. But personal data is much more transparent online.

According to the famous German philosopher Jurgen Habermas, its most vigorous advocate, the public sphere stands and falls with the question of universal access. Because of this open to all principle, the privileged form of public speaking is rational, critical, consensus-oriented expression. Because of that the most vocal critiques of the public sphere concept object to the absence of those forms of expressions which are more pertinent to structurally de-favored such as women or non-western citizens. The same issue echoes in the context of global communication with the conclusion that the globalized and de-westernized public sphere needs a broader perspective on diversity, including on various forms of public expression.

The recently initiated and ongoing debate about the end of multiculturalism also touches upon this problem. Those who proclaim the death of multiculturalism propose that a new encompassing idea of public life should simultaneously negotiate the right to be different and apply it both contextually and globally. They say the issue is not any more how to enlarge the public sphere globally, but the problem is how to find its new common normative center. The question is whether such a global public sphere is at all possible. And if not, if global public communication is only possible as multi-centered, will that also mean that various traditional forms of exclusionary and discriminatory practices will be tolerated in the name of cultural sensitivity?

During the past decade contradictory developments complicated this dilemma even further. More freedom and opportunities were accompanied by a strong backlash from anti-liberal, conservative and right-wing forces globally. Defenders of “traditional values”, “national heritage” and “cultural exceptionalism” easily connected with right-wing extremists to undermine science, secularism and liberal values in many countries. The media became increasingly polarized and weaponized in the ongoing cultural wars against the gains of the emancipatory movements and inclusive policies of the late 20th century.

Also, increased visibility did not bring about the fundamental changes expected by those who argued that more and better media coverage would directly lead to more power on the part of the represented. Media representation alone is not enough to empower people or to correct previous injustices. The recent global democratic decline inevitably reduces the spaces available for expressing and respecting differences. The spread of authoritarianism, populism, hate speech and conspiracy theories helps right-wing forces to use the right to be different argument to completely twist the diversity narrative into a defense of their lost privileges. This conservative backlash is like no other before as it utilizes language representing liberal approaches to promote antidemocratic policies and make non-democratic claims. Using the language of difference, proponents of the backlash in fact only advocate freedom of expression to justify attacks on marginalized and oppressed groups.

Digital, mobile and social media that are transforming audience habits and user choices bring new challenges to diversity. Diversity defenders therefore face a new situation in the virtual space beyond traditional borders: differences are visible and articulated but people are still being marginalized and repressed. It seems that inclusion on its own is not enough and the case for diversity needs to be reinforced globally.

Dr Safi Naciri

Dr Safi Naciri is a journalism professor at University Hassan 2 and at ISIC, Higher Institute of Information and Communication in Morocco. He holds a PhD in Political Science from the University of Tangier, with research on media and democracy. Naciri is a former Editor-in-Chief at SNRT, Moroccan national radio, where he presented several radio shows. He is a regular contributor to public debates and discussions and has published several publications including The History of far left in Morocco (2004). Naciri is a member of the Arabic Network for the Study of Democracy (ANSD) in Beirut.

THE STORYTELLING TIMES

Salah is one of the guests I hosted on "Zaman Al-Haky" (The Storytelling Times), the talk show I hosted for years on Moroccan radio. The program hosted a significant segment of the elite, but my interview with Salah was different. Every time I listen to it, I burst into tears.

Salah was in his twenties when he was abducted, and he spent nearly nine years in secret detention alongside five comrades. They spent two years handcuffed and blindfolded. Then, suddenly one day at dawn, they were loaded onto a bus surrounded by soldiers on all sides. Perhaps they are on their way to be executed?! How could this be happening to teenagers for just distributing secret leaflets? The journey continued, and the hours passed until they finally arrived at another secret detention centre in the middle of nowhere in the desert. They were housed in dark cells that were closed all the time, during the freezing winters and scalding summers. It was like a corner in hell, where hunger, filth, diseases, and brutal beatings were their daily morning routine. They felt disconnected from place and time. They lost any contact with their families, who knew nothing about their whereabouts. Every passing day reinforced the feeling that they would die and be buried there without anyone knowing about them.

Salah told me all that, but he told much, much more as well. My words are powerless to describe the hellish torture that Salah and his comrades endured, the sadism of the executioners, who enjoyed torturing their victims. Language fails us miserably in such situations.

One morning, they were released. The young men couldn't believe they were free. They were in a state of bewilderment. For months, they had difficulty believing they had been released. Upon his release, Salah was given a single banknote to arrange for his transportation from this remote point in the desert to the capital, and then to his family's house.

He arrived in the capital at night; it was winter, and his spring clothes were unable to protect him from the bitter cold. It was too late at night to find any transportation. But Salah began to wonder in confusion, was his family still living in the same house? Nine years had passed. Was his mother still alive? What about his father? His siblings? He was afraid that if his mother opened the door and found him after these years, she might not be able to bear the shock and would be struck by calamity. So, what should he do? His thoughts were scattered.

Salah decided at first to knock on the door and wait, or rather, sneak a peek inside the house. If he noticed that she was the one heading to open the door, he would run away and disappear somewhere. It was past midnight, but a light emanated from one of the lower windows. He summoned all of his strength and knocked gently. His nerves were at their highest level of tension. His heartbeat was racing. He saw that a woman was heading to open the door. Was it his mother? Should he flee and hide somewhere? But bewilderment paralyzed his ability to think and move. She opened the door and asked, "Who are you?" He replied, "I am your son." She was stunned. "My son from where?" "Your son Salah," he said. She stared at him, and it seemed that she was unable to speak or even think. After a while, she turned around and left him standing there. She left the door open and entered her sleeping children's rooms, shouting, "Wake up! Someone says he is your brother!" Salah took a few steps inside the house.

They gathered around him. He had difficulty recognizing them. When he was abducted, they were just little children, and now they were young men, some of them with beards and mustaches. They, in turn, stared at this stranger, thin as a thread, pale, and sad. In a split second, the eldest threw himself on him, cheering and yelling, "This is my brother Salah! This is my brother Salah!" The brothers were hugging each other. The mother yelled, "I know my son's body. He has a mole on his left shoulder." She removed his shirt, saw the mole, and then collapsed in tears.

Salah told me that afterward, he could no longer understand what was happening around him, and everyone became engaged in heartfelt collective weeping.

WHEN THE BERLIN WALL FELL...

I was born in a village on the outskirts of Casablanca, where I first attended school. My memories still hold onto aspects of the farmers' lives, especially their folk songs. Their sincere and unpretentious singing expressed a plethora of emotions, including nostalgia, pain, love - life with all its harshness and mystery. My father was a farmer, but after his death, when I was a little child, we moved to the city, where I became involved in political work at an early age. The leftist revolution of the 1970s swept up my generation and left many victims in its wake. The "Years of Lead," as they were called in Morocco, saw tens of thousands of people imprisoned, exiled, or killed during popular uprisings. I spent a short period in prison, but my experience pales in comparison to those who were sentenced to death or life imprisonment, or who were forced into exile.

This painful period ended, but its scars continue to linger in the individual and collective memory. When the Berlin Wall fell, the Moroccan government declared that it wanted to turn a new page and achieve historical reconciliation. It acknowledged the violations of human rights committed in the past and sought to compensate the victims and offer apologies. It also sought to reconcile with women by passing laws that would protect their rights, and to recognize the Amazigh language and culture and provide ways to promote and integrate them into the media and public life.

When the Berlin Wall collapsed, I--like many others--felt a sense of disappointment and despair. The dreams of revolution, which had opened our eyes, had evaporated. All our ideas and expectations were scattered. In these circumstances, I decided to return to the classroom. After completing a law degree, I enrolled in a journalism institute in Rabat. That's how I entered journalism from the field of politics. In early 1993, during my time as a journalism student, the National Conference on Media and Communication was held. The state wanted to use this conference to emphasize its commitment to accepting democratic reforms within certain limits. The debate was attended by the Minister of the Interior and Media, who had great power and influence in the government. Ironically, the ministry combines two sets of government functions that should be kept completely separate. The discussion was also attended by leaders and representatives from opposition parties, and by editors of party-affiliated newspapers. Dozens of journalists and civic activists also attended, although their presence was not given equal weight to that of the government and opposition representatives.

At the opening of the conference, the Minister of the Interior and Media read a royal message calling for "developing the national media and making it keep pace with the political changes." The message also emphasized that since the end of the Cold War and the ideological conflict between East and West, communication had become increasingly important for the aspirations of the world's peoples for freedom, security, and peace. The message stressed that the conference was held "under favorable conditions for our democratic process, characterized by dialogue, exchange of ideas, and service of the public good, at a time when the rule of law is strengthened, and the reputation and position of Morocco are enhanced on the world stage."

After the reading of the royal message, the opposition leaders attending as journalists strongly appealed for separating responsibility for the media from the interior ministry in order to ensure the independence of media institutions and provide legal and institutional conditions that would enable journalists to perform their duties in an atmosphere of freedom and security, and away from all forms of state pressure and control. They emphasized that all of this would help develop democratic life.

However, politicians spoke without giving journalists the floor. This indicated that the event, at its core, was political and had political implications. Nonetheless, this negative aspect could be overlooked when we think about the recommendations that resulted from the debate, which can be viewed as a political vision with professional content on how to reform the media. Overall, the event served as a milestone in the process of reconciliation between the government and the opposition.

It is natural for a country aspiring to democratic transformation to be dominated by political concerns, which was noticeable during the "debate." Therefore, the central focus of its recommendations was political, or had political dimensions that were not hidden, such as talking about freedom and lifting the government's and its agencies' control over public media. Secondarily, the recommendations addressed the need to consider the country's political and cultural diversity, and the importance of supporting regional media and those that speak the Amazigh language. The recommendations did not include a comprehensive discussion of media diversity as a concept.

In Morocco, the media is part of politics, as is the case in all North African and Middle Eastern countries. I transitioned to journalism from politics, carrying my dreams and idealistic values. Politicians draw the lines of liberation and control, while journalists execute them. It took me some time to discover this bitter truth. After graduating and becoming involved in professional practice, I had to learn how to utilize every single opportunity to help me escape from the domination of politics and its agendas. I found refuge in memories, in the forgotten, marginalized, and excluded. I published my first book, which was called "The Farthest Left in Morocco - A Noble Struggle Against the Impossible." Then, years later, I created my radio program, called: "Zaman Al-Haky" (The Storytelling Era).

MOROCCO: A COUNTRY OF DIVERSITY

Throughout its history, Morocco has been a diverse country. It is a geographical crossroads, where Africa meets Europe. While sitting in a café in Tangier, you can easily see with the naked eye the Spanish town of Tarifa across the water. The Mediterranean Sea has had a profound cultural impact on the country. This is the land of Tamazgha, which extends eastwards to the Egyptian borders, and southwards to the coastal countries, and even includes the Canary Islands. This is Morocco, a mix of Arab, Amazigh, Islamic, Hebrew, Andalusian, African and Mediterranean identities.

When France occupied Morocco in the early twentieth century, they wanted to ignite conflict between these different elements, especially through what was called "the Amazigh policy". However, the opposite happened, as a national movement was formed from the entire society with their different ideologies and backgrounds, and the desire for unity in confronting the colonizers prevailed. It was emphasized that Morocco has one identity based on its Arabic and Islamic foundations, which led to the erasure of all manifestations of diversity.

But after the declaration of independence in 1956, and the birth of the modern state, this unifying approach, which reduced the national identity to its Arab and Islamic aspects, became a constraint on the development of a more openly diverse society. The oppressed and marginalized groups began to express themselves, albeit tentatively, through limited media outlets. There was a dominant radical left at universities and in youth circles, a cultural movement that sought to restore popular culture, and the formation of the first Amazigh associations and the first nucleus of the women's movement. This cultural and political process continued from the early 1970s until the fall of the Berlin Wall in 1989 and was accompanied by widespread repression.

At the beginning of the 1990s, the state made limited amendments to family law and committed to teaching Amazigh in primary schools and broadcasting television news in the Amazigh language. These were modest steps. The state's main concern was to position itself in a post-Cold War world and promote slogans about democracy and human rights. The authorities attempted to settle serious violations of human rights in order to encourage opposition groups, particularly the Socialists, to participate in the government. The Amazigh and women's issues, although they began to gain media attention, seemed secondary compared to the direct political issues. However, overall, spaces of freedom began expanding, and public debates started to touch on the prohibited and forbidden, especially when the second channel 2M and independent newspapers began to emerge.

By the end of the 1990s, these massive transformations led to the ascendence of the socialist leader Abderrahmane Youssoufi, whose aim was to achieve a democratic transition. Then a royal speech fully recognized the Amazigh as a national language and culture. A new family code was then issued, leading to the formation of the Equity and Reconciliation Commission, which was responsible for investigating serious human rights violations. Hearings for the victims of these violations were held and were broadcast live on radio and television channels.

In this atmosphere, I joined the national radio and experienced all this political and media transformation, with all its noise and contradictions. I was part of the trend that sought to expand the spaces of freedom and establish professional practices that respected the intelligence of the news audience and represented a break from the old sterile, empty, and opportunistic official discourse. However, it was not always easy.

Even with the departure of Abderrahmane Youssoufi, who was considered a failure in the attempt at a democratic transition, the dynamics of political and media openness continued, whether through independent journalism or public media, albeit to a lesser extent. Media attention was particularly focused on the issue of serious human rights violations. Within this dynamic, the audiovisual sector was liberalized, allowing private individuals to establish radio channels, and new channels were added to public media, most notably the Amazigh channel.

MEETING WITH MILICA

One evening, I received a call from a friend who suggested that I meet with a British citizen who was visiting Morocco. That's how I met Milica, and from there began my journey with the Media Diversity Institute. Over the years, I worked alongside the Institute, which was to me like a great school from which I learned a lot and gained lots of experience. MDI has left a remarkable mark on the Moroccan media landscape through its training courses, which were provided to hundreds of young journalists, and through various other activities and events it organised and hosted. The Institute was able to bring a part of the Anglo-Saxon media culture, especially as it relates to media diversity, to Morocco.

I remember when Milica, along with the king's advisor and the minister of communication, inaugurated an international conference organised by MDI in Rabat to mark the launch of their activities. Dozens of media experts and journalists from Morocco, Europe, and the Arab world were there. Years later, I sadly recall the evening when a young journalist called me and told me that a headline on the front page of a newspaper read: "Organisation Advocating for LGBTQ+ Rights is About to Form a Partnership with National Radio." I rushed out and bought the newspaper. The article was clear in its condemnation of the partnership that MDI and the radio were preparing to sign.

When we investigated, we found that the minister of communication—the same person who attended MDI's opening event--was behind the article, as well as subsequent articles. The minister was a member of the Islamist party that rode the wave of the Arab Spring to reach the government. About a year before assuming his powerful position, he participated in a study trip to London organised by the MDI itself for the benefit of directors of the most important Moroccan media outlets. The delegation visited the BBC, Channel Four, and The Guardian, and attended meetings with British journalists whose focus was on media diversity.

When I met the minister weeks later, I said to him, "You know the Media Diversity Institute well." In an attempt to evade the topic, he replied, "The partnerships are up to the minister, not the radio director!"

WOMEN AND WOMEN

After the fall of the Berlin Wall and the tumultuous 1990s in Morocco, the central elite was preoccupied politically, which is understandable in a country striving for a complete democratic transition. This was reflected in the media landscape, where politicians - mostly men - dominated radio and television broadcasts, and their activities and statements dominated the front pages of newspapers. Since then, increasing recognition of societal diversity has been closely connected with the development of progress toward democracy, as demonstrated by the women's and Amazigh movements. We can say that the recognition of the Amazigh language and culture as an official language alongside Arabic in 2001, and its inclusion in the 2011 constitution, represented a qualitative leap in the development of Moroccan society—a leap that was gradually echoed in media coverage, albeit not to the desired level. The same applies to the issue of women, as after the modest amendments to the Family Law in 1993, the bolder amendments of 2004 followed. Then the 2011 constitution acknowledged in its nineteenth chapter the equality between men and women, the pursuit of parity, and the need to combat all forms of discrimination. However, the presence of women, especially in political talk shows discussing political issues, remains very limited.

I hugged Kenifra and cried together
Mountains and nation sing forever
For dwarves to delve

The city of Khenifra is located in the midst of the Atlas Mountains, which are crossed by the Oum Er-Rbia River. Most of the population in the area are Amazigh speakers. Here are the Zayanes tribes that bravely resisted French colonization, but they did not benefit from the blessings of independence.

In the early 1970s, when a wing of the radical leftist opposition decided to launch an armed revolution, they chose the Middle Atlas Mountains as their base. When the leader of the revolution, Mahmoud, and his comrades were besieged inside one of the houses, they refused to surrender. They fought until their ammunition ran out and chose to die standing.

I pulled over the car on the road from Rabat to Marrakech. I turned on the radio and the voice of Al-Hassania came out. Whenever I listen to her songs, I am reminded of the Middle Atlas Mountains, Khenifra, Imilchil, and of all the forgotten and marginalized mountainous regions of Morocco. Even though I speak Arabic and don't understand Amazigh, I can perceive from the voice of Al-Hassania the expression of pain and longing, and I can discern a collective lamentation from the screech of the violin.

I assume that Al-Hassania was born in the early 1970s, and she surely hasn't experienced those painful events that befell the Middle Atlas Mountains after the failure of the revolution and the subsequent comprehensive repression. Thousands of members of the tribes in the area were arrested and abducted, even though most of them did not participate in the movement, which was crushed in its infancy. Many died under torture in secret detention centers. After three decades, the Equity and Reconciliation Commission recognized the state's responsibility for gross human rights violations. But certainly, even though Al-Hassania didn't experience the ordeal, she should have heard a lot about it. I imagine some of the collective memory wounds of the Middle Atlas Mountains find a place in the voice of Al-Hassania and in her melodies.

I continue to drive on the highway, and my memory continues its journey. I cherish the shadow of a woman I once loved, and I recall the touch of her fingers. Al-Hassania's voice blends with the sorrowful features of that woman's face. Then, Salah's face comes to my mind as he stands frozen at the door of his house in that dark night. His mother asks, "Who are you?" - "I am your son." - "Which son?" - "Salah!" Then, she shouts at her sleeping children, "Wake up, there is someone at the door who says he is your brother." Why do all these images flood my memory now? And what does it mean to escape to the past?

I presented the program "Zaman Al-Haky" (The Storytelling Era) on Moroccan radio for nearly nine years. I hosted those who took up arms against the colonizers. I hosted "Brika," an elderly woman who, along with her husband, sheltered the resisters in her house. She still remembered the arrests and those who died under torture. I hosted men and women who tasted the agony of years of gunfire, politicians, intellectuals, and artists from all walks and directions.

This is the rich and wounded memory.

A CONVERSATION WITH REEM

In contrast to my nostalgia for the past and its wounds, I find my daughter, Reem, singing about what's happening in the world today. Her fluency in English helps her in that regard. The world is a small village to her. We discuss the recent statements made by the Tunisian President, Qais Saied, about a conspiracy theory that a certain group is planning to change the demographic composition of the country by encouraging immigrants from the South Sahara to come to Tunisia. I am surprised when I watch a conversation on France 24 in which a university professor dares to defend the foolishness and delusions of the Tunisian president.

A social media campaign with the slogan "No to the Africanization of Morocco" has emerged. This campaign has led to clashes in Casablanca with immigrants from the South Sahara. Concerning issues related to personal freedom, such as eating during Ramadan, consensual sexual relationships outside of marriage, homosexuality, or single motherhood, Moroccan media tends to promote stereotypes and preconceived judgments. This issue has been exacerbated by the growing influence of social media.

As I speak to Reem, my opera singer daughter, about diversity and the media, I hear the mournful voice of Al-Hassania emanating from the radio.

Dr Verica Rupar

Dr Verica Rupar is a professor of journalism at the School of Communication Studies, AUT, New Zealand, and a Chair of the World Journalism Education Council. Her academic work includes studies of the epistemology of journalism, the relationship between journalism, media and democracy, as well as communication practices around key social issues relevant to the promotion of social inclusion. Her publications include *Inclusive Journalism*; *Journalism: Themes and Critical Debates*; *Getting the facts right: reporting ethnicity and religion*; *Scooped: Politics and Power of Journalism in Aoteraoa New Zealand* and *Journalism and meaning-making*. She is a former journalist.

John Owen

John Owen is professor emeritus of journalism at City University where he taught the post-graduate international journalism course for over 13 years. He created the Freedom Forum European Centre in London and was its executive director. He was also the founding executive producer of the international broadcast conference NewsXChange. He was executive producer for programmes for the Al Jazeera English Channel in Washington and London. Owen spent twenty years with the Canadian Broadcasting Corporation and served as its chief news editor (head of news) in Toronto and also its chief of foreign bureaux in London. He was one of the founders of the London-based Frontline Club for journalists and media and served for many years as its chairman.

JOURNALISM, DIVERSITY AND FACES OF CHANGE

Dr Verica Rupar in Conversation with John Owen

The story about media and diversity for many of us starts with the question of whom journalists should listen to. The answer seems obvious: they should listen to people if they are to serve the public interest. The image of journalists as custodians of the public interest has been heralded by generations of reporters and reinforced in the public imagination, but the evidence is there for everyone to see; the actual work of a journalist often differs from the imagined version.

Many books, commentaries, movies and documentaries have been produced on the subject. The most recent one, *Journalism Manifesto*, one of the most radical academic works on the discrepancy between what journalists should do as opposed to what they actually do, argues that in the 20th century, mainstream journalism was driven by elites, written by elites and consumed by elites. Not with people in mind. The authors see the practice of contemporary journalism as outdated, disconnected from ordinary people, alienated from its audience, and losing touch with those that practice contemporary journalism. What follows is a bold statement: journalism is at crossroads, and if it does not change it will simply die.

The calls for journalism to listen and understand social needs, to adapt and transform, and to be led by ideas of public good, have been strong for a long time. Among the most powerful voices calling for this change has been the Media Diversity Institute which was established 25 years ago.

It seems appropriate to start this conversation with John Owen by discussing the ongoing need for change in journalism. John was the European Director of the international journalism foundation The Freedom Forum when MDI was established, and he and his organization provided much-needed support for the MDI work we celebrate today. He is a lifelong journalist who worked as a reporter, writer, producer, and editor for more than four decades. He served as chief news editor at CBC TV News in Canada and as an executive producer of programming for Al Jazeera English. He is a professor emeritus of journalism at City University, where he taught the post-graduate international journalism class for 13 years. He was chairman for many years of The Frontline Club, a centre for journalists and media in London, and a co-editor of and contributor to the journalism textbook *International News Reporting: Frontlines & Deadlines*, published by Wiley-Blackwell. He is also co-editor of *Dying to Tell the Story: The Iraq War and the Media. a Tribute*, published by the International News Safety Institute. He has devoted considerable time and energy to educational and charitable journalism and media projects that have helped improve journalism practice around the world. John was an MDI Trustee in the early 2000s, significantly contributing to the programme direction at the time.

It took a couple of weeks to set up a Zoom meeting. We both knew from the beginning it wouldn't be just an hour or so of casual chit-chat. We both took the questions and issues we wanted to discuss seriously: there were emails exchanged, links forwarded, and comments shared - the type of encounter one misses in intellectually isolated New Zealand, where I live, and the States, where John resides.

We go to the heart of the matter first:

People tend to talk about journalism and change in the context of the digitization of news, noticing the shifts in how journalism is produced, distributed, and consumed. That is certainly important, but do you think it covers the whole story? Thinking of your own career, what were these 'crossroad moments' that made you change your way of doing journalism?

My real start as a reporter was in Milwaukee, Wisconsin, in 1968. Unlike many in my own generation, I started not in newspapers but actually in broadcast. I joined a radio and television station, a very good one, thanks to my very experienced and well-connected graduate journalism professor at Indiana University. I got hired and I got a chance but after a year or so I became quite disillusioned with daily commercial news in broadcasting. I migrated to the public service broadcaster. In the US, these were the early days of PBS [Public Broadcasting System] journalism.

What were you disillusioned in?

The same things that I still loathe about local commercial TV News--the "If it bleeds, it leads" approach to covering communities. I disagreed with how local news covered racial issues that reinforced racial stereotypes and provoked more conflict. When the local PBS station, WMVS [in Milwaukee, Wisconsin], decided to create a new weekly current affairs programme, I applied for the executive producer position and was hired. It was demanding and exhilarating producing, reporting, and hosting the programme plus also doing documentaries and hosting a new weekly interview programme. I was able to do lengthy, prime-time reports and discussion programmes about race, housing, transportation, and lead-paint poisoning afflicting children living in the inner city.

I later moved on to a PBS station in Rochester, New York, where I created, produced, and hosted a new alternative nightly news programme. That eventually led me to Toronto and CBC Canada.

When we were in Egypt, participating in one of the MDI academic mentoring programmes, ten or so years ago, we talked about how journalists moved from being interested in individual people, people with names, homes, professions and lives to be told, to viewing people as members of groups, and individuals as representatives of groups. What changes in journalism would you say were the most significant ones in the last 25 years?

All the obvious ones--the Internet revolution, legacy media decline, the emergence of social media, Twitter, Facebook, TikTok, the iPhone revolution, and the shutting down of local newspapers. In the US context, there was certainly the weakening of FCC [Federal Communications Commission] regulation, the killing of the Fairness Doctrine in 1987 [the Fairness Doctrine required broadcasters to provide balanced coverage of controversial issues and to give equal time to opposing candidates for public office], the launch of cable television and the creation of Fox News. One should add the power and influence of the owner of Fox News, Rupert Murdoch. This development led to the end of impartiality in American broadcast news and the path to "fair and balanced" Orwellian language and eventually to where we are now in the world of Trump's "fake news", Kellyanne Conway's "alternative facts", [Kellyanne Conway served as senior counsellor to President Trump] and the mantra deployed by autocrats of journalists as "the enemy of the people".

Where we are today in terms of who tells the truth and whose truth is it anyway? Trump lied 30,573 times, according to one study. In 1976, in the post-Watergate and post-Vietnam War era, 72% of Americans trusted the news media. Today the figure is 34%. Amongst Republicans, 14%.

At the same time, the attacks on journalists and media increased...

The attacks on journalists increased dramatically once reporters and TV news teams gained freedom and independence in a post-Berlin Wall world, in post-Soviet Union countries and in the former Yugoslavia, and in African countries no longer under the control of imperial powers. And of course, in the always explosive Middle East against the backdrop of Israel vs Arab countries, and in Latin America, the Fidel/Cuban legacy and vicious conflicts in Nicaragua and El Salvador.

In the post-daily journalism world that I've lived in for much of the 25 years MDI has been in existence, I've made one of my greatest priorities trying to champion and support training and protection for journalists and media trying to cover conflicts, wars, as well as embattled local journalists trying to report on corruption and human rights abuses.

One of my takeaways - reflecting on this period - is that no amount of journalism craft training and skillset improvement or specialised safety training and protection can lift or transform the quality of journalism and media in transitional countries [i.e., post-conflict countries] unless civil society reforms have ensured a commitment to the rule of law.

Reporters can't expose wrongdoing and corruption if they are attacked physically, and their attackers are not arrested and brought to justice. If there is accepted impunity for those who harm or threaten journalists, then only the bravest journalists backed by committed news organisations will stay the course and also be able to fight off defamation suits and other legal challenges.

Working under threats produces far too much self-censorship than is healthy for robust democratic societies. It's all about the stories not pursued, not considered because of fear of the consequences after publication or posting. Today journalists who work online are under attack. My own daughter was subjected to a vicious bullying assault by an accredited right-wing, wannabe Alex Jones vid-blogger while covering the CPAC [Conservative Political Action Conference], a Trump-loving conference in Texas. He got a million hits out of trying to bully my daughter. No one stepped in to help her. Instead, MAGA zealots simply crowded around and recorded video on their phones so they could post this humiliation.

The Media Diversity Institute came about in part because of Milica Pešić's own experience in Serbia of being abused for publicly opposing Slobodan Milosevic's call for patriotism over professionalism. She left Belgrade and took refuge in London. At that time, you were working for the Freedom Forum. How did the two of you meet?

I took the job at the Freedom Forum in 1996. We were created at a time of great turmoil in the Balkans, Chechnya and in the former Soviet Union. There was a lot going on in Europe at that time, and what was heavily on my mind was the question of how to support responsible, free and independent journalism and the quality of the press emerging from state control.

One day, a bright, young woman from Serbia, Milica Pešić, came into my office looking for a job to be an office assistant. She was impressive but, in my view over-qualified for what was a junior office assistant position. Milica likes to remind me of that rejection. But I was very interested in her own background and perspectives on how and why nationalist state-controlled media were driving these conflicts in her native Serbia and throughout the Balkans. She was doing some freelance work for the US-based Center for War, Peace, and the News Media at NYU. We engaged in discussions that ultimately led to Milica organising a major international conference at my centre that helped kickstart the development of what became the Media Diversity Institute. She became its inspirational and tireless leader--creating an amazing network in the Balkans, Serbia, Kosovo, Montenegro, Albania and then Central Europe, Caucuses and elsewhere.

Our Freedom Forum office in London was also becoming a hotbed of independent media. The independent Belgrade-based radio station, B92, under enormous pressure from Milosevic, had a workspace in our office. Also, we established free drop-in computer workstations for freelance and exiled journalists who couldn't afford to access the Internet.

The onsite work of MDI was significant, but it became visible to the wider audience only with widespread access to the Internet. Those who participated in the MDI programmes joined a wonderful new community, they stayed in touch as colleagues and friends, but the real social impact came with the presence in the digital world. I started teaching media and diversity 20 years ago in New Zealand. At that time the only online material on the subject that could be found was on the MDI website. David Tuller's Reporting Diversity Manual was the first I used in the class and is still one of the best collections of case studies and tips that support teaching and training. You wrote the forward for that book--do you mind if we look at it again and see what still stands?

I don't mind at all. Here's what it says:

"The Media Diversity Institute believes that in struggling democracies journalism has too often been a negative force, publishing stories filled with half-truths, misinformation, and racial slurs.

Its founding Director, Milica Pešić, argues passionately that with proper training and re-training, a new breed of enlightened and responsible journalists can turn hateful communities into productive and tolerant democracies.

It's not as though Pešić and the Media Diversity Institute are trying to turn journalists into social workers bent on reforming their societies. They are challenging them to practice good fact-based, fair and impartial journalism that informs rather than misinforms.

Where I wholeheartedly agree with Milica Pešić is that the journalism of diversity is not a problem, a millstone hanging around the neck of beleaguered editors and reporters. Smart, savvy editors will recognise that a poorly served or neglected part of the population can be added to the ranks of new readers. 'Diversity Sells' is a sign that ought to be plastered all over editorial offices."

I would sign this forward today. Its relevance is still there.

What has changed meanwhile is the emergence of social media. The explosion of new journalism forms on different media platforms is liberating in terms of reconnecting with the audience, but also terrifying when one thinks about the absence of fact checking and verification, and most of all the amount of misinformation disseminated. Where is it going, do you think?

My loathing of American cable TV news and its endless white noise of partisan commentary and empty-headed analysis that I watch far more than is good for my health, always bring back the question of how to keep and develop journalism that matters. Public service broadcasting is in trouble. I can't believe that Brits will allow the BBC to be destroyed or killed by a thousand financial cuts. Yet, just this week[1], it killed off its Arabic World Service broadcasts. My old CBC in Canada is also fighting for its life and needs to recommit to remaining a broadcaster committed to public service broadcasting principles. Although, I have to add, I'm proud of a former student who has just been appointed the executive producer of its flagship investigative current affairs series "The Fifth Estate".

I start my day reading various newsletters and blogs before moving on to my digital media must reads - Heather Cox Richardson, Robert Hubbell, Timothy Snyder, James Fallows, Semafor, or wonderfully engaging new podcasts such as The News Agents & the Rest is Politics, The Daily, Maddow's Ultra historical series, Pod Save America, Pod Save the World, Ezra Klein, etc. Plus of course all the wondrous multimedia storytelling that we see in the *NY Times* with amazing visualisation.

Indeed, where is all of this going and what do I make of it? I am having trouble understanding some of the trends. The most recent of Ben Smith's posts for Semafor confused me. It tries to explain what "The News Movement", created by ex-FT editor Will Lewis and ex-BBC Editor Kamal Ahmed in London, is attempting to do. Do these bright,

[1] The interview was held on February 20, 2023

experienced journalists really believe their own hyper rhetoric about trained journalists doing substantive reporting in pieces to the camera of TikTok length? That context and explanation will be possible there? I get their urgent need to exploit what they see as an opportunity to get GenZers who get 60% of their information from social media to sign up, but others have tried and failed to cash in on youth markets. Even Rupert Murdoch lost millions investing in Vice News, which sold itself as the new media gateway to youth viewers and online consumers.

Flashy devices enabled us to stay tuned with the outside world, but the constant flow of news and information that mimics news sometimes fragments our understanding of the world instead of enriching it.

The new ecosystem shattered the trust in news, that is a real problem.

The trust in the media has been declining for a while. How did you approach it as a professor of journalism, teaching a cohort of international students?

The education of future journalists in stable societies where journalism is well established centres around knowledge and skills. I used to bring prominent journalists into the class because these people were really speaking about key journalistic issues. Hearing about their experiences is really important for the careers of journalists from all over the world. Talking about the kind of risk they would be expected to take, or how do you determine whether or not a story is true in a post-conflict period or, you know, all the things we know about now but didn't know before. Teaching digital tools is important, and we all have so much fun playing with it, but fundamental issues of thinking, being open and curious, and asking the right questions do not change.

But things have changed, and changed for the better?

What has changed dramatically from the time when MDI started is the diversity of newsrooms. They are more women, persons of colour, openly gay people and trans people. We see this on our screens and hear their voices in North America and Europe and certainly in the Middle East and Africa.

The language has changed too. The mainstream media, even The Sun, would be reluctant to use the misogynistic or homophobic terms they used 25 years ago. Because what is acceptable in public talk has changed--that has improved. The manifestation of our respect for diversity changed over time, and you have more people from different backgrounds on TV.

Media Diversity Institute has played an important role in promoting this tangible evidence of diversity. What is its legacy?

First and foremost, it has survived. No small accomplishment in the world of NGOs and journalism and media foundations. Few that were in existence 25 years ago have survived in a such robust fashion.

Truth be told, MDI has flourished because of the terrible developments related to hate speech and abusive social media. Milica and the backers of MDI have exploited the demands by governments and corporations - especially in the EU and the US - for projects, studies, training programs, online courses that help support newspapers, broadcasters, news agencies, and online publications trying to fight back against antisemitism, Islamophobia, and anti-LGBTQ posts. The “Get the Trolls Out” [GTTO] project that you helped to create has been a significant success in this regard. Bravo, Verica!

Thank you, John. It is the people that make successful projects and the GTTO team has been fantastic in developing new forms of media monitoring. Same could be said for the master's programme Diversity and the Media, run jointly with Westminster University. I helped set it up 12 years ago and am fascinated with its development. It attracts students from around the world.

I think that tells us that there is still plenty of work to do in societies that are fracturing due to ethnic, religious, gender and other differences. Michael Ignatieff's quote from Freud in his keynote remarks to the first ever MDI conference at the Freedom Forum 25 years ago is still incredibly relevant. He talked about the "narcissism of minor difference" that disrupted societies and was exploited by hateful state media. We see that happening in Hungary, in the way Orban's state-controlled media are covering the openly gay U.S. ambassador to Hungary. MDI still faces enormous challenges and its programmes and projects are still urgently needed.

Dr Anbin Shi

Dr Anbin Shi is currently Ministry of Education Endowment Professor of Global Media and Communication Studies with the School of Journalism and Communication, and Director of the Israel Epstein Center for Global Media and Communication, Adjunct Professor of Global Media and China, Schwarzman College, Tsinghua University, China. His research interests include intercultural communication, global communication, public communication, press and politics. He has published six books and over 200 articles in Chinese and English academic journals, the latest entitled *China's International Communication and Relationship Building* (2022, Routledge), and *China's Media Go Global* (Routledge, 2017). In addition, Professor Shi is now serving as the special consultant and guest professor for the State Council's Information Office and has completed the training of more than 10,000 government spokespersons and press officers at central, municipal and provincial level. He also frequently appears on CGTN (CCTVNEWS), The New York Times, The Washington Post, Newsweek and Al Jazeera to comment upon contemporary China's press and politics.

MEDITATING CULTURAL DIVERSITY IN THE QUEST FOR A DYNAMIC CHINESENESS IN THE ERA OF GLOBALISATION: A CONCEPTUAL OVERVIEW AND SOME AUTOETHNOGRAPHIC REFLECTIONS

As a constantly changing yet productive concept over different historical periods, the discursive formation of "Chinese-ness" remains central to constructing Chinese modernity and postmodernity. The single English word "Chinese" is both complicated and intriguing, for there is no single corresponding equivalent in the Chinese language that can encompass its denotations. There exist a cluster of terms in both spoken and written language to reflect its different attribute of "Chinese": racial (*zhongguoren/huaren,* or the Chinese people); cultural (*zhonghua/huaxia*, or the Han/Huaxia civilization); ethnic (*hanzu/hanren*, or the Han people), and citizenry (*zhongguoji*, or the Chinese citizenship). Such a multi-layered concept of "Chinese-ness" therefore serves as an illuminating index of the complications of Chinese identities.

In the self-reliant and isolated "Middle Kingdom" of the past five millennia, such conceptual frameworks as "Chinese" or "Chinese-ness" remained vague and insignificant. All the Chinese emperors held a steadfast yet naïve belief that they were the one and only ruler of the entire world. Consequently, the modernist concept of "Chinese" and "Chinese-ness" were not developed until China's confrontation with the Western world during the Sino-British Opium War (1839-42). In the face of a national crisis, Chinese intellectuals' two-fold mission of enlightenment and national salvation mandated the development of a clear-cut definition of Chinese ethnicity and/or national identity. To pursue this project, they were obliged to deal with such imported concepts as nation, state, sovereignty, citizenry, race, ethnicity, and national/cultural identity. The definition of Chinese-ness had therefore become part and parcel of the agenda of constructing Chinese modernity. The modernist notion of a unified, homogeneous, and unquestioned Chinese identity as represented by the People's Republic of China (PRC) since 1949, the socialist Party-state, was emblematic of the consummation of the quest for Chinese modernity.

As Confucius aptly put it, "to maintain diversity in the midst of diversity is the gentlemen's way of life." In this light, the Maoist endeavor for a unified Chinese-ness sparked the quest for cultural diversity in terms of class, gender and ethnicity. The most relevant understanding of "diversity" in the Chinese context emerged in tandem with the evolution of cultural diversity standards in the PRC over time. The Party-State-led pursuit of diversity was organized to serve grand political goals, most notably the promotion of ethnic diversity.

Since 1949, 56 ethnic groups in China were identified and named under the aegis of a unified Chinese-ness. Han Chinese constitute the majority, accounting for 94% of the population. One of the most crucial ways China promoted ethnic diversity was by preserving the uniqueness of minority groups and the provision of regional autonomy. Following Mao's political agenda, the central government granted 55 ethnic minority groups the right to use their own languages and practice their customs, traditions and religious beliefs, and even assist those who lacked their own scripts to further research their past cultural traditions. While clearly advocating for the development of cultural education in each ethnic group's own language and writing, Mao also proposed that all ethnic groups learn each other's languages and scripts on a voluntary basis, and specifically demanded Han cadres working in minority areas to learn the languages of the local ethnic groups.

In addition, the government encouraged minority participation in politics and administration at all levels and promoted cultural exchange and communication between various ethnic groups based on the needs of political, economic and cultural development.

During this period, we can see a large number of novels, films, dramas and popular songs with ethnic minorities as the hero or heroine, in stark contrast to pre-1949 China, when limited number of art works were mostly written by western adventurers and journalists and merely captured exotic scenery to satisfy the Euro-American imagination. Suffice it to mention one example, more accurate and diverse media representation with 15 feature films with ethnic minority heroes and heroines were produced between 1957 and 1966. The most well-known is the musical *Liu Sanjie* (The Third Sister Liu) focusing upon Zhuang nationality's culture in southwestern China produced in 1961, and later exported and became highly popular in Southeast Asian counties.

The Reform and Opening-up Policy has resulted in a rapid polarization of China's social classes since the 1980s, when many Chinese scholars who had studied abroad at Western universities, particularly in the UK and the US, started to import multiculturalism and identity politics into China. A hybrid approach to cultural studies is being developed in China by combining Western cultural theories and methodologies with Chinese traditional culture and philosophy. Due to the profound influence of culture studies in the Chinese social sciences academic field, scholars began to regard "identity" as a dynamic and constantly negotiated sense of self, rather than a fixed or predetermined attribute, through cultural practices and social interactions involving media, art, literature, and popular culture. In response to the growing belief that diversity should be a fundamental component of human societies, media outlets began critically examining the imbalance between the "minority" and the "majority" with the complex interplay between various identities, including gender, class, sexual preference, and nationality.

In point of fact, news media play a central role in promoting cultural diversity in the quest for a more fluid, dynamic definition of Chinese-ness. For example, in 2005, China Central Television (CCTV) produced and aired an in-depth documentary featuring the Chinese gay community and “closeted gay men’s wives”. For the first time, Chinese mainstream media covered LGBTQ+ issues, emphasizing that this crucial social issue had long gone unnoticed and unaddressed. In the documentary, it was revealed that members of the gay community in China, far from being able to openly “come out”, had felt ashamed about their sexual orientation because they also felt an obligation to produce newborns to continue the family line. The lack of open discussion of same-sex relationships and the fear of rejection or ostracism may make LGBTQ+ individuals unwilling to reveal their sexuality or gender identity. Homosexuals were therefore unable to be honest about their sexual preferences. They sometimes had to pretend to be interested in pursuing a heterosexual relationship when interacting with family, friends and colleagues. Such dilemmas forced more and more Chinese gay men into “shadow marriage” without their spouses knowing the truth, resulting in a huge population of “closeted gay men’s wives”.

Situations have changed again in the 21st century with the advent of the Internet and social media. Promoting cultural diversity has become a more effective way of mobilizing the “netizen power” in China. The de-stigmatization of Hepatitis B virus (HBV), a viral ailment that mostly affects the liver and is particularly prevalent in China with an estimated 100 million affected, is another example of changing social attitudes influenced by news coverage. Yet, many Chinese communities discriminated against and stigmatized those who had HBV at the beginning of the twentieth century, making it challenging for them to get the care they needed and lead normal lives. Zhang Xianzhu, an HBV-positive man, applied for a public service position in 2003 and gained first place in the competition among hundreds of applicants in both the written test and the interview. But he was not hired because of his infection. He decided to file an administrative complaint against the city's Employment Department after sharing his tale on an online forum for HBV patients. This decision quickly attracted media attention. Many incidents of people being denied access to jobs, education, and even medical care because of their HBV condition were highlighted in related news reports. This media attention raised public awareness of the problem and made many people more conscious of the prejudice experienced by those with HBV. Over time, advocacy groups and organizations began to emerge in China that sought to raise awareness about HBV discrimination and promote greater understanding among the public, including public education campaigns, media outreach, and direct advocacy with policymakers and other stakeholders. In 2007, the Chinese Ministry of Human Resources and Social Security, the Ministry of Education and the Ministry of Health issued regulations to protect the employment rights of HBV carriers.

Admittedly, the year 2016 witnessed a sudden U-turn around the world for the sweeping trend toward capitalist globalization, which had been growing since the 1980s. Both the Brexit vote in the UK and the advent of the Trumpian "America First" policy inaugurated a new era of the "post-West", "post-order" and "post-truth" world, as succinctly summarized by these tag words of the 2017 annual Munich Security Conference (MSC). Notably, the MSC's chosen theme in 2021 turned into a more desperate tag of "West-less-ness" in the aftermath of the Covid-19 pandemic and the Trumpian "infodemic". The backlash of ultra-right nationalism, isolationism and protectionism in the Western countries has paved the groundwork for the crushing power of anti-globalization, or worse still, de-globalization, in the foreseeable future.

At this historic juncture, it is even more ironic that a die-hard Communist Party commissar, as stereotyped in the Western media, instead of a leader from the "free world", made a strong case for advancing economic globalization and rejecting trade protectionism in a keynote speech at the 2017 annual meeting of the World Economic Forum in Davos, Switzerland. In lieu of chanting a similar "China First" slogan or reiterating his famous slogan of "Chinese Dream", Xi advocated a more cosmopolitan ideal of building "a community with shared future for mankind" (hereafter CSF) in a speech delivered in the United Nations Office at Geneva just one day after the Davos talk. Both speeches positioned Xi as the new standard-bearer of globalization, and showcased China's blueprint for mapping out a feasible alternative to the omnipotent Pax Americana through the Belt and Road Initiative (BRI).

In its ambitious blueprint, BRI covers more than 100 countries in Asia, Europe, Africa, North America, and Oceania, estimated to include 64% of the world's population and 30% of the global GDP (World Bank 2018). A predecessor, the Euro-American-centric Marshall Plan, smacked of Cold War mentality and did not transcend the age-old dichotomy of the West vs. the East, or of nationalism vs. neo-liberalism. Therefore, the Marshall Plan pursued a parochial yet highly ideology-laden agenda of building a free world to combat the Eastern bloc in the service of America's national interest.

By contrast, BRI is more cosmopolitan in the sense of engaging the least developed countries and bridging the economic gap between the Global North and the Global South, mapping out an alternative route to reshaping the order of global communication with little resort to economic, cultural, or ideological warfare. Under the framework of BRI, the historical legacies of the "middle kingdom" have been transformed into a new role of the "Global Middle", or more precisely, the "global mediator", as evinced by the most recent reconciliation, in March 2023, between Saudi Arabia and Iran via China's diplomatic efforts.

With regard to the macro-level global environment, this 'new era' reflected a power shift among major global players, such as China, US, EU, and Russia, and therefore called for the necessity and urgency of revising, if not reshuffling, a new geopolitical order. Incessant crises such as the Sino-US trade war, the 'chip war' and high-tech competition, as well as the Russo-Ukraine warfare since February 2022, unveiled a new era for globalization. The backlash of ultra-right nationalism, isolationism, and protectionism in Western countries also paved the solid groundwork for the crushing power of anti-globalization, or worse still, de-globalization, in the foreseeable future.

The new positioning of a 'global China' does not just constitute a theoretical and practical innovation from that of the West but also evokes a brand-new identity in terms of what constitutes 'being Chinese' in the new era. Scholarly discussion should be focused on the framing of identity (re)formation in China's media discourses, wherein in the midst of increasingly transcultural exchange and social integration worldwide, a fluid and dynamic identity is, by and large, replacing the monolithic and essentialist conceptualization of 'Chinese-ness'.

A case analysis can help illustrate these points. Eileen Gu (Gu Ailing) is an American-born Chinese Olympic champion in freestyle skiing and the first foreign-born naturalized athlete to win gold medals for Team China in the Olympics. More importantly, she is a social media influencer or KOL both on Weibo, China's equivalent of Twitter, and Instagram, attracting millions of followers around the world as the new icon of 'global China.'

Yet, the popularity of Eileen Gu has raised a highly controversial issue, athlete naturalization, as China is known for perhaps the strictest immigration policies. This issue has become more prominent as officials resort to naturalization as a quick fix to the pressure they face to perform well in such global competitions as the 2022 Beijing Winter Olympics. Before July 2022, China had fielded 42 naturalized athletes in eight Olympic events that were considered weak spots for Team China, including soccer and ice/snow sports. Efforts to improve the country's Olympic achievements resulted in eleven non-ethnic Chinese gaining Chinese citizenship. As postulated by Coakley, the social and cultural environment provides an ideal entry point to study how people make sense of self through the medium of sports.

Conversely, sports may also provide a venue in which many individuals can articulate their own cultural identity. In an interview with *The South China Morning Post*, a Hong Kong-based English-language newspaper, Eileen Gu said, 'I am fully American and look and speak the way I do. Nobody can deny I'm American. When I go to China, nobody can deny I'm Chinese because I'm fluent in the language and culture, and completely identify as such'. This quote is a perfect illustration of how sports, as a medium of international communication in the era of neo-globalization, redefine and integrate the concept of national identity, instead of dividing it. The so-called 'third culture individuals' (TCI) are raised in a culture other than their parents' or the culture of their country of nationality and live in a different environment during their childhood and adolescence.

Aside from asserting a new vision of being Chinese, Eileen Gu's articulation via social media platforms also functioned to consolidate the ideal of promoting multiculturalism and social/ethnic equity in the post-Trumpian world. Her multi-ethnic identity as a daughter of California and an active participation in such online campaigns as the #StopAsianHate helped highlight efforts to combat the backlash of racial discrimination in the aftermath of Donald Trump's quasi-white-supremacy advocacy and the 'infodemic' around Chinese or even Asian immigrants in the wake of the Covid-19 pandemic.

Notably, TCI has become an emergent force in the sphere of global media culture, with more emerging Chinese-originated movie and sports icons asserting their fluid and dynamic identities, including the Oscar-winning female director Zhao Ting; the first Marvel hero of Asian origin Liu Simu, a Canadian citizen born in northeastern China; the US Open Tennis champion Emma Raducanu, a British national whose mother emigrated from China; and the Olympic gold medalist of men's figure skating Nathan Chan from Team USA, among others.

Predictably, TCI's prevalence in the realm of global social media culture further evinced the potency and relevance of "platform cosmopolitanism", echoed by President Xi Jinping's call for constructing 'a community of shared future for mankind'. In the foreseeable future, as a global China surges and takes the spotlight on the world stage, the mission of China's global communication is not only to make China known to other global players, but also to map out a new vision and new order of global communication. This new vision and order bridge the information gap and digital divide between the Global North and the Global South and reconcile the age-old cultural and ideological contestation between the West and the Rest.

On March 15, 2023, President Xi Jinping proposed "Global Civilization Initiatives", an effort that reinforces the Party-State's belief in and advocacy for cultural diversity and inclusiveness. Chinese-ness in the context of globalization should be constructed on the basis of a dynamic relationship between China and the West. Their politico-economic and cultural dialogue, communication, and interaction have become both permissible and desirable in the post-Cold-War era. What Chinese intelligentsia should keep a critical eye on is any form of politico-economic and cultural hegemony, be it native or foreign, rather than Western culture *per se*. Moreover, modernization or globalization is not identical to Westernization.

More importantly, the reconstruction of more "globalized" Chinese identities also requires more intensive intercultural communications with China's allies in Asia, Africa and Latin America. The successful China-ASEAN and China-Africa summits in 2006 are emblematic of China's rising impact upon the non-West world. To redefine a dynamic Chinese-ness therefore plays an important role, if not the decisive one, in the construction of Chinese modernity, an ongoing process of incessant global/local encounter, conflict, and negotiation.

As my genealogical overview and auto-ethnographic reflections have shown, Chinese-ness remains a nexus of meaning whereby national identity and cultural subjectivity can be reasserted not merely as a discursive formation of radical otherness, but also as a locale wherein difference, disjunction, and displacement between class, race, gender, and ethnicities can be incorporated and coordinated into a dynamic, organic entity. It is precisely due to "dynamic" Chinese-ness as such that we can never settle into "being" Chinese but will be always "becoming" Chinese. As such peripheral colonies as Hong Kong and Macao have been handed over to the PRC, as the reunification of Taiwan may be accomplished ideally by peaceful negotiation in the future, as the Chinese "diaspora" all over the world (particularly in North America and Oceania) has become a significant socio-cultural phenomenon, the problematic of Chinese-ness will remain at the core of the prospering fields of Chinese media and cultural studies, wherein every journalist and scholar will play an active part.

The author wishes to acknowledge his research assistant Ms. Yu Yayun for her help with collecting data and preparing parts of the draft.

Dr Anida Sokol

Dr Anida Sokol is a media researcher, coordinator of media research projects and trainer from Mediacentar Sarajevo, Bosnia and Herzegovina. She is the deputy editor of Mediacentar's online magazine Media.ba dedicated to journalism and the media. She is the author of various research studies on the media in BiH and the Western Balkans, including on regulation of harmful content online, media financing from public budgets, media trust, propaganda, disinformation and hate speech. She holds a PhD from the Faculty of Political Science, Sapienza University Rome.

Anida has worked as a lecturer on Politics and the Media and Political Communication at the Sarajevo School of Science and Technology and Burch University in Sarajevo. She holds training courses on verification of information, media literacy, hate speech, solutions journalism and ethical standards in journalism. She writes articles on journalism and the media for Media.ba.

THE ROLE OF MEDIA IN REPORTING LGBTIQ+ RIGHTS IN BOSNIA AND HERZEGOVINA

These are the recollections of three members of Mediacentar Sarajevo about the first Sarajevo Queer Festival, which was held in September 2008.

Long-time journalist and Mediacentar director Boro Kontić was a participant in the festival and the person who opened the doors of this organisation to the guests and organizers. Slobodanka Dekić, an associate of Mediacentar Sarajevo and the group's former project coordinator, was one of the organisers of the festival and an activist with the Q association, the first organization of LGBTIQ+ people in Bosnia and Herzegovina (BiH). Marija Arnautović, the chief editor at Mediacentar Sarajevo, reported on the preparations for the festival and devoted many years of journalistic work to reporting on minority groups.

It is worth noting that Mediacentar Sarajevo issued its first manual to help ensure more professional reporting on these topics, "The Right to Diversity", in 1999. The manual addressed the issue of how to report professionally on sexual minorities almost 25 years ago. We developed it in cooperation with the Media Diversity Institute. That productive collaboration has now lasted for more than two decades.

MEDIA AND THE LGBTIQ+ COMMUNITY: STORIES OF MEDIA REPRESENTATIVES AND ACTIVISTS FROM SARAJEVO

Billboards announcing the first queer festival in Bosnia and Herzegovina, scheduled for September 2008, appeared on the streets of Sarajevo the month before. They were very simple, with a figure and the headline "Queer Sarajevo Festival". Slobodanka Dekić, one of the organizers, remembers that, with the announcement of the festival, the media rush also began. The Bosniak print magazine *SAFF* and the daily newspaper *Dnevni avaz* were at the forefront and portrayed the festival primarily as anti-Bosniak, with headlines such as: "Who Is Forcing the Queer Festival on the Bosniaks?" and "Gays in Sarajevo on the Night of Laylat Al-Qadr". All the journalists were asking the same question: "Why is the festival being held during Ramadan?" Slobodanka Dekić says that it was a legitimate question, and in hindsight, she regrets not providing a "smarter" answer: "Maybe we should have said it was precisely because it was Ramadan and we wanted everyone to celebrate the beautiful holiday, even the non-believers."

The organisers had been receiving death threats for weeks before the opening of the festival. The media were completely polarized, and only a few had come to the defence of the festival and LGBTIQ+ people. These included the Sarajevo magazine *Dani* and the public service broadcaster of the Federation FTV, recalls Slobodanka. In some media, this support came as a result of the individual efforts of journalists and editors who supported LGBTIQ+ rights, such as Kristina Ljevak, who worked at FTV. On Internet forums, users called for the lynching of the organizers, media outlets that sponsored the festival received threats, and posters with homophobic content were distributed and put up all over the city. Certain politicians and religious leaders propagated intolerance against LGBTIQ+ people, thereby further spreading hatred.

Almost every day, the *Dnevni Avaz* published homophobic statements by political and religious leaders and headlines suggesting that homosexuals were insulting Muslims. One cover featured the statement of a religious official as a headline: "Freedom should not be used to promote that garbage from the West." The cover also included a sub-title: "They are doing it on purpose during Ramadan because the mosques are full."

The festival was originally scheduled for September 9, but due to the media frenzy a large number of places where exhibitions and screenings were supposed to take place cancelled because the owners were afraid that their premises would be the target of hooligan attacks. The festival was rescheduled for September 24.

In the lynching atmosphere, open threats targeted the media that supported the festival. Threatening letters signed by "war veterans of Sarajevo" were sent to the editors of *Dani* magazine, the student radio EFM and *Radio Sarajevo*. "From this moment in which you have condemned yourself, you will not be at peace in the endless future...", they wrote to the newsrooms. Those three media outlets were the few that openly supported the festival as patrons. The rest either reported about it in an inflammatory manner or often asked inappropriate questions under the guise of objective journalism, Slobodanka Dekić recalls fourteen years later.

According to Boro Kontić, the director of Mediacentar Sarajevo, there was also a negative reaction from the Union of War Veterans, leading Bosniak politicians and religious representatives. The city was plastered with posters that directly called for violence with slogans like "death to fags".

As the opening day of the Queer Festival approached, the threats became more and more severe and frequent, with daily media incitement. The organizers decided to hold the festival anyway. Two days before the opening, Marija Arnautović, the current editor of Mediacentar Sarajevo, interviewed the organizers about the threats for *Radio Free Europe*. She also talked with some of the editors of the newsrooms that had been threatened. She asked politicians why, in a constitutionally secular state, an atmosphere of hatred is being created and what the relationship between the arts festival and the month of Ramadan should be. Although the question was not whether he was looking forward to the festival, a representative in the State Parliament, Bakir Izetbegović, answered, "I am not happy about it at all. A reminder of Sodom and Gomorrah on the day of the 27th night, a noble night that Muslims celebrate, I am not happy about it at all."

Although she didn't spend much time thinking about it back then, she nonetheless believed that it was important for all those who understood why this kind of festival was important to be as loud as possible. Maybe we were naive, says Arnautović today, but even with all those threats, we believed that nothing bad would happen. She says that they trusted the police to prevent possible riots, but also viewed Sarajevo as a tolerant city. After everything that happened on September 24 in front of and around the building of the Academy of Fine Arts, according to Arnautović, it became clear that some blatant and intentionally aggressive journalistic misconduct, and perhaps some clumsy but unintentional journalistic errors, were largely responsible for the heated atmosphere before the first queer festival.

THERE WILL BE A FESTIVAL

It was the end of September 2008, but a warm evening, remembers Boro Kontić. The long footpath along the Miljacka, usually deserted, was packed with people. He almost had to fight his way into the building of the Academy of Fine Arts, the large exhibition hall on the ground floor where the opening of the first Queer Sarajevo Festival was being held. More precisely, the evening represented the first public appearance of lesbian, gay, transgender, and intersex persons in Bosnia and Herzegovina.

It seemed to him, Kontić says, that everything would pass without incident because, a few hours before the opening ceremony, only a small group of citizens, including several Wahhabis, showed up at the scheduled protest against the queer festival. In the invitation to the anti-festival rally in the centre of Sarajevo, Kontić says, "conscientious citizens were asked to express their protests against the deviant ideas that are trying to be presented as normal and acceptable to the Bosnian public, our children and future generations." The appeal ended with a slogan: "Stand Up Sarajevo."

Mediacentar, under the leadership of Kontić, was actively involved in supporting the festival in accordance with their policy of respecting diversity and advocating for the protection of freedom of expression and human rights. The least he could do, he says, was to appear at the opening and express solidarity with the participants.

According to Slobodanka Dekić, about 200 people attended the event. A group of about 70 hooligans gathered across the street from the Academy, on the other side of the Miljacka. They started insulting the festival visitors and throwing stones. They followed some visitors and physically attacked them.

The media reported that festival participants were attacked. While watching television coverage of the events, Marija Arnautović recognised a friend of hers, who was describing how "a girl was attacked over there" and how a group of people who blocked the entrance to the Academy of Fine Arts building were harassing and insulting people. Arnautović knew that some of her friends and colleagues were inside the building. She tried to find out what was going on by texting them. A colleague wrote that she could not leave the Academy building, and others reported that groups of people were waiting for festival participants in the streets of Sarajevo. The most painful thing, Arnautović says, was finding out that a "witch hunt" was going on in the streets of Sarajevo, which continued in the coming days as well.

During these events, fear and uncertainty reigned in the Academy of Fine Arts building. The security managed to take the organizers out of the building and, as Dekić remembers, "put them in a taxi". They went to the emergency room because the festival selector Andrej Viskochis was seriously injured and needed emergency medical assistance. After that, they went to the police to give their statements. Another group of volunteers tried to get home by taxi, miles away from the Academy building, and a group of hooligans intercepted them and broke the window of the taxi with a gun in order to drag them out and beat them.

After the opening of the exhibition of portraits by the photographer Irfan Redžović and an address from the ambassador of the Kingdom of the Netherlands, all the guests left the premises of the Academy. Boro Kontić, together with several journalists from *Dani* magazine, set off on the footpath towards the city. On the other side of the Miljacka river, from the stone fence in front of the Faculty of Law, a large group of people loudly shouted slogans, of which, he says, he only caught: 'Fags, we will find you tonight'. They were passing through a barrage of people, among them several Wahhabis, who were watching them, as he says, with the kind of interest one would see in, say, a zoo. They were agreeing on which pub to stop by and when they started down the street that leads north from the Čobanija bridge, only ten meters away, he sensed something happening behind him. He turned and saw journalists Peđa Kojović on the ground and Emir Imamović wrestling with a couple of young men. "We ran to them and someone shouted: 'Police!!' A few uniformed people appeared and everything quickly calmed down. The attackers ran away, one was still caught, and Peđa and Emir went to give statements."

What were the stats of that night? A total of eight people were injured, and seven were arrested. The Danish selector of the festival's film program, Andrejs Viskochis, suffered the most serious injuries and was operated on and kept in the hospital. The attackers approached him from behind, knocked him to the ground and kicked him. Several festivalgoers were literally dragged out of a taxi and beaten. More attacks happened miles away from the event venue.

The festival was effectively cancelled, but certain programs continued in changed locations. Mediacentar provided space to continue at least some of the activities, says Boro Kontić. A media conference was also held in the Mediacentar hall the day after the attacks. The president of the Helsinki Committee for Human Rights, Srđan Dizdarević, called the events in Sarajevo scandalous, unacceptable and anti-civilization, pointing out that the fascist rhetoric triggered the violence.

"Should we fear that in the future the cultural and public life of Sarajevo will be regulated by paramilitary gangs that will determine which exhibitions we can visit, which movies we can watch and which swimming pools we can swim in?" asked the editor of *Dani* magazine, Senad Pećanin, who witnessed the hooligan attack on his colleagues Kojović and Imamović.

After the attack, the Queer Sarajevo Festival continued with its activities, but without public gatherings and promotions, and in a new location. With so many doors closed for them, says Slobodanka Dekić, they still needed a place to gather people because a lot came from outside Sarajevo, and Mediacentar opened theirs. First of all, she says, people who worked there were not afraid, and also truly open-minded.

The feeling of acceptance and security, which Mediacentar provided to the organizers after everything that had happened, was extremely important for her. Mediacentar, she says, is a big company, a company that is not in any way explicitly associated with the LGBTIQ+ community, although they called themselves a gay centre in the days of the festival. But that's where she found herself experiencing a sense of security at a time when it was vitally necessary.

At that time, she did not know that she would soon become part of the Mediacentar team. Before the festival itself, she was being screened for a job and her task was to design a conference about feminism and prepare a budget. While she was performing this task, she received information on her mobile phone that her email had been hacked and that various messages were being sent from her address. "I said, 'Wait, just let me finish the budget!'" she recalls, so eager was she to pursue the position. She found out that she got a job at Mediacentar after the festival, in a taxi, when a Mediacantar employee who was also a member of the festival's organising committee said to her: "Boba, I completely forgot to tell you. You got a job at Mediacentar." She started working with a team in which, as she says, different people work, but the principle is that everyone must feel comfortable and respect each other.

The festival continued for a short time at Mediacentar. The organizers were receiving threats and they got a round-the-clock police escort, as did other festival participants. There was a "hunt" for the participants, visitors were followed, and groups of Wahhabis and hooligans visited the planned festival locations. On Thursday, September 25, they were spotted hanging around Mediacentar, and the next day near the Meeting Point cinema, as reported by *Dani* magazine. In the meantime, a video was published on YouTube – an open death threat against one of the organizers, Svetlana Đurković, with an animation of a knife cutting off the head of the figure pictured on the official festival poster. After much thought and discussion with the police, it was decided - the festival was cancelled.

The following year, the festival was reduced to virtual presentations, posters and video messages in different media.

The next year, in 2010, there was only a single discussion about "how to revive the queer movement in BiH," Boro Kontić remembers. It was said that there was no association or non-governmental organization for the representation of queer rights in Bosnia and Herzegovina, nor was it possible to find a single person from public life, especially from the government, who would be willing to get engaged in this segment of human rights. According to organizers from the Sarajevo Open Centre, who hosted the meeting, it was closed to the public to avoid the possibility of more violence.

VIOLENCE AS THE RESULT OF MEDIA INCITEMENT

The violence that happened in 2008 at the first queer festival in Sarajevo was largely the result of media coverage, says Slobodanka Dekić. In that situation, the media demonstrated their potential for producing fear-mongering journalism. Hiding behind the guise of objective journalism, the media asked inappropriate questions, omitted certain key information, failed to regulate comments that publicly called for lynching, and sent a clear message – that they do not approve of the Queer Sarajevo Festival being held in the month of Ramadan. The most frequently asked question was why the festival was being held during Ramadan.

According to Dekić, the inflammatory media coverage brought the most trouble to people who were not among the festival organizers but were nonetheless now visible in the media. "Suddenly now everyone knew what queer was – before that, no one had any idea what it meant," said Dekić. One of her gay friends agreed to give an interview to the Sarajevo magazine *Dani,* including his photograph and full name. He says that he insisted on this sort of visibility out of his sense of anger and revolt in the moment, even though the journalist who interviewed him was aware of the possible consequences. That interview brought him serious negative consequences, including threats directed not only at him but at his entire family because, as Dekić says, violence never stops at one person.

As a festival organizer, she was not prepared for how the media reacted, nor did she even think about the media scene beforehand. "That was a big lesson for later," she says. "Now I understand what visibility means and that you have to have control over how communication flows to the public and what information goes out at all times."

Today, Marija Arnautović believes that journalists were not ready or sensitized to the issue, even those who believed that the festival should take place as a promotion of diversity. "We should have thought from the very beginning about the need to protect the identities of the organizers," she says. To reveal their identities was to put a target on their foreheads and they had to live in fear for their safety for months before and after the festival.

The Press and Online Media Council, after complaints by the organizers of the festival, determined that *Dnevni avaz* violated provisions of the Press Council Code, including the provisions against incitement and discrimination. The organizers of the Sarajevo Queer Festival then also announced that they would be filing criminal charges against certain media outlets, including *Dnevni avaz*, as well as individuals who propagated hatred towards people of a different sexual orientation through public speeches and writings. The editor of *Dnevni avaz* at the time said that such threats of filing reports against the media were characteristic of the era of totalitarianism and conformity, that the times have passed when journalists could be threatened for their writing, and that *Dnevni avaz* only reported the statements of people they spoke to about the event.

Certain television and radio stations were penalised for transmitting homophobic text messages that had been submitted as answers to television survey questions. The Communications Regulatory Agency, for example, fined the OBN Television 30,000 convertible marks because homophobic text messages were published in the *Mimohod* television programme answering the survey question: "Gay parade in Sarajevo?"

FIRST PRIDE PARADE - LESSONS LEARNED

After a long break, the first Pride Parade was held in Sarajevo under the name "No life within four walls" only nine years later, in September 2019, with the support of the new cantonal government and without the participation of nationalist parties. According to Boro Kontić, almost 2,000 people gathered, passed through Sarajevo's main street, and listened to several speeches in front of the Bosnian and Herzegovinian Assembly building.

Eleven years after the Sarajevo Queer Festival, Marija Arnautović reported on this first Pride Parade. The procession, with strong police protection, passed without incident, but the participants still remembered the violence that had occurred at the earlier event. They feared that the violence could be repeated. But news coverage was much fairer this time around, inappropriate comments on social media were deleted more often, and most media reported on the parade just like they would report on other daily events in the city.

Slobodanka Dekić also believes that media reporting has improved, but that this improvement has mainly consisted of changes in the words and phrases used to describe minority groups but not to fundamentally different attitudes toward them among the media. She says that there is a lack of reporting about peer violence against children with different gender identities or about LGBTIQ+ people who were, during the pandemic, forced to live in confined spaces with parents who do not accept them.

"Now I always look at the younger people who organize the parades and I always wonder if it's the same for them," says Dekić. "It's terrible because you are completely unprotected and because you know that most people think that everything that happens to you is well-deserved."

Today, when Arnautović conducts training sessions for journalists on how to report on marginalized social groups, she always uses examples of unprofessional media reporting on the LGBTIQ+ community.

In the patriarchal and conservative society of Bosnia and Herzegovina, resistance to this group and to any topics concerning sexual minorities, gender issues, and women's rights is still very powerful. High-quality, professional and engaged media reporting on these issues is very important for helping to overcome these traditional attitudes and for improving the rights of minority groups. But the media of BiH devote little or no time to investigating and reporting on the discrimination that LGBTIQ+ people experience in healthcare, education, and employment.

There was no violence or incidents on the streets during the first or subsequent Pride Parades in Sarajevo, but hate speech in the comments sections of articles on online portals and social networks, as well as malicious statements by politicians denying support for basic human rights, continued.

Actions sometimes speak louder than words. While the line of participants of the first Pride Parade - waving rainbow flags and holding banners expressing solidarity, love and defiance - was turning the corner near the BiH Presidency building, Boro Kontić remembers, local utility company workers had already thoroughly washed Sarajevo's main street with hoses, as if they wanted to disinfect the streets, starting from the point where the Pride parade began.

POST SCRIPTUM

During the preparation of this text, on March 18, the members of the Organizing Committee of the BH Pride March were attacked by hooligans during an informal meeting on the Banja Luka premises of Transparency International, the international anti-corruption organization. Three people were injured, including two journalists who came to report on the matter after they heard that the police threw the activists off the NGO's premises, declaring that they had to leave for their own safety and that the police could not protect them. After the police left, the activists were violently attacked by 30 hooligans. The members of the Organizing Committee of the BH Pride March stated that the attack was planned and that the police handed them to the hooligans.

The attack was preceded by inflammatory and hateful statements from leading political figures in Republika Srpska, Milorad Dodik and Draško Stanivuković, who asked the police to prevent the organization of an LGBTIQ+ cultural event that was scheduled to take place on 18th of March. They also said that they don't approve of such an event and that Banja Luka should defend its traditional values. After their statements, the Ministry of Interior of Republika Srpska forbade the public event that was scheduled to take place on March 18th, a screening of a film and a panel discussion on the premises of the cultural center Incel.

This announcement came on the same day the event was supposed to be held. Since many activists were already in Banja Luka, they decided to hold an informal meeting at a site that was known only by the police. The BH Pride March organisers and international organizations and media organizations connected the violent attacks with the hate comments of the leading political figures in Republika Srpska and called for their prosecution. Milorad Dodik, the president of Republika Srpska, continued with hate speech, stating that Republika Srpska will introduce a law according to which LGBTIQ+ persons will not be allowed to attend schools and universities. Many media outlets in Republika Srpska republished these statements without criticism and some also spread disinformation. Overall, the media failed to report on hate crimes, on LGBTIQ+ rights, and on the violation of the right to peaceful assembly; instead, they focused on the attack and the violence. This most recent incident reminded many of the attacks during the Queer Sarajevo Festival many years ago.

Dr Haiyan Wang

Dr Haiyan Wang is an Associate Professor in the Department of Communication, University of Macau. She received her Ph.D. from the Chinese University of Hong Kong, MA from University of Westminster, UK., and BA from Fudan University, China. Before becoming an academic, she was an award-winning investigative journalist in Southern Metropolitan Daily, China. Her academic interests include the impact of digitization on media and journalism, and women in media. She is the author of *Disrupting Chinese Journalism: Changing Politics, Economics and Journalistic Practices of the Legacy Newspaper Press* (2023, Routledge) and *The Transformation of Investigative Journalism in China: From Journalists to Activists* (2016, Lexington Books).

GENDERED JOURNALISM IN CHINA: FROM NEWSROOMS TO CLASSROOMS

I still remember the first week I was a journalist. I was 22, freshly graduated from college. I had moved from Shanghai on the east coast of China to Guangzhou by the southern sea and joined a metropolitan newspaper there that was established not long before in the wave of media commercialization reform. It was 1999, seven years after the reformist leader Deng Xiaoping made his famous "South Tour Talk" to call for the suspension of ideological struggle and the liberalization of a market economy following the 1989 crisis. Guangzhou was one of the frontline cities Deng Xiaoping had chosen to experiment with his new policy, and it was in that context that the newspaper I came to join was established. The newspaper developed very fast and soon became recognized nationwide as one of the most liberal and influential media outlets in the country. But at the time I joined it, it was in its early stages. Its influence hadn't yet grown, and the newsroom, which was very small indeed, was filled with journalists migrating from inland regions to pursue fortune and life-changing opportunities in this coastal city, the so-called "land of hope".

I was the only college graduate to join this newspaper that summer. I looked different, fresh, and perhaps exciting to my colleagues. First because I was a woman, and a young woman - so young that a taxi driver who took me to the site of a fire asked whether I was a "high-school student". Second, I held a formal journalism degree from an elite university while most of my colleagues at that time didn't even attend college. I looked like an "oddball" in this newsroom. So, my colleagues decided to give me a "test" to see whether I could fit in. They called me to a common room. The door was closed. There were five to six people, mostly men. Obviously, they were enjoying some winding-down time in the late afternoon before rushing to finish their reports of the day. The air was thin, filled with the smell of cigarettes and alcohol. In the middle of the room, there was a tea table, scattered with a pack of cards. The others led me to the table. One male colleague pointed to a puddle of glue they had intentionally poured on the edge of the table, and asked me, "what is it?" (You need to know that in the old days the glue used in most workplace was made out of thick rice milk and looked a lot like semen). I immediately understood what they wanted from me. I didn't give them a straight answer, like "it is glue", because it seemed unplayful. Instead, I went the sensational way. I covered my face with both hands and called out, "Aha! Disgusting!" Apparently, my colleagues were satisfied by my reaction. "She knows it!" The room busted into a round of laughter.

After that, I worked for nine years in that newsroom.

As I reflect back now on my journalist's career, I often come to revisit this moment. I ask myself why I reacted in that way, and would it have been different if I had reacted otherwise, such as turning cold-faced and telling them it was a bad joke and not funny? I try to analyze myself. I come to a resolution with myself. Understandably, for a newcomer in the workplace, social pressure is often something unavoidable. Perhaps I just wanted to show my colleagues that I didn't want to be an "oddball", I wanted to be part of them, I was playful just like them, and I could take jokes, even is such a blatantly sexist joke. Looking back from today, I realize I may have appeared to be too eager, too cooperative, and too quick to let go of my principles. But subconsciously maybe I knew that

I had to be strategic in order to be accepted by my colleagues. Perhaps that was the "right" attitude that allowed me to stay in the job for nearly a decade.

In my later career as a journalism researcher and educator, I interviewed many women journalists about their experiences in newsrooms. I came to realize that my encounters were not exceptional. I was told again and again that in order to survive in the newsroom, the ability to navigate in the sexist environment was an essential skill. I heard stories that were far more disturbing than mine. For instance, a mid-career reporter who also worked in Guangzhou told me that she hated the frequent "going-outs" with colleagues after work but had to appear willing to participate and act as if she enjoyed these occasions. The "going-outs", usually organized in the evening in a restaurant, a tea house or a bar near the office area, were not just about eating and drinking, but more about forming special bonds with the editors and getting important assignments and opportunities for promotion. Ambitious as she was, she often felt obliged to join the party, even though it meant that she had to play a role she didn't like and take part in the flirting games. Her cooperation didn't gain her the promotion she deserved, but yielded some opportunities for her to cover important news stories, such as the National People's Congress meeting in Beijing, among others.

But not every woman is as flexible and "lucky" as she is. I also heard stories from women journalists who refused to cooperate even though they faced huge social pressure. As a journalist who had just left the profession told me:

> When they made sexist jokes to me, I often returned a cold face. I didn't want to react in the way they expected, like... laughing, returning another joke.... But gradually I noticed the consequences. They saw me as a boring and uninteresting person, because I am not playful. I felt I was isolated. It was getting very hard. So, I quit. (quoted in H. Wang, 2016, p.501)

What these women's experiences have taught me is that sexism is not just about a culture of peer-socialization, but also a gender-based politics and a mechanism of inclusion or exclusion in the newsroom. Like other scholars have discovered in the Western context, newsrooms are often like a "blokes club" (North, 2016), and women are routinely under the pressure to become "one of the boys" (van Zoonen, 1998). You accept, you are in. You refuse, you are out. That is the dominating logic in the workplace, and the middle path is only available to the few who have access to social, financial or political capital (Djerf-Pierre, 2005). Not to mention that, in the Chinese context, there is a deep-rooted conception that women are men's objects. Even though they have become independent working women, part of their perceived job in the workplace is to create a delightful working environment for their male colleagues, especially the powerful ones. As a male journalist told me when I interviewed him about his views on his female colleagues:

> They should make the boss feel it is pleasant to have them around. This way, they will have good chances in their careers even though they can't make good journalism. (quoted in H. Wang, 2016, p.501)

His comments expressed the explicit gender-based discrimination confronting women, but he was completely non-reflexive about this. Even though he knew that the interviewer in front of him, me, was formerly a woman journalist too, he had no intention of shying away from his contempt. Sadly, it is not only him. This kind of unsympathetic and disrespectful view of women is common in newsrooms, as well as in the general society in China.

II

Back to my journalism career, I encountered more and more such "jokes" from my colleagues as time went by. Sometimes it was a picture of a naked woman model that they invited me to view. Sometimes they shared with me a comment on the body or bodily movement of a female colleague. I was mostly cooperative, never thought it was necessary to take a more serious approach. Even worse, I didn't see any problems. Even though I was uncomfortable when such jokes were made at my expense, I thought it was standard and normal. I thought, in a mixed-gender and often times stressful working environment, some jokes could soften the tension and light up the atmosphere. It seemed there was nothing wrong, and no need to feel offended.

Like most of my colleagues at that time, I hadn't developed a sensitivity about gender issues, hadn't had the critical mindset to question why most of the "jokes" are about women and directed to women. I had been totally blind to sexism, not having been able to recognize it, not having had the guts to challenge it.

I am not alone. I am just a typical example of a generation of journalists in China who joined newsrooms during the same time period, the 1990s, which happened to be the start of the so-called "golden age" of Chinese journalism (H. Wang, 2021). We were all so busy breaking news, pursuing explosive stories that would sell newspaper copies and getting established in the industry that we took no time to look inwardly, reflect on own values and actions, and examine whether anything was wrong in our own backyard.

The limitations I had were almost universal for those of my generation, and were produced by the set of political, economic, social and cultural conditions in which we lived. I came from a small town in Hubei Province in the central part of China. I grew up in an environment where, by tradition, the fathers were the breadwinners and the mothers were the homemakers. Even though I was the older child in the family, I was raised to believe that my brother, who is two years younger, was more important than me, and that I, as a girl, should always put his interests before mine. In my whole childhood and even young adulthood, I remember one thing my parents, especially my mother, kept telling me: "You are a girl." She reminded me of that over and over.

The implication was that a girl should always do a girl's deed. For instance, she should always be virtuous and caring, always be humble and tolerant, never challenge men or outshine them, behave properly according to what the society thinks is right for a girl or woman. Those are powerful, almost sacred, social expectations, so powerful that for many years I worried that if I became "not like a girl", I would not only disappoint my family, but also destroy myself and would never be redeemed. Nobody explained to me that there was something called a "gender stereotype", and that I might be another victim suffering from its damaging effects.

Neither had the professors taught me in this regard when I went to college. As one of the top students in the high school in my hometown, I was admitted to the journalism school in Fudan University in Shanghai. I was thrilled about going to college and being in the big city. But I felt nothing in particular about the fact that most of my classmates were men and most of our professors were men also. These were facts I was only to "discover" or take notice of years later after leaving the college.

In college, both practice-based and theory-based courses were offered to prepare us to become competent future journalists, but as far as I can recall, none of the courses discussed gender or any issues related to diversity. I don't remember anything ever being taught on this subject during the four years of courses. In our minds (as well as the professors' minds), "gender" was a biological given, it was non-questionable. The idea that gender is a social construction was beyond our horizon. What's more, the word meaning "gender", *xing*, also means "sex".

Talking about *xing* could be easily taken as talking about sex. Therefore, it could sound shameless, disrespectable, immoral and at the same time anti-Communist, as the ruling Communist Party subscribed to a kind of asexual ideology.

In short, at that time, sexism didn't exist in our vocabulary, and gender was not an issue. The only relevant conceptual tool we possessed was the self-congratulatory idea of "state-feminism". According to official policy, women and men were equal. But in practice, the state turned a blind eye to the hurdles preventing women's liberation. As Z. Wang (2015, p. 519) commented, it was in effect a kind of "state patriarchy", "often with vacillation and inconsistency".

III

The landscape of journalism education in China is very different today. In 1998, just one year before I graduated from Fudan, the Ministry of Education officially granted journalism (and communications) the status of a first-tier discipline in the social sciences, a recognition that spurred the rapid expansion of journalism education across the country. The number of journalism programs increased from just over a thousand in the late-1990s to more than 1,500 in the 2020s, enrolling some 14,000 students at the undergraduate level and 7,000 students at the graduate level each year (CAHJC, 2021; Hu & Leng, 2016; Guo & Chen, 2017; R. Wang, 2020). Such a massive increase in student enrollment calls for education reform regarding the recruitment of teaching faculties, structure of the curriculum, design of the syllabus and course outlines, and publication of textbooks (Chen, 2020). Relevant actions have been taken, but unfortunately many of the blind spots in the journalism educational system continue to persist. One of those blind spots has been the lack of sensitivity to gender and diversity issues.

Take journalism curriculum as an example. Journalism curriculum in China is usually divided into four categories: GE (general education) compulsory courses, GE elective courses, specialization compulsory courses and specialization elective courses. The GE courses aim to provide students with general social science knowledge, and the specialization courses target professional training, which includes skills like news-gathering, interviewing, writing and editing, media management, media ethics, content curation and design, lab practice, internship practice, and so on. In a study I did for MDI in 2022, I surveyed the undergraduate journalism curricula currently used in five journalism schools in Guangdong province[1]. I found that among the overall 600+ courses listed in their catalogues, only two directly addressed the issue of gender. The first was the "Media and Gender" course at Shantou University (STU), and the second was "Gender Justice and Media" at South China University of Technology (SCUT). The other three universities (Sun Yat-sen University, Shenzhen University, and Jinan University) had no such courses listed.

While the STU students I interviewed said they cherished the opportunity to take the "Media and Gender" course, the SCUT students told me that their "Gender Justice and Media" course only existed in name and has not been offered for many years. I asked why, and their answers were, "It was offered in our final year. Our credits are already full and no need to have extra" (H, interviewed on 20 March 2022), or, "very few students elected the course. It didn't meet the minimum criteria of student enrollment" (G, interviewed on 20 March 2022). All of the reasons the students gave sounded understandable. It seemed that it could almost have been an "accident" that they didn't end up taking any gender-related courses.

[1] The five schools are the Changjiang Journalism School at Shantou University (STU), the School of Journalism and Communication at South China University of Technology (SCUT), the College of Communication at Shenzhen University (SZU), the School of Journalism and Communication at Jinan University (JNU), and the School of Communication and Design at Sun Yat-Sen University (SYSU).

But it was an inevitable "accident" if we consider a comparison with the "Marxist theory of journalism" course, which all five universities listed in their journalism curricula. This course is required by the government as part of an effort to strengthen political education in the journalism discipline, and exists not only in the universities I studied but also in almost every J-school in China. This course is classified as "specialization compulsory", and the course policy states that students won't be granted a graduation certificate if they don't take it. All five universities offered the course in the first year of study, and allowed students to make it up in subsequent years if by any chance they missed it initially.

On the contrary, the gender course is "specialization elective". The offering of the course depends on the availability of the faculty, and taking the course depends solely on the availability and interests of the students. There are no structural arrangements—like requiring all students to take it—to guarantee its stability. Not to mention that most J-schools don't even have a gender-related course. This contrast indicates how marginal the gender concept is in the overall structure of journalism education. It also raises the deeper concern that journalism students--our future journalists--have little opportunity to be educated about gender issues in their formative years in college.

More worryingly, journalism educators don't consider this absence to be a pressing problem. In a study based on interviews with 16 faculty members at the major J-schools in China, the interviewees were asked to list the courses that they think should be included when revising their curricula. A total of 64 new course titles were proposed. More than half of these were on journalism and new media skills, but none was related to gender or other diversity issues (Chen, 2020). In other words, gender education in Chinese J-schools suffers from a dual blindness: one being its absence in the curriculum, and the other being the ignorance of or indifference to this absence on the part of journalism educators.

Given this deficit, the intervention of activist groups such as MDI is critical. As a long-time member of MDI's international community of journalism researchers and educators, I have been honored to participate in various activities organized by MDI, including talks, workshops and visits. The concept of "media diversity" has deeply influenced my thinking, which in turn has benefited my teaching and been expressed in the changes I have seen in my journalism students. One of the most unforgettable experiences was in 2016, when I invited and hosted five MDI experts, who came from the U.K., Australia and New Zealand to spend a week each with me and my students in Guangzhou. It was a never-before (and perhaps never-again) experience for my students. It gave them an opportunity to be immersed in an intellectual world that is totally different from what the mainstream journalism education in China offered them. It opened their eyes to a variety of diversity issues (i.e. gender, age, religion, migration, race and ethnicity, etc.), which they had seldom questioned before. It made them reflect on the privileges they have enjoyed and have taken for granted for so long. It also made them think about hard questions regarding diversity, inclusivity and equality and what they might do in their future careers as journalist to promote social justice, especially that of marginalized social groups. I am glad to see that many of them have already begun to shine in reporting about diversity in their media jobs. I firmly believe that MDI has contributed to making this change.

REFERENCES

- CAHJC (The Chinese Association for History of Journalism and Communication). (2021). Yearbook of China's Journalism and Communication Education (Zhongguo xinwen chuanbo jiaoyu nianjian). *Wuhan University Press.*
- Chen, C. (2020). Journalism Education in the 21st Century: How to Cultivate Innovative Talents? *Journalism Research (Xinwen Daxue), 173* (9), 10-21.
- Djerf-Pierre, M. (2005). Lonely at the top: Gendered media elites in Sweden, *Journalism, 6*(3), 265–290.
- Hu, Z. & Leng, S. (2016). The employment opportunities and difficulties of journalism and communication graduates (Xinwen chuanbo xuelei xuesheng jiuye xianzhuang he nandian). *The Press (Xinwen Zhanxian)*, (06), 27-30.
- Guo, K., & Chen, P. (2017). The changing landscape of journalism education in China. *Journalism & Mass Communication Educator, 72*(3), 297-305.
- North, L. (2016). Still a "blokes club": The motherhood dilemma in journalism, *Journalism, 7*(3), 315–330.
- van Zoonen, L. (1998). One of the girls? The changing gender of journalism. In: Carter C, Branston G and Allan S (eds.) News, gender and power. *Routledge*, pp. 33–46.
- Wang, H. (2016). "Naked swimmers": Chinese women journalists' experience. of media commercialization. *Media, Culture & Society, 38*(4), 489–505.
- Wang, H. (2021) Generational change in Chinese journalism: Developing. Mannheim's theory of generations for contemporary social conditions. *Journal of Communication, 71*(2), 104-128.
- Wang, R. (2020). Challenges of journalism discipline and changes in journalism education (Xinwenxue mianlin de tiaozhan yu xinwen jiaoyu biange). *China Publishing Journal (Zhongguo chuban)*, (14), 10-14.
- Wang, Z. (2005). "State feminism"? Gender and socialist state formation in Maoist China. *Feminist Studies, 31*(3), 519–550.

Dr David Tuller

Dr David Tuller, DrPH, is Senior Fellow in Public Health and Journalism at the Center for Global Public Health at the University of California, Berkeley. He received a masters degree in public health in 2006 and a doctor of public health degree in 2013, both from Berkeley. He was a reporter and editor for ten years at The San Francisco Chronicle and served as health editor at Salon.com. He has written regularly about public health and medical issues for The New York Times, the policy journal Health Affairs, and many other publications.

INSTEAD OF CONCLUSIONS

In the fall of 1994, I was living in Moscow and gathering material for what eventually became a book called *Cracks in the Iron Closet: Travels in Gay and Lesbian Russia.* With my friend Ksusha, I attended a three-day "les-bi-gay" workshop conducted by three American activists. This was their third visit to Russia for the purpose of engaging in "community building," they told the dozens of us gathered.

The phrase immediately triggered my cynical skepticism; everyone from the West seemed to be engaged in some kind of "building" activity in Russia. Mormons and Jesus-lovers were "building religion." Business consultants were "building capitalism." There were no end of Americans involved in "democracy building." Many of these efforts struck me as inappropriate, naïve in the extreme, pathetically ineffective. The les-bi-gay community building effort seemed no different.

The first session, on Friday evening, drew about 50 people to a stuffy basement in an outlying Moscow district. The three Americans droned on and on about identity politics, self-love, coming out, group process, and yada yada yada. They lost the audience quickly. The participants giggled at random moments and seemed a bit bewildered by the goings-on. By the third session on Sunday, only about 15 attendees remained in the les-bi-gay seminar.

A couple of days later, I met with two of the American seminar leaders to discuss their work. An American friend of mine, Laurie, a sociology grad student gathering material for her doctorate on gender issues in Russia, accompanied me. Alma, one of the seminar leaders, told us that they'd engaged in an invaluable "needs assessment" before the seminar. They had learned, she said, all about the coercive Soviet method of ideological indoctrination.

"You really should check that out!" she advised us enthusiastically. "There's been a lot of dysfunctional group behavior that causes people to have a lot of shit and pain around groups and leadership!"

Laurie and I glanced at each other. These people were engaged in "community building" here, and had just realized that Russians had "a lot of shit and pain" around groups? Had they heard of Stalin?

A few days later, I was hanging out with Ksusha and our friend Sveta. Ksusha began ranting about the ridiculousness of the whole enterprise.

"Really, Sveta, it was like kindergarten, just like kindergarten," she said. "Imagine telling Russians that they have to be in some stuffy basement room at 10 am on the weekend and stay for ten hours, when they could be at the beach! Maybe if these Americans had held it in the woods or somewhere outside..."

She leaned toward me, waved her arms, and launched into a diatribe against "collectives." "David, we were always in collectives, in groups—at work we'd gather once a week, once a month for ideology lectures. Russians hate that. What do we need it for? Maybe Americans need that, but we don't. We need places to meet—bars, cafes, discos. Just to meet, to see each other. Maybe after we have these places for a while then we'll want to gather in groups and talk about ourselves."

Sveta seized the opportunity to have the last word. "Well, Americans think they can save us," she chortled. "They think that they're the Messiah. Or Superman. And as for the American gays and *lesbianki*, they think they are the Supergays and the Superlesbianki!"

I couldn't disagree with her analysis.

This and related experiences during the time I lived in Moscow served me well when I became involved in the journalism training world. In 1998, after almost a decade as a reporter and editor at the SF Chronicle, I received a fellowship from the Knight Foundation to spend nine months in St Petersburg. I would be working with a new media diversity program being created by Milica Pešić, a Serbian journalist living in London, under the auspices of New York University's Center for War, Peace, and the News Media. I'd taught some undergraduate journalism courses in San Francisco, and obviously I'd lived in Russia, but beyond that I wasn't sure what I was supposed to be doing or how I was supposed to do it.

I was very aware that the countries scattered across the post-Soviet landscape were teeming with US and Western advisors in all spheres of activity—banking, public health, legal systems. Perhaps some of these efforts were useful, but others were infused with undeniably imperialistic impulses. In my travels, I had recognized the extent to which this overbearing approach had been pursued even in the domain of gay and lesbian rights. (In those days, no one would have understood "LGBTQ"!) I didn't want to repeat the pattern in journalism. I tried to approach the work with caution and humility.

Milica and I bonded during our first trip together—two weeks in Albania in February of 1998. She impressed me with her charisma, her humor, her boundless energy, and her dedication to her work. During these first workshops, I generally followed her lead until I gradually got my footing. Later that year, we traveled together to a media diversity gathering in Ohrid, Macedonia. In 2003, we conducted nine days of training in Armenia, Georgia, and Azerbaijan--the three former Soviet Caucasus republics. I also wrote some reporting diversity training materials for MDI, which were then translated into multiple languages.

Milica took our responsibilities seriously but also loved turning everything into an adventure. In Georgia, we decided—with the approval of the participants--to move the workshop from Tbilisi, the capital, to the ski resort in the mountains. We skied during the day and held our seminars in the evenings. That worked out great for everyone. In Baku, when I saw a beautiful red antique carpet in the market, I returned later in the day with Milica, who gave a brilliant performance as my financially savvy wife. The sellers understood quickly that she controlled the family budget. They smiled at me knowingly and immediately agreed to lower the price. (That red carpet still graces my living room floor in San Francisco. When I look at it, I smile and think of Milica.)

I worked as well for other journalism training programs sponsored by either US or European funders. When accepting these assignments, I always sought to work alongside local trainers, who had a more pragmatic and realistic take on what was feasible for the journalists in our groups. They were obviously much more familiar with the facts on the ground—what was feasible in terms of reporting strategies, and what was not. I could offer suggestions or ideas, but I accepted that some would be dismissed as irrelevant or as impossible to execute, for whatever reason, and that some participants would likely reject everything I said just because I was American.

I also recognized that journalists in the post-Soviet and former Eastern bloc countries, including workshop participants, often maintained financial arrangements with advertisers. Some American trainers expressed shock at learning that journalists sometimes wrote ad copy for money—even as they covered news stories about the advertisers paying them. Or they engaged in other actions that would be grounds for immediate firing in the U.S. I didn't share the outrage I saw some of my compatriots expressed. I was aware that our local colleagues lived in their reality, not mine. They had to feed their children, not me. So they had to make the decisions they needed to make in order to survive. I couldn't judge their choices.

In any event, I was a bit hesitant when Milica asked me to review and edit the essays for this book. Editing is often a thankless job. Most people are understandably sensitive about having their writing assessed—I certainly am. And not surprisingly, journalists generally pride themselves on their ability to communicate; in my experience, they don't always take kindly to rigorous editing. Taking on the task of dealing with dozens of essays about controversial issues involving diversity and the use and misuse of media and language seemed like a daunting prospect fraught with pitfalls and possibilities for conflict.

Moreover, most of the authors were not writing in their native languages but in English. I speak two other languages—Russian and French. But while my spoken fluency is pretty good, I am very aware that I am incapable of writing a serious paper in either language. I dread to think of someone having to edit whatever I would come up with.

I assumed that many or most of the authors would be translating in their heads as they were composing their articles. Words and phrases in translation, even when technically accurate, do not necessarily carry the same valence as in the original language. Sometimes the translated word is more powerful and aggressive than in the original, sometimes less so. Shades and nuances of meaning can also get lost. This certainly happens with slurs, whether they involve race, gender, sexual orientation, religion, citizenship status, or other demographic categories. They can be translated, of course, but they resonate differently—the weight of the opprobrium they carry does not necessarily come across, or it comes across with even greater force.

Would corrections I might make to awkward phrasing be accepted as offered, as well-meaning suggestions from a journalism colleague? Or would they be viewed with concern and suspicion, coming as they did from a white American guy in his 60s? I didn't know. (I suppose I get exemptions for being gay and Jewish, but I think my point is clear.) I was concerned that suggestions or changes made for linguistic or grammatical reasons related to English usage or style would or could be misinterpreted as efforts to censor or silence.

I fretted about all these things before accepting the job. But I figured someone was ultimately going to have to edit the essays, so it might as well be me.

In each case, I did my best to retain the writer's voice even as I fiddled with some of the phrasing or suggested trims or asked questions about various references or statements. Some of my responses undoubtedly arose out of my limited awareness and understanding of particular local contexts, historical events, and regional trends. But as an editor I tend to be nit-picky and detail-oriented. If I find myself confused or lost, I assume some other readers might as well, so I always feel it is my responsibility to alert the authors. The trick is in being able to broach every issue with care and sensitivity while remaining alert to the possibility of offense arising from linguistic misunderstandings.

I hope that, for the most part, I was able to perform this task respectfully, and that no one felt my edits were designed or intended to undermine or deflate the meaning they wanted to convey. My goal in all cases was to try to help them get their points across as clearly as possible—not to distort their message or impose my own ideas or thoughts or political viewpoint. I really enjoyed the exchanges I had with some of the authors via the comment bubbles on Word documents, often extending through two and three revisions.

That's a long way of saying that editing these essays was a challenging job! But it was definitely a rewarding one.

As I read these powerful, heartfelt, and probing accounts, I was surprised at how much I learned. For one thing, they provided me with a window, or multiple windows, onto MDI's history. I knew bits and pieces from what Milica had said and what I'd picked up during my own involvement with the organization. But given the diversity and range of the essays, reading them helped fill in many of the pieces. I hadn't realized, for example, that MDI started off working only with reporters and then expanded to include media owners and decision-makers. Later on, I learned, Milica recognized the importance of working with non-governmental organizations that represented disadvantaged groups and ethnic minorities, training them on how to get the word out and reach media organizations with their messaging, as well as with academic institutions seeking to develop curricula and programs on media and diversity.

In fact, before I accepted this assignment, I was actually unaware of the vast reach of MDI's efforts, especially in the last 10 or 15 years. After working on the MDI training manuals years ago, I had devoted most of my time to study and then work at the School of Public Health at the University of California, Berkeley. Milica and I maintained our friendship, but I had little ongoing professional relationship with MDI. So in reviewing the essays, I was blown away by how many programs

MDI had sponsored in far-flung regions, how many local journalists it had impacted, and how many initiatives it had pursued. I was impressed all over again by Milica's energy and vision as well as her ability to bring together media professionals from everywhere to discuss and debate these critical issues.

I was also immensely moved by the passion expressed by all the authors, no matter their perspectives, as well as their shared commitment to the notion that journalism and all forms of media can and must be used as tools for positive change. Many of the authors grew up in extremely harsh and oppressive circumstances, yet they have managed to retain their humor, their humanity, and their desire to promote inclusion, tolerance and diversity. I find myself immensely inspired by this resilience.

In other words, despite my initial trepidation about taking on the project, in the end I felt humbled, honored and touched to review these brief but revealing glimpses into MDI's past and present and into the lives of people invested in its core mission. I hope, and expect, that the essays will provoke a similar range of reactions among this book's readers.